First World War
and Army of Occupation
War Diary
France, Belgium and Germany

46 DIVISION
138 Infantry Brigade
Lincolnshire Regiment
4th Battalion.
1 March 1915 - 30 January 1918

WO95/2691/1

The Naval & Military Press Ltd
www.nmarchive.com
Published in association with The National Archives

Published by

The Naval & Military Press Ltd

Unit 10 Ridgewood Industrial Park,
Uckfield, East Sussex,
TN22 5QE England
Tel: +44 (0) 1825 749494

www.naval-military-press.com

www.nmarchive.com

This diary has been reprinted in facsimile from the original. Any imperfections are inevitably reproduced and the quality may fall short of modern type and cartographic standards.

© **Crown Copyright**
Images reproduced by permission of The National Archives, London, England, 2015.

Contents

Document type	Place/Title	Date From	Date To
Heading	WO95/2691/1		
Heading	46th Division 138th Infy Bde 4th Bn Lincoln Regt Jan 1916-Jan 1918		
Heading	138th Inf. Bde. 46th Div. Battn. Disembarked Havre from England 1/3.3.15 War Diary. 4th Battn. The Lincolnshire Regiment. March 1915 Attached: Battn. Operation Orders Nos. 1, 2, 3, 4, 5		
War Diary		01/03/1915	31/03/1915
Heading	Battalion Operation Orders Nos. 1, 2, 3, 4 & 5		
Operation(al) Order(s)	Operation Order No. 1. by Lt. Col. J.W. Jeush Commanding 1/4th Bn Lincolnshire Regiment.	09/03/1915	09/03/1915
Operation(al) Order(s)	Operation Orders No. 2. by Lt. Col. J.W. Jeush Commanding 1/4th Bn Lincolnshire Regt.	11/03/1915	11/03/1915
Operation(al) Order(s)	Operation Orders No. 3. by Lt. Colonel J.W. Jeush Commanding 1/4th Bn Lincolnshire Regt.	16/03/1915	16/03/1915
Operation(al) Order(s)	Operation Orders No. 4. by Lt. Colonel J.W. Jeush Commanding 1/4th Bn Lincolnshire Regt.	26/03/1915	26/03/1915
Operation(al) Order(s)	Operation Orders No. 5. by Lt. Col. J.W. Jeush Commdg 1/4th Bn Lincolnshire Regt.	30/03/1915	30/03/1915
Heading	138th Inf. Bde. 46th Div. War Diary 4th Battn. The Lincolnshire Regiment. April 1915		
War Diary		01/04/1915	30/04/1915
Heading	138th Inf. Bde. 46th Div. War Diary 4th Battn. The Lincolnshire Regiment. May 1915		
War Diary		01/05/1915	31/05/1915
Heading	138th Inf. Bde. 46th Div. War Diary 4th Battn. The Lincolnshire Regiment. June 1915		
War Diary		01/06/1915	30/06/1915
Heading	138th Inf. Bde. 46th Div. War Diary 4th Battn. The Lincolnshire Regiment. July 1915		
War Diary		01/07/1915	31/07/1915
Heading	138th Inf. Bde. 46th Div. War Diary 4th Battn. The Lincolnshire Regiment. August 1915		
War Diary	In Trenches	01/08/1915	03/08/1915
War Diary	Zillebeke Dugouts	04/08/1915	04/08/1915
War Diary	Barracks Ypres	05/08/1915	10/08/1915
War Diary	Trenches	11/08/1915	16/08/1915
War Diary	E Huts	17/08/1915	22/08/1915
War Diary	Trenches	23/08/1915	28/08/1915
War Diary	Embankment Dugouts	29/08/1915	31/08/1915
Heading	138th Inf. Bde. 46th Div. War Diary 4th Battn. The Lincolnshire Regiment. September 1915		
War Diary	Embankment Dugouts Cruisstrant	01/09/1915	02/09/1915
War Diary	In The Trenches 9.50 Ai.2.T.3	03/09/1915	08/09/1915
War Diary	In Huts. H 26b Sheet 28 1/40000	09/09/1915	13/09/1915
War Diary	In Huts	14/09/1915	14/09/1915
War Diary	In The Trenches 79.50. A 1.2.3	15/09/1915	20/09/1915
War Diary	Brigade Reserve	21/09/1915	26/09/1915
War Diary	In The Trenches.	26/09/1915	26/09/1915
War Diary	In The Trenches 19.55.A 1.2.3.R1	27/09/1915	30/09/1915

Heading	138th Inf. Bde. 46th Div. War Diary 4th Battn. The Lincolnshire Regiment. October 1915 Attached : Appendices.		
War Diary	In The Trenches	01/10/1915	01/10/1915
War Diary	Dickebusch Huts	02/10/1915	02/10/1915
War Diary	Busnettes	03/10/1915	06/10/1915
War Diary	Hesdigneul	07/10/1915	14/10/1915
Miscellaneous			
Miscellaneous	White cards were received by the following : 2367 Pte F. Gilliat.		
War Diary	Reserve Trenches	15/10/1915	15/10/1915
War Diary	Hesdigneul	16/10/1915	26/10/1915
War Diary	Verquin	27/10/1915	31/10/1915
Miscellaneous	Appendices.		
Operation(al) Order(s)	Operation Order No. 14 by Brig-Genl. G.C. Kemp. Commanding 138th Infantry Brigade.	11/10/1915	11/10/1915
Miscellaneous	Appendix "A"		
Miscellaneous	Instructions For Use of Smoke. Appendix "B"		
Miscellaneous	Time Table Of Gas And Smoke.		
Miscellaneous	Divisional Squadron.	10/10/1915	10/10/1915
Miscellaneous	46th Division. G.C. 104	15/10/1915	15/10/1915
Miscellaneous	138th Infantry Brigade.	15/10/1915	15/10/1915
Heading	138th Inf. Bde. 46th Div. War Diary 4th Battn. The Lincolnshire Regiment. November 1915		
War Diary	Verquin	01/11/1915	05/11/1915
War Diary	Verquin Robecq	06/11/1915	30/11/1915
Heading	138th Inf. Bde. 46th Div. War Diary 4th Battn. The Lincolnshire Regiment. December 1915		
War Diary	In The Trenches.	01/12/1915	02/12/1915
War Diary	King's Billets	03/12/1915	03/12/1915
War Diary	Le Sart	04/12/1915	14/12/1915
War Diary	Le Sart Billets	15/12/1915	19/12/1915
War Diary	Thiennes Billets	20/12/1915	29/12/1915
War Diary	Thiennes	30/12/1915	31/12/1915
Heading	1/4th Lincols Regt. Jan Vol IX		
War Diary	Thiennes	01/01/1916	06/01/1916
War Diary	Marseilles	07/01/1916	09/01/1916
War Diary	At Sea	10/01/1916	12/01/1916
War Diary	Alexandria	13/01/1916	14/01/1916
War Diary	Shallufa	15/01/1916	29/01/1916
War Diary	Sidi-Bishr	30/01/1916	31/01/1916
Heading	1/4 Lincoln Regt Feb Vol X		
War Diary	Sidi Bishr	01/02/1916	03/02/1916
War Diary	On Boued Ship	04/02/1916	09/02/1916
War Diary	On Train	10/02/1916	11/02/1916
War Diary	Ailly	12/02/1916	20/02/1916
War Diary	Boisbergues	21/02/1916	29/02/1916
Heading	1/4 Lincoln Regt Vol XI		
War Diary	Boisbergues	01/03/1916	01/03/1916
War Diary	Doullens	02/03/1916	06/03/1916
War Diary	Houvin	07/03/1916	09/03/1916
War Diary	Villers Chatel	10/03/1916	10/03/1916
War Diary	In The Trenches	11/03/1916	21/03/1916
War Diary	Camblain L'Abbee	22/03/1916	27/03/1916
War Diary	In The Trenches	28/03/1916	31/03/1916
Heading	1/4 Lincoln Regt Vol XVII		

War Diary	In The Trenches	01/04/1916	14/04/1916
War Diary	Camblain L'Abbee	15/04/1916	18/04/1916
War Diary	In The Trenches	19/04/1916	22/04/1916
War Diary	Averdoingt	23/04/1916	28/04/1916
War Diary	Maroeuil	29/04/1916	09/05/1916
War Diary	Sus St Leger	10/05/1916	20/05/1916
War Diary	Humbercamps	21/05/1916	31/05/1916
Miscellaneous	1/4th Battn. Lincs. Regt.	14/07/1916	14/07/1916
War Diary	Humbercamp	01/06/1916	05/06/1916
War Diary	Fonquevillers	06/06/1916	18/06/1916
War Diary	Humbercamp	19/06/1916	25/06/1916
Miscellaneous	A Form. Messages And Signals		
War Diary	Humbercamp	26/06/1916	27/06/1916
War Diary	Fonquevillers	28/06/1916	30/06/1916
Miscellaneous	4th Lincoln Regt.		
Miscellaneous	A Form. Messages And Signals		
Miscellaneous	O.C. 4th Lincoln.	27/06/1916	27/06/1916
Operation(al) Order(s)	Operation Order No. 29. by Lt. Col G.J. Barrell Commanding 1/4th Battn, Lancs Regt. In The Field. 20.6.1916	20/06/1916	20/06/1916
Miscellaneous			
War Diary	Fonquevillers	01/07/1916	01/07/1916
War Diary	Hannescamp	02/07/1916	08/07/1916
War Diary	Bienvillers	09/07/1916	11/07/1916
War Diary	Lacauche	12/07/1916	14/07/1916
War Diary	Berles	14/07/1916	16/07/1916
War Diary	Bules	17/07/1916	18/07/1916
War Diary	Pomier	19/07/1916	22/07/1916
War Diary	Bules	23/07/1916	28/07/1916
War Diary	In The Trenches Berks.	29/07/1916	30/07/1916
War Diary	Bienvillers	31/07/1916	31/07/1916
Miscellaneous	C Form (Duplicate). Messages And Signals.		
Miscellaneous	C Form (Original). Messages And Signals.		
Miscellaneous	C Form (Duplicate). Messages And Signals.		
Operation(al) Order(s)	Operation Order No. 30 by Lt. Col. G.J. Barrell Cnzdg, in The Field. 1/4th Battn. Lines Regiment.	03/07/1916	03/07/1916
Operation(al) Order(s)	Operation Order No. 31. by Lt. Col. G.J. Barrell Cnzdg. 1/4th Battn Lincolnshire Regiment.	06/07/1916	06/07/1916
War Diary	Bienvillers	01/08/1916	03/08/1916
War Diary	Trenches	04/08/1916	09/08/1916
War Diary	Pommier	09/08/1916	14/08/1916
War Diary	Trenches	15/08/1916	21/08/1916
War Diary	Bienvillers	22/08/1916	27/08/1916
War Diary	Trenches	27/08/1916	31/08/1916
War Diary	Trenches (Berles)	01/09/1916	02/09/1916
War Diary	Pommier	03/09/1916	07/09/1916
War Diary	Trenches (Berles)	08/09/1916	14/09/1916
War Diary	Bienvillers	15/09/1918	20/09/1918
War Diary	Trenches (Berles)	21/09/1916	26/09/1916
War Diary	Pommier	27/09/1916	30/09/1916
Miscellaneous	138th. Inf. Bde.	15/09/1916	15/09/1916
Miscellaneous	Bombardment Phase I		
Miscellaneous	Phase II		
Miscellaneous			
War Diary	Pommier	01/10/1916	01/10/1916
War Diary	La Cauchie	02/10/1916	02/10/1916

War Diary	Trenches	03/10/1916	05/10/1916
War Diary	Trenches (Berles)	05/10/1916	08/10/1916
War Diary	Bienvillers	09/10/1916	12/10/1916
War Diary	Trenches (Berles)	14/10/1916	22/10/1916
War Diary	Pommier	23/10/1916	24/10/1916
War Diary	Trenches (Berles)	25/10/1916	29/10/1916
War Diary	Mondicourt	30/10/1916	31/10/1916
Operation(al) Order(s)	Operation Order No. 1 by Capt. E.N. Marris Commdg A Coy, 1/4th Bn. Lincolnshire Regt.	03/10/1916	03/10/1916
Operation(al) Order(s)	Operation Order No. 46, by Major G.A. Yool, Commanding 1/4th Bn. Lincolnshire Regiment.	04/10/1916	04/10/1916
Operation(al) Order(s)	Operation Order No. 52 by Lieut-Col. G.A. Yool, Commanding 1/4th Battalion Lincolnshire Regiment.	01/11/1916	01/11/1916
Operation(al) Order(s)	Operation Order No 48 by Lieut-Col. G.A. Yool, Commanding 1/4th Battalion Lincolnshire Regiment.	21/10/1916	21/10/1916
Operation(al) Order(s)	Operation Order No 49 by Lieut-Col. F.S.N. Savage Armstrong D.S.O. Commanding 1/4th Battalion Lincolnshire Regiment.	24/10/1916	24/10/1916
Miscellaneous	Battalion Orders by Lieut-Col. F.S.N. Savage Armstrong, Commanding 1/4th Battalion Lincolnshire Regiment.	24/10/1916	24/10/1916
Miscellaneous	Orders For Wiring Fatigue	24/10/1916	24/10/1916
Operation(al) Order(s)	Operation Order No 50 by Lieut-Col. F.S.N. Savage Armstrong, D.S.O., Commanding 1/4th Battalion Lincolnshire Regiment.	29/10/1916	29/10/1916
Operation(al) Order(s)	Operation Order No 51 by Major R.M. Earl Commanding 1/4th Battalion Lincolnshire Regiment.	31/10/1916	31/10/1916
Miscellaneous	46th Division. VIIth Corps GS 1113 46th Division 2084/G.	07/10/1916	07/10/1916
Miscellaneous	Report on Raid Carried out by 4th Lincolns on night 5th/6th October.	07/10/1916	07/10/1916
Operation(al) Order(s)	Report on Operations on 5th October, 1916 by 138th Inf. Bde.	06/10/1916	06/10/1916
Miscellaneous	1/4th Lincolnshire Regiment.	05/10/1916	05/10/1916
War Diary	Mezrolles	01/11/1916	01/11/1916
War Diary	Maison Ponthieu	02/11/1916	02/11/1916
War Diary	Agenvillers	03/11/1916	10/11/1916
War Diary	Neuilly L'Hopital	11/11/1916	21/11/1916
War Diary	Beaumetz	22/11/1916	22/11/1916
War Diary	Bonnieres	23/11/1916	24/11/1916
War Diary	Halloy	25/11/1916	30/11/1916
Operation(al) Order(s)	Operation Order No. 55 by Lieut-Col. G.A. Yool, Commanding 1/4th Bn. Lincolnshire Regiment.	21/11/1916	21/11/1916
Operation(al) Order(s)	Operation Order No. 56 by Lieut-Col. G.A. Yool, Commanding 1/4th Bn. Lincolnshire Regiment.	24/11/1916	24/11/1916
Operation(al) Order(s)	Operation Order No. 57 by Lieut-Col. G.A. Yool, Commanding 1/4th Bn The Lincolnshire Regiment.	05/12/1916	05/12/1916
Operation(al) Order(s)	Operation Order No. 58 by Lieut-Col. G.A. Yool, Commanding 1/4th Battalion Lincolnshire Regiment.	10/12/1916	10/12/1916
Operation(al) Order(s)	Operation Order No. 59 By Lt. Col. G.A. Yool, Commanding 1/4th Bn. Lincolnshire Regt.	16/12/1916	16/12/1916
War Diary	Halloy	01/12/1916	05/12/1916
War Diary	Bienvillers	06/12/1916	10/12/1916
War Diary	Trenches (Fonquevillers)	11/12/1916	16/12/1916
War Diary	Souastre	17/12/1916	19/12/1916
War Diary	Trenches (Fonquevillers)	20/12/1916	24/12/1916

War Diary	Bienvillers		25/12/1916	28/12/1916
War Diary	Trenches (Fonquevillers)		29/12/1916	01/01/1917
War Diary	Souastre		02/01/1917	05/01/1917
War Diary	Trenches (Fonquevillers)		06/01/1916	09/01/1916
War Diary	Bienvillers		10/01/1917	13/01/1917
War Diary	Trenches (Fonquevillers)		14/01/1917	25/01/1917
War Diary	Bienvillers		26/01/1917	29/01/1917
War Diary	Trenches (Fonquevillers)		30/01/1917	31/01/1917
War Diary	Fonquevillers		01/02/1917	03/02/1917
War Diary	Souastre		04/02/1917	06/02/1917
War Diary	Hannescamps		07/02/1917	10/02/1917
War Diary	Bienvillers		11/02/1917	13/02/1917
War Diary	Hannescamps		14/02/1917	18/02/1917
War Diary	Souastre		19/02/1917	22/02/1917
War Diary	Hannescamps		23/02/1917	26/02/1917
War Diary	Bienvillers		27/02/1917	28/02/1917
War Diary	Fonquevillers		01/03/1917	01/03/1917
War Diary	St Amand		02/03/1917	17/03/1917
War Diary	Essarts		18/03/1917	18/03/1917
War Diary	Quesnoy Fm		19/03/1917	19/03/1917
War Diary	Douchy		19/03/1917	19/03/1917
War Diary	St Amand		20/03/1917	21/03/1917
War Diary	Bertrancourt		22/03/1917	22/03/1917
War Diary	Arqueves		23/03/1917	23/03/1917
War Diary	Mirvaux		24/03/1917	24/03/1917
War Diary	Glisy		25/03/1917	27/03/1917
War Diary	Estree Blanche		28/03/1917	31/03/1917
Operation(al) Order(s)	Operation Order No 97 by Lieut. Col. G.A. Yool, Commanding 1/4th Battalion Lincolnshire Regiment.		10/04/1917	10/04/1917
Operation(al) Order(s)	Operation Order No 99 by Lieut. Col. G.A. Yool, Commanding 1/4th Battalion Lincolnshire Regiment.		15/04/1917	15/04/1917
Operation(al) Order(s)	Operation Order No 100 by Lieut. Col. G.A. Yool, Commanding 1/4th Battalion Lincolnshire Regiment.		19/04/1917	19/04/1917
War Diary	Estree Blanche		01/04/1917	15/04/1917
War Diary	Vendin Lez Bethune		16/04/1917	19/04/1917
War Diary	Cite St Pierre		20/04/1917	28/04/1917
War Diary	Lievin		29/04/1917	30/04/1917
Operation(al) Order(s)	Operation Order No 96. by Lieut. Col. G.A. Yool, Commanding 1/4th Bn. Lincolnshire Regiment.		08/04/1917	08/04/1917
War Diary	Loos (Harts Crater)		01/05/1917	06/05/1917
War Diary	Bully Grenay		07/05/1917	11/05/1917
War Diary	Lievin		12/05/1917	25/05/1917
War Diary	Bully Grenay		26/05/1917	27/05/1917
War Diary	Bouvigny		28/05/1917	31/05/1917
Operation(al) Order(s)	Operation Order No 107 by Lieut. Col. G.A. Yool, Commanding 1/4th Bn. Lincolnshire Regiment.		01/05/1917	01/05/1917
Operation(al) Order(s)	Operation Order No 118 by Lieut. Col. G.A. Yool, Commanding 1/4th Battalion Lincolnshire Regiment.		28/05/1917	28/05/1917
War Diary			28/05/1917	28/05/1917
War Diary	Bouvigny Boyeffles		29/05/1917	06/06/1917
War Diary	Cite Des Bureaux Lievin Cite Des Riaumont.		07/06/1917	08/06/1917
War Diary	Chateau (Lievin)		09/06/1917	09/06/1917
War Diary	Aix Noulette		10/06/1917	10/06/1917
War Diary	Lievin Bn. H.Q. M22d.65.15		11/06/1917	14/06/1917
War Diary	Lievin Bn H.Q. M22b 20.w		15/06/1917	18/06/1917
War Diary	M 22b 20.10 Lievin		18/06/1917	18/06/1917

War Diary	M 22d 65.15	19/06/1917	22/06/1917
War Diary	Fosse 10	23/06/1917	27/06/1917
War Diary	Cite Des Garennes	28/06/1917	30/06/1917
Miscellaneous	Report on Operation Of 28th June-2nd July 4th. Lincs. Regt.	28/06/1917	28/06/1917
Miscellaneous	Operations of July 1st-2nd.		
Operation(al) Order(s)	1/4th Battalion Lincolnshire Regiment Order No. 123	27/06/1917	27/06/1917
Operation(al) Order(s)	Operation Order No 119 by Lieut. Col. G.A. Yool, Commanding 1/4th Battalion Lincolnshire Regiment.	06/06/1917	06/06/1917
Operation(al) Order(s)	Operation Order No. 120 by Lieut. Col. G.A. Yool, Commanding 1/4th Battalion Lincolnshire Regiment.	10/06/1917	10/06/1917
Operation(al) Order(s)	Operation Order No. 121 by Lieut. Col. G.A. Yool, Commanding 1/4th Bn Lincolnshire Regiment.	26/06/1917	26/06/1917
War Diary	Cite Des Garennes	01/07/1917	02/07/1917
War Diary	Houvelin	03/07/1917	20/07/1917
War Diary	Verquin	21/07/1917	21/07/1917
War Diary	Mazingarbe.	22/07/1917	27/07/1917
War Diary	Trenches	28/07/1917	28/07/1917
War Diary	Trenches. Loos-Hulluch Sector	01/08/1917	03/08/1917
War Diary	Trenches	28/07/1917	03/08/1917
War Diary	Fouquires	04/08/1917	15/08/1917
War Diary	Philosophe	16/08/1917	25/08/1917
War Diary	Trenches	26/08/1917	28/08/1917
War Diary	Fouquieres	29/08/1917	01/09/1917
War Diary	Trenches	03/07/1917	09/09/1917
War Diary	Philosophe	10/07/1917	10/07/1917
War Diary	Trenches (St. Elis Right Subsector)	16/07/1917	21/07/1917
War Diary	Fouquieres	22/09/1917	29/09/1917
War Diary	Trenches	30/09/1917	02/10/1917
War Diary	Philosophe	03/10/1917	14/10/1917
War Diary	Fouquieres	15/10/1917	20/10/1917
War Diary	Trenches	21/10/1917	27/10/1917
War Diary	Philosophe	28/10/1917	31/10/1917
Operation(al) Order(s)	1/4th Battalion Lincolnshire Regiment Order No. 149	20/10/1917	20/10/1917
Operation(al) Order(s)	1/4th Bn. Lincolnshire Regiment. Order No. 150	26/10/1917	26/10/1917
Operation(al) Order(s)	1/4th Battalion Lincolnshire Regiment Order No. 151	30/10/1917	30/10/1917
Miscellaneous	Raid 4th Lincolns. 5/6 11 17		
War Diary	Philosophe	01/11/1917	05/11/1917
War Diary	Trenches	06/11/1917	08/11/1917
War Diary	Fouquieres	08/11/1917	15/11/1917
War Diary	Trenches	16/11/1917	25/11/1917
War Diary	Vaudricourt	26/11/1917	30/11/1917
Operation(al) Order(s)	1/4th Bn. Lincolnshire Regiment Order No. 161	20/11/1917	20/11/1917
Map	1/4th Lincolnshire Regt. Operation Orders.		
Operation(al) Order(s)	1/4th Bn. Lincolnshire Regt. Operation Orders. No. 153	04/11/1917	04/11/1917
Operation(al) Order(s)	1/4th Battalion Lincolnshire Regiment. Order No. 152	01/11/1917	01/11/1917
Operation(al) Order(s)	1/4th Bn. Lincolnshire Regt. Order No. 155	07/11/1917	07/11/1917
Miscellaneous	Report On Raid By 1/4th Lincolnshire Regiment Immediately North Of Vermelles-Hulluch Road On Night 5th/6th November, 1917	05/11/1917	05/11/1917
Miscellaneous	Headquarters G 46th Division.	06/11/1917	06/11/1917
Miscellaneous	Quarries		
Map	Quarries (2)		
Miscellaneous	Quarries		
Miscellaneous	G.742/234		

Type	Description	Date From	Date To
Miscellaneous	Artillery Arrangements for Raid of 138th: Infantry Brigade on Night of 5th:/6th: November.		
Miscellaneous	46th Division. No. 154. G.O. 10th November, 1917	10/11/1917	10/11/1917
Miscellaneous	46th. Division. G.	07/11/1917	07/11/1917
Miscellaneous	G.C. "K" Special Company, R.E.		
Miscellaneous	Headquarters, 46th. Division.	06/11/1917	06/11/1917
Miscellaneous	Report on Raid By 1/4th Lincolnshire Regiment Immediately North Of Vermelles-Hulluch Road On Night 5th/6th November 1917	05/11/1917	05/11/1917
Map	Hulluch (2)		
Miscellaneous	137 Bde Raid. Hulluch (2)		
Map			
Miscellaneous	138th. Inf. Bde No. G. 146/7		
Operation(al) Order(s)	138th. Infantry Brigade Order No. 175/2	04/11/1917	04/11/1917
Operation(al) Order(s)	138th. Infantry Brigade Order No. 175/1	03/11/1917	03/11/1917
Miscellaneous	G.742/233		
Miscellaneous	G. 742/229		
Miscellaneous	G.742/228		
Miscellaneous	138th. Inf. Bde. No. G. 146/6	03/11/1917	03/11/1917
Operation(al) Order(s)	138th. Infantry Brigade Order No. 175	01/11/1917	01/11/1917
Operation(al) Order(s)	To accompany 138th. Infantry Brigade Order No. 175	01/11/1917	01/11/1917
Operation(al) Order(s)	46th Division Order No. 259	02/11/1917	02/11/1917
Miscellaneous	G.O.C. Force.		
Operation(al) Order(s)	K Special Company R.E. Operation Order No. 21	01/11/1917	01/11/1917
Miscellaneous	G.742/195		
Miscellaneous	G.742/192	23/10/1917	23/10/1917
Miscellaneous	Headquarters, 46th Division.	22/10/1917	22/10/1917
Miscellaneous	A Form. Messages And Signals		
Miscellaneous	C Form. Messages And Signals.		
Miscellaneous	A Form. Messages And Signals		
Miscellaneous	46th Div. G.		
Miscellaneous	Headquarters, R.A. I Corps.	15/10/1917	15/10/1917
Operation(al) Order(s)	48th Division Order No. 251	17/10/1917	17/10/1917
Miscellaneous	Headquarters, 138th Infantry Brigade. G. 742/174	15/10/1917	15/10/1917
Miscellaneous	138th. Inf. Bde. G. 146	13/10/1917	13/10/1917
Miscellaneous	Approovel		
War Diary		01/12/1917	06/01/1918
War Diary	Trenches	07/01/1918	13/01/1918
War Diary	Annequin	14/01/1918	16/01/1918
War Diary	Trenches	17/01/1918	19/01/1918
War Diary	Bethune	20/01/1918	21/01/1918
War Diary	Cantrainne	21/01/1918	23/01/1918
War Diary	Busnes	24/01/1918	30/01/1918
Operation(al) Order(s)	1/4th Battalion Lincolnshire Regiment Order No. 171		
Operation(al) Order(s)	1/4th Bn. Lincolnshire Regiment Order No. 172	12/01/1918	12/01/1918
Operation(al) Order(s)	1/4th Bn. Lincolnshire Regiment. Order No. 173	15/01/1918	15/01/1918
Operation(al) Order(s)	1/4th Battalion Lincolnshire Regiment Order No. 174	16/01/1918	16/01/1918
Operation(al) Order(s)	1/4th Battalion Lincolnshire Regiment Order No. 175	20/01/1918	20/01/1918
Operation(al) Order(s)	1/4th Battalion Lincolnshire Regiment Order No. 176	20/01/1918	20/01/1918
Operation(al) Order(s)	1/4th Battalion Lincolnshire Regiment. Order No. 177	23/01/1918	23/01/1918

(0,156,0)/256m

(0,156,0)/256m

46TH DIVISION
138TH INFY BDE

1/-4TH BN LINCOLN REGT

JAN 1916 — ~~DEC 1917~~
JAN 1918

To 39 DIV 118 BDE

No trace of ~~Dispatch~~ prior to 14 JAN

138th Inf.Bde.
46th Div.

Battn. disembarked
Havre from England
1/3.3.15.

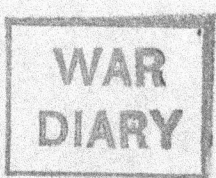

4th BATTN. THE LINCOLNSHIRE REGIMENT.

M A R C H

1 9 1 5

Attached:

Battn. Operation
Orders Nos. 1, 2, 3,
4 & 5.

WAR DIARY

4th & 8th Lincolnshire Regt.

INTELLIGENCE SUMMARY.

(Erase heading not required.)

Army Form C. 2118.

Hour, Date, Place		Summary of Events and Information	Remarks and references to Appendices
March 12th 1915.		Right half Battalion disembarked again at 10 am, went to rest camp till 3 p.m. then went into billets at TRINITY SCHOOLS and DISPENSARY HALL for the night. Left half Batt? in the RESTCAMP at HAVRE. Transport arrived HAVRE early in the morning and went to REST CAMP.	
" 2nd			
		Right half Batt? embarked on DUCHESS OF ARGYLL at 3 p.m. Sailed at 5:45 p.m. Left half Bn. in the REST CAMP at HAVRE. Two platoons entrained at 6 p.m. for CASSEL.	
" 3rd			
		Right half Batt? arrived HAVRE at 12.55 am. Disembarked at 7 am, and went to shed no 6 PONDICHERY till 3 p.m. Whole Batt? less 2 Platoons entrained at 3.30 & left HAVRE at 6.29 p.m. One horse died en route.	
" 4th			
		Arrived ARNEKE at 2.30 p.m. Detrained and marched 4 miles to ZUYTPEENE. Went into billets.	
" 5th		In billets at ZUYTPEENE.	
" 6th		In billets at ZUYTPEENE.	
" 7th		In billets at ZUYTPEENE.	
" 8th		In billets at ZUYTPEENE.	
" 9 "		Left ZUYTPEENE 9.40 am and arrived STRAZEELE at 3 p.m. Went into billets.	Operation Order No 1 attached.
" 10 "		In billets at STRAZEELE.	

Army Form C. 2118.

WAR DIARY
4 E Batt: Lancashire Regt.
INTELLIGENCE SUMMARY.

(Erase heading not required.)

Instructions regarding War Diaries and Intelligence Summaries are contained in F.S. Regs., Part II. and the Staff Manual respectively. Title pages will be prepared in manuscript.

Hour, Date, Place	Summary of Events and Information	Remarks and references to Appendices
March 11th 1915	Orders received to leave at 11.5 am. Arrived SAILLY SUR LA LYS at 9 pm. Went into billets.	Operation Order No 2 attached.
12th	In billets at SAILLY SUR LA LYS.	
13th	In billets at SAILLY SUR LA LYS.	
14th	Standing by ready to move at 2 hrs notice. Church parade.	
15th	Standing by ready to move at 2 hrs notice. In same billets.	
16th	Left SAILLY SUR LA LYS at 10.30 a.m. and marched to LE KIRLEM. Operation orders No 3 attached.	
17th	Was STEENWERCK and went into billets.	
18th	In billets at LE KIRLEM. Training in attack & defence.	
19th	9 hrs shewing bayonet fighting & musketry training.	
19th	ditto.	
20th	ditto.	
21st	ditto.	
22nd	Church parade.	
23rd	Brigade defence scheme in the afternoon.	
24th	Training in defence and attack of trenches, bomb throwing.	
25th	Brigade attack scheme in the morning. Bomb throwing and bayonet fighting in the afternoon.	
26th	Rents, merrie, bayonet fighting and bomb throwing. Left LE KIRLEM at 2.30 pm. Arrived PLOEGSTEERT at 6 pm. Went into billets. 36 coolas unable coming up at LE KIRLEM. 1 Offr + 47 men from STAFFORDSHIRE Bat attached to Batts also for instructions.	Operation Order No 4 attached.

Army Form C. 2118.

4/13th Lincolnshire Regt.

WAR DIARY
INTELLIGENCE SUMMARY.
(Erase heading not required.)

Instructions regarding War Diaries and Intelligence Summaries are contained in F. S. Regs., Part II. and the Staff Manual respectively. Title pages will be prepared in manuscript.

Hour, Date, Place	Summary of Events and Information	Remarks and references to Appendices
March 27th 1915	In billets at PLOEGSTEERT. Battalion attached to the 11th Infantry Brigade, and to the SOMERSET LIGHT INFANTRY for instruction in trench duties. 280 all ranks employed during the day at R.E works and 80 all ranks at night. One Company in the trenches for 24 hours.	One man wounded.
March 28th —	In billets at PLOEGSTEERT. 220 all ranks employed under the R.E in digging &c during the day and 80 at night. Three platoons in SOMERSET L.I. trenches & 3 with LONDON RIFLE BRIGADE for 24 hours duty in the trenches.	One man wounded.
March 29th —	In billets at PLOEGSTEERT. 280 all ranks employed under the R.E. in digging &c during the day & night. Three (3rd) platoons in SOMERSET L.I. trenches and 3 with LONDON RIFLE BRIGADE for 24 hours duty in trenches.	
March 30th —	In billets at PLOEGSTEERT. 120 all ranks employed under the R.E in digging, making wire entanglements &c. Company in the trenches about 8 p.m.	
March 31st —	Left PLOEGSTEERT at 8.50 a.m. Arrived LE KIRKEM 11.25 a.m. Outpost line billets.	Operation orders no 5 attached.

A.M.Johnson Capt. Adjt.
1/4 Bn Lincolnshire Rgt.

BATTALION OPERATION ORDERS NOS. 1, 2, 3, 4 & 5.

Operation Orders No 1.   Copy No 8
by
Lt. Col. J.W. Jessop
Commanding 1/4th Bn Lincolnshire Regiment.

Ref. 1/100,000 Sheet No 5A.   ZUYTPEENE.
                                       9. March 1915.

1. The Brigade will march to a new area.

2. The Battalion will pass the starting point — bridge over PEENE BECQUE, 200 yds NE of ZUYTPEENE at 9.30 a.m. in the following order: Signallers, Companies (B leading). ~~Machine gun Section~~.
Route: Bridge 400 yds NE of ZUYTPEENE — CASSEL — CAESTRE — STRAZEELE.

The transport will proceed by a different route & will pass the starting point (Level crossing, one mile W of BAVINCHOVE at 11.30 a.m. following in rear of the STAFFORDSHIRE BRIGADE. Route: BAVINCHOVE — QUEUE DE BAVINCHOVE LES OISEAUX — LE BREARDE — road running E from cross roads ½ m. South of LE BREARDE.

3. Detail. All stores to be loaded on wagons by 8.45 a.m.
   Water bottles to be filled before leaving.
   Fur coats will be at the Q.M. Stores at 7.30 a.m. & will be taken to new billets by bus.

4. The M. Gun will proceed with the Transport.

5. Reports to head of Battalion.

Issued at 6.30 a.m. to Company Orderly Sgts.
   Copy No 1 Bde. Hd Qrs.
    " " 2-5 O.C. Companies.
    " " 6 Transport Officer.
    " " 7 Machine gun Officer.
    " " 8 War diary.
    " " 9. Retained.

A.M. Johnson Capt & Adjt.
4th Bn Lincolnshire Regiment.

Copy No 8

Operation Orders No 2.
by
Lt. Col. J.W. Jessop.
Commanding 1/4th Bn Lincoln Regt.

Ref. 1/100,000 Sheet 5ᴬ.   STRAZEELE. ST.
                                             11. 3. 15.

1. The Brigade will march to a new billetting area.

2. The Battalion will pass the starting point Level crossing at STRAZEELE STATION at 11.45 a.m. in the following order :- Signallers, Companies C. leading, Machine Gun Section, Transport.
   Route :- Road junction 400 yds south of the Z of STRAZEELE — MERRIS — Road junction W of BLEU — road angle 200 yds S. of D of DOULIEU — R of TROU BAYARD — SAILLY SUR LA LYS

3. Detail. All stores to be loaded on wagons by 10 a.m.
   Fur-coats will be left under a small guard of 1 N.C.O + 3 men at the black shed near Railway Station.
   The G.O.C. wishes every man to have a full meal before starting.

4. Reports will be sent to the head of the Battalion.
   Issued by cyclist orderly at 9. a.m

   Copy no 1 Bde Hd Qrs.
   Copies nos 2 - 5 O.C Companies.
   Copy no 6 Transport Officer.
   —   — 7 Machine gun officer.
   —   — 8 War diary.
   —   — 9 Retained.

                                    A.B. Johnson Capt + Adjt.
                                    1/4th Bn Lincolnshire Rt.

Copy no 8.

Operation Orders No 3.
by.
Lt. Colonel J.W. Jessop.
Commanding 1/4th Bn Lincolnshire Regt.

Ref: 1/100,000 Sheet 5A.

SAILLY SUR LA LYS.
16th March 1915

1. The Brigade will move to a new area.

2. The Battalion will pass the starting point, road junction 400 yds W of the B of BAC ST MAUR at 11 a.m. in the following order: Signallers, Companies, D leading, Machine Gun Section, Transport. The Bn will follow the 4th Leicestershire Regt.
The Battalion Billetting Party consisting of Capt M STANILAND Interpreter, 2 NCOs per Coy, 2 NCOs per Hd Qrs + 5 cyclists will report to Capt Viccars at 7 a.m. at Bde Hd Qrs.

3. Detail. Attention is directed to N.M.D. War Standing Orders page 21 para 5.
All stores to be loaded up at the O.C. Int Stores at 10 a.m.

4. Reports to be sent to the head of the Battalion.

Issued by Cyclist Orderly at 7.30 a.m.
Copy No 1 Hd Qrs L.L. Bde.
"   Nos 2-5. O.C. Companies.
—   No 6 Transport Officer.
—   " 7 Machine Gun Officer.
—   " 8 War Diary.
—   " 9 Retained.

A.B. Johnson Capt + Adjt.
4th Bn Lincolnshire Rgt.

Copy No 8.

Operation Orders No 4
by
Lt. Colonel J.W. Jessop.
Commanding 1/4th Bn Lincolnshire R¹.

Reference Map. Bel & Fr. (B series) Sheet No 36
Scale 1/40,000

LE KIRLEM
26th March 1915.

1. The LINCOLN and LEICESTER Brigade (less 5th Bn LEICESTERSHIRE REGIMENT) will be attached to various Brigades of the 4th Division from the 26th to the 31st March.

2. The Battalion will be attached to the 11th Infantry Brigade and be billeted in the vicinity of PLOEGSTEER BREWERY.

3. The Battalion will pass the starting point, entrance to Transport field at 2.25 p.m. in the following order: Signallers, Companies (D leading) Machine gun Section, Transport. Route: cross roads 1000 yds South South West of STEENWERCK CHURCH — LE VEAU — T of RABOT

4. Detail. Any surplus stores not actually required during this attachment will be left at the farm near the E of LE KIRLEM. A guard will be formed over them from men of No 8 platoon.

5. Reports to head of Battalion.

Issued by cyclist Orderlies at 10 am.
  Copy No 1. Hd Qrs L & L Bde.
  — — Nos 2 - 5 O.C. Companies.
  — — 6. Transport Officer.
  — — 7. Machine Gun Officer
  — — 8. War Diary.
  — — 9. Retained.

A.B. Johnson Capt & Adjt
1/4th Bn Lincolnshire R¹.

Copy No 8.

Operation Orders No 5
by
Lt Col J.W. Jessop.
Cmmdg 1/4th Bn Lincolnshire Regt

Reference HAZEBROUCK 5A.
1:100,000.

PLOEGSTEERT BREWERY
30.3.15.

1. The Battalion will return tomorrow to its billets in LE KIRLEM and will pass the starting point, Battalion Hd Qrs, at 8.50 a.m. in the following order:- Signallers, Companies (D leading), Machine Gun Section, Transport. The measle contact cases of B Company will follow in rear of C. Company. The platoon of the 1/5th S. Staffordshire Regt will follow in rear of the Battalion and leave it at the cross roads immediately North of the R in RABOT. The two platoons of C. Company and Machine gun section will form up at the West end of the track leading to their billets and move off in their proper order as the Battalion passes. The Battalion will move off from the starting point by double platoons at intervals of 200 yards.
Route: PLOEGSTEERT cross roads — ROMARIN — T of RABOT Cross roads North of R in RABOT — STEENWERCH STATION — STEENWE[

2. The Transport Officer will be responsible that the Transport which are ready to move out of their field at 10.15 a.m. They will no move out until the Battalion has passed and will then follow in rear as usual in their proper order. He will ensure that 1 G.S. Wagon is at Battn Hd Qrs at 6 a.m. and the remainder at 7 a.m.

3. Detail. All blankets, officers' valises, surplus Company stores &c must be sent to the Q. Mrs Stores by 7.30 a.m.

4. Reports will be sent to the head of the Battalion.

Issued by Orderlies at 6.30 p.m. to:-
Copy No 1. --- Bde Hd Qr.
Copies Nos 2-5 -- O.C. Companies.
Copy No 6 --- Transport Officer.
— No 7 --- Machine gun Officer
— No 8 --- War Diary.
— No 9 --- Retained.

A.B. Johnson Capt & Adj
1/4th Bn Lincolnshire Regt

138th Inf.Bde.
46th Div.

WAR DIARY

4th BATTN. THE LINCOLNSHIRE REGIMENT.

A P R I L

1 9 1 5

Army Form C. 2118.

WAR DIARY
1/4th Battalion of Leicestershire Regt.
INTELLIGENCE SUMMARY.

(Erase heading not required.)

APRIL

Instructions regarding War Diaries and Intelligence Summaries are contained in F. S. Regs., Part II. and the Staff Manual respectively. Title pages will be prepared in manuscript.

Hour, Date, Place	Summary of Events and Information	Remarks and references to Appendices
April 1st 1915.	Battalion in billets at LE KIRLEM. Latrine Recovery.	
2nd —	In billets at LE KIRLEM. Church parade.	
3rd —	In billets at LE KIRLEM. Route march. Practice in rapid fire, bestomes.	
4th —	In billets at LE KIRLEM. Church parade.	
5th —	Battalion marched to BAILLEUL and went into billets there. Left LE KIRLEM 8.45 a.m. and arrived BAILLEUL 10.15 a.m.	
6th —	Left BAILLEUL 1.30 p.m. Senior officers all rode into town then marched by 5th LEICESTERS for 24 hours. Battalion in billets at DRANOUTRE.	
7th —	Battalion in billets at DRANOUTRE.	
8th —	Battalion in billets at DRANOUTRE.	
9th —	The Battalion left DRANOUTRE at 6.45 p.m. and relieved 5th LEICESTERS in the RIGHT SECTOR. Relief completed by 11.15 p.m. Trenches occupied as follows. 15 A.Coy. 15 S. A.Coy. 14/14S. S.P.1 & E.4. D.Coy. COOKERS C. Coy. POND & PACKHORSE B.Coy. H.Q. at FRENCHMANS.	
10th —	In the trenches. Quiet day throughout.	
11th —	In the trenches. Quiet day throughout.	
12th —	In the trenches. Quiet day throughout.	
13th —	Germans shelled FRENCHMANS and POND farms. No damage at farms. LIEUT STANILAND + 3 ptes. Killed + 6 wounded by shells at POND. Relieved by 5th LEICESTERS in the evening. Relief completed by 11.15pm. Battalion marched back to billets 3 M. N. of DRANOUTRE for rest.	

WAR DIARY
1/4th Battalion of LINCOLNSHIRE Regt.
INTELLIGENCE SUMMARY.
(Erase heading not required.)

Army Form C. 2118.

Month: APRIL

Hour, Date, Place	Summary of Events and Information	Remarks and references to Appendices
April 14th 1915.	Battalion resting in huts at DRANOUTRE.	
15th	Battalion resting in huts at DRANOUTRE.	
16th	Battalion resting in huts at DRANOUTRE.	
17th	Battalion moved off to relieve 5th LEICESTERS but receiving the order to return to billets and stand by. Operation against HILL 60.	
18th	Battalion relieved 5th LEICESTERS in the evening. Relief completed by 11.30 p.m.	
19th	In the line chos. Distribution as follows:- 14Pl.14.S.P.I.+ E.4, B Coy. - 15. 13.5, C Company. COOKERS, A Coy. COBB and PACKHORSE, D Coy. Head Qrs. at COBB farm. Drawing water at PACKHORSE.	
20th	In the line chos. Verdes at 11.15 am J.A. Or. N.M.D.	
21st	In the line chos. Lt W.B HIRST killed. Quiet day and no fire.	
22nd	German H.E. shells found our COBB and PACKHORSE shelling our battalion near LINDENHOEK road. No damage done. Relieved by 5th LEICESTERS. Battalion stored by at LINDENHOEK.	
23rd	Arrived back in billets at 5 am. Standing by all day. 14 officers + 400 men of R. Dublin Fusiliers billeted in our hut for the night.	
24th	Dublin Fusiliers left 5 am. for YPRES. Our Company (C) on fatigue laying cable between REGENT ST. and PICCADILLY.	
25th	In huts at DRANOUTRE. Quiet day.	

Army Form C. 2118.

WAR DIARY
1st 4th Battalion of LINCOLNSHIRE Regt.

INTELLIGENCE SUMMARY.
(Erase heading not required.)

APRIL

Hour, Date, Place	Summary of Events and Information	Remarks and references to Appendices
April 26th 1915.	Relieved 5th LEICESTERS in the evening. Relief completed 10.45 p.m.	
27th —	In the trenches. Distribution as follows:— Firing Line A Coy. 15.1.S. one platoon B Coy. with bombing party. 16.14.S. S.P.I + E.L. D Coy. COOKERS, 3 platoon B Coy. PACKHORSE 2 platoon C Coy. + During Jackson. COBB 2 platoon C Coy + Head Quarters.	
28th —	In the trenches. Quiet day + night.	
29th —	In the trenches. Visited by G.O.C. N.M.D. 11 am. Quiet day + night.	
30th —	In the trenches. Relieved by 5th LEICESTER Regt 11 p.m.	

A.M. Johnson Capt Adjt.
for O.C. 1st 4th Bn Lincolnshire R.

138th Inf.Bde.
46th Div.

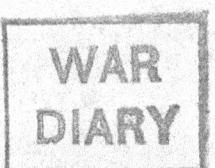

4th BATTN. THE LINCOLNSHIRE REGIMENT.

M A Y

1 9 1 5

WAR DIARY
4th Battalion Lincolnshire Regt
INTELLIGENCE SUMMARY

(Erase heading not required.)

Army Form C. 2118.

MAY

Hour, Date, Place	Summary of Events and Information	Remarks and references to Appendices
May 1st 1915.	Battalion in huts at LOCRE. Interior Economy.	
2nd —	In huts at LOCRE. A & D Coys on digging fatigue all night.	
3rd —	In huts at LOCRE. Interior Economy.	
4th —	Battalion relieved 5th LEICESTERS in evening. Relief completed 11.30 p.m.	
5th —	In the trenches. Bn. H.Q. COB FARM. Quiet day.	
6th —	In the trenches. Quiet day. Weather hot.	
7th —	In the trenches. All night whole of front was wired. Completed 2.45 a.m.	
8th —	In the trenches. Quiet day. Fire at R.E. Farm 8 p.m.	
	Relieved by 5th LEICESTERS at midnight.	
9th —	In huts at LOCRE. Lt Hall + Lt Fox rejoined from 9th LINC. Regt. Church Parade at 6 p.m.	
10th —	Left LOCRE at 7.45 p.m. & relieved 5th Bn. SHERWOOD FORESTERS at LINDENHOEK at midnight. Bn. H.Q. at LINDENHOEK CHALET. Trenches occupied as follows F4 F6 - C Coy. F5 - A Coy. G1, 2 + 6 D Coy. S, P.3 - A Coy. In reserve B Coy.	
11th —	In the trenches. Quiet day.	
12th —	In the trenches. Quiet day.	
13th —	In the trenches. Enemy shelled our front line during afternoon & early evening. At 7 p.m. they fired trench mortars (7) against G1 & 2 salient. They then directed machine guns on the breach made in our trench & shelled remainder of line. Under cover of this, they sent across a party estimated at 20 men with bombs & explosive cylinders, to G2 which were afterwards found at bottom of mine. The Bat? stood to all night & 5th LEICESTERS re-informed us with 1 Coy. 1 Sarmain (9th Batt Regt) was left dead in G1. Nothing further took place.	

1247 W 3299 200,000 (E) 8/14 J.B.C. & A. Forms/C. 2118/11.

WAR DIARY
1/4 Battalion of Lincolnshire Regt.
INTELLIGENCE SUMMARY
MAY

Army Form C. 2118.

Instructions regarding War Diaries and Intelligence Summaries are contained in F.S. Regs., Part II. and the Staff Manual respectively. Title pages will be prepared in manuscript.

(Erase heading not required.)

Hour, Date, Place	Summary of Events and Information	Remarks and references to Appendices
May 14th 1915.	In the trenches. Quiet day	
15th -	In the trenches. Enemy shelled our cross roads in morning	
16th -	In the trenches. Reprisals carried out in G trenches at 7.30 pm	
17th -	Relieved by 5th LEICESTERS at night. Completed 1 a.m. In huts at LOCRE. Zeppelin observed at 5 am moving S.E. (This probably the one which dropped bombs on RAMSGATE)	
18th -	In huts at LOCRE. A B C Coys + part of D Coy on digging fatigue.	
19th -	In huts at LOCRE. Interior economy	
20th -	In huts at LOCRE. II Corps Commander (Sir Chas Fergusson) visited us in the morning. He relieved 5/LEICESTERS at night.	
21st -	In the trenches. Distribution as follows: Ft F6-C Coy. F5.F3 Coy. G1.2.+6-A Coy. SP3 D Coy. In reserve D Coy. GOC sent for Capt Tebbs + offered him post as 2nd in command of 4/LEICESTERS which he accepted	
22nd -	In the trenches. Quiet day. Minor lightening storm at night	
23rd -	In the trenches. Enemy shelled F4 + 5 in morning - no damage done.	
24th -	In the trenches. Relieved by 5/LEICESTERS at night.	
25th -	In huts at LOCRE. Interior economy	
26th -	In huts at LOCRE. Very hot day. Interior economy	
27th -	In huts at LOCRE. B Coy on digging fatigue in morning. D Coy on same fatigue in afternoon. Very mild colors.	

Army Form C. 2118.

WAR DIARY
1/4th Battalion or LINCOLNSHIRE Regt.
INTELLIGENCE SUMMARY
MAY.

(Erase heading not required.)

Instructions regarding War Diaries and Intelligence Summaries are contained in F.S. Regs, Part II. and the Staff Manual respectively. Title pages will be prepared in manuscript.

Hour, Date, Place	Summary of Events and Information	Remarks and references to Appendices
May 28th 1915.	In huts at LOCRE. C.O, 2nd Maj. & Adjt inspected all Coys with respirators in the morning. Church parade at mid-day. The Battn relieved 5/LEICESTERS by night completed by 11.15 p.m. Distribution F4. F6. D Coy. F5. B Coy. G.1.2.+6. C Coy. S.P.10. A Coy. in reserve A Coy.	
29th —	In the trenches. Germans killed 3 children in KEMMEL square this afternoon. B Coy 7th RIFLE BRIGADE (new army) arrived at 9.15 p.m. for instructions in trench duties. Our Adjutant employed in making map of Brigade trench area.	
30th —	In the trenches. Quiet day. Great fire at YPRES visible.	
31st —	In the trenches. Zeppelin reported to N. moving N.W at 8 p.m. D Coy 7th RIFLE BRIGADE arrived 9.15 p.m & relieved their B Coy. Quiet day.	5-8-15.

A.B. Johnson Capt & Adjt
4/6 Lincolns Regt

138th Inf.Bde.
46th Div.

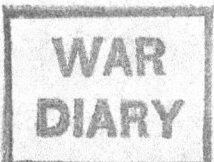

4th BATTN. THE LINCOLNSHIRE REGIMENT.

J U N E

1 9 1 5

WAR DIARY
1/4th Battalion Lincolnshire Regt.
or
INTELLIGENCE SUMMARY

JUNE 1915 Army Form C.2118.

(Erase heading not required.)

Hour, Date, Place	Summary of Events and Information	Remarks and references to Appendices
June 1st 1915	In the trenches. Officers of 2nd Rifle Brigade came round trenches. 1st C.H. Elliott killed by rifle bullet.	
2nd	In the trenches. Quiet day. Relieved by 5/Leicesters. Battn. in huts at LOCRE.	
3rd	In huts at LOCRE. Interior economy.	
4th	Battn. in huts at LOCRE. Capt. Hampson (R.C.) left for hospital & thence to England. O.E. Battn. Col. Joseph was killed by a shell at WINNEL while visiting dugouts of 5/Leicesters with Major Barrell & Major Cooper — all were officers, three were killed.	
5th	In huts at LOCRE. Col. Jessop was buried at DRANOUTRE at 3 p.m. G.O.C. Division, Staff were present.	
6th	In huts at LOCRE. Interior economy.	
7th	In huts at LOCRE. B & part of A Coy. on digging fatigue.	
8th	In huts at LOCRE. We relieved 5/Leicesters in new line. Distribution: G 1,2,6 — B Coy. G 3,4,4a — A Coy. H 1,2 — D Coy. SP 11 — D Coy. Reserve — C Coy. Bn. H.Q. at Doctor's House.	
9th	In the trenches. Major P. 5th Oxford & Bucks L.I. visited trenches.	
10th	In the trenches. A Coy. 5/Ox. & Bucks L.I. came up for instruction.	
11th	In the trenches. Our area heavily shelled during afternoon.	
12th	In the trenches. Relieved by 5/Leicesters.	
13th	In huts at LOCRE. Church Parade.	
14th	In huts at LOCRE. Interior economy. A Coy. on digging fatigue.	
15th	In huts at LOCRE. Practice move. Order received at 12 noon to be ready to move — with 1st line transport. Confirmn reported ready at 12.10 p.m. Wind Brigade all ready at 12.25 p.m. D Coy. on digging fatigue.	

Army Form C. 2118

WAR DIARY
1/4 Battalion Lincolnshire Reg¹
INTELLIGENCE SUMMARY
JUNE 1915
(Erase heading not required.)

Instructions regarding War Diaries and Intelligence Summaries are contained in F.S. Regs., Part II. and the Staff Manual respectively. Title pages will be prepared in manuscript.

Hour, Date, Place	Summary of Events and Information	Remarks and references to Appendices
June 16th 1915	Bn in huts at LOCRE. Relieved 5/Leicesters in trenches. A Coy. 10/Durham L.I. attached for instruction.	
17th	In the trenches. Distribution: G 1, 2, 6 – D Coy. + 1 Platoon D.L.I.; G 3, 4, 4a – "A Coy. + 1 Platoon D.L.I.; H 1, 2, – C Coy. + 1 Platoon D.L.I.; SP 11 – C Coy. + ½ Platoon D.L.I.; Reserve – B Coy. + ½ Platoon D.L.I.	
18th	In the trenches. A & C Coys. 10/D.L.I. attached to us. Our C & D Coys withdrawn to reserve.	
19th	In the trenches. Orders received for move to fresh area on night of 22/23. Quiet day.	
20th	In the trenches. Quiet day. Demonstration by 137th & 138th Brigades at night.	
21st	In the trenches. Battalion was relieved by the 9th D.L.I. at night.	
22nd	In huts at LOCRE. The Battn. was inspected by G.O.C. II Corps, who strongly commended the work done by the division. The Battn. left LOCRE at 9 p.m. & arrived near OUDERDOM at 11.15 p.m. & went into bivouac.	
23rd	In bivouac. A few shells burst on N. side about ½ mile away	
24th	In bivouac.	
25th	In bivouac.	
26th	In bivouac.	
27th	In bivouac. Dugouts commenced.	
28th	In bivouac. G.O.C. II Army came to Brigade H.Q. saw C.O.s at 2.0 p.m. Draft of 89 men arrived from England.	

Army Form C. 2118.

WAR DIARY
1st Battalion Lincolnshire Regt
INTELLIGENCE SUMMARY
JUNE 19/15

(Erase heading not required.)

Hour, Date, Place	Summary of Events and Information	Remarks and references to Appendices
June 29th 1915	In bivouac. G.O.C. inspected the draft. The Batln. relieved 1/Norwood Fusiliers. Distribution S/Pt A, B, C, E — A Coy.; Dugouts SANCTUARY WOOD — D. Coy., MAPLE COPSE — B & C Coys.	(Strength 16 Officers 297 N.C.O. & men)
30th —	In dugouts. Constant shelling during day. We relieved 1st Lincolns & S. Lancs at night. Distribution B4 — A Coy. B5 — C Coy. & 1 Platoon D Coy. B6 — D Coy. less 1 Platoon in support — B Coy. Brigade H.Q. were shelled in evening with gas shells.	

G J Darell Lt Col
Comdg 1/Lincoln Regt

138th Inf.Bde.
46th Div.

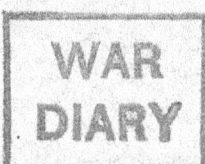

4th BATTN. THE LINCOLNSHIRE REGIMENT.

J U L Y

1 9 1 5

Army Form C. 2118.

JOC4.

WAR DIARY
1/4th Batt^n or Lincolnshire Regt.
INTELLIGENCE SUMMARY

(Erase heading not required.)

Instructions regarding War Diaries and Intelligence Summaries are contained in F. S. Regs., Part II. and the Staff Manual respectively. Title pages will be prepared in manuscript.

Hour, Date, Place	Summary of Events and Information	Remarks and references to Appendices
July 1st 1915.	Battalion in trenches E of SANCTUARY WOOD. Took over Hd.Qr. of St Lawrence Regt. Trenches occupied B4. C B8. One Coy in support in wood on 2nd line.	
July 2nd —	In trenches.	
July 3rd —	In trenches. Capt W.S. Johnson wounded.	
July 4th —	In trenches.	
July 5 th —	In trenches Relieved by 6th Bn. N. Staffordshire Regt. Relief completed 11.30 a.m.	
July 6th —	Went into bivouac near OUDERDOM.	
July 7th —	In bivouacs at OUDERDOM.	
July 8th —	In bivouac at OUDERDOM. 4 shells fired over camp, 1 man wounded.	
July 9th —	In bivouacs at OUDERDOM. 4.20 a.m. digging near KRUISSTRAAT.	
July 10th —	In bivouacs at OUDERDOM.	
July 11th —	In bivouacs at OUDERDOM. C.O. Adj. & 2 Coy Commanders went to look at our trenches th taken over on HILL 60. Trenches	
July 12th —	Battalion taken over from 1st Bedfordshire Regt. on HILL 60. Trenches 38. to 42.S. Relief completed 1.20 a.m.	
July 13th —	In the trenches.	
July 14th —	In the trenches. Shelled by whiz bangs.	
July 15th —	In the trenches. Shelled by whiz bangs.	
July 16th —	In the trenches.	
July 17th —	In the trenches. Bde. H.Q. moved from ZILLEBEKE lake to KRUISSTRAAT.	

Army Form C. 2118.

WAR DIARY
INTELLIGENCE SUMMARY
(Erase heading not required.)

Instructions regarding War Diaries and Intelligence
Summaries are contained in F. S. Regs., Part II.
and the Staff Manual respectively. Title pages
will be prepared in manuscript.

Hour, Date, Place		Summary of Events and Information	Remarks and references to Appendices
July 18th	1915.	In the trenches. Relieved by 6. S. Staffordshire Regt in trenches 38 & 41 A + by 5th Leicesters in 42. S. Relief completed midnight.	
July 19th	1915.	Battalion arrived in bivouac at GOED MOET MOULIN at 3 am.	
July 20th	—	In bivouac.	
July 21st	—	In bivouac.	
July 22nd	—	In bivouac. Battn found digging fatigue of 400 at KRUISSTRAAT.	
July 23rd	—	In bivouac. " " " 200 " "	
July 24th	—	In bivouac. Few shells near camp. Relief postponed	
July 25th	—	In bivouac. Transport moved to new ground near VLAMEATINGE. B" relieved 8th 13th Leicestershire Regt in line over 30 to A7. Relief completed 12.15 am. Company of Yorkshire Regt attached for instruction.	
July 26th	—	In the trenches. Shelling all day.	
July 27th	—	In the trenches. Company D Yorkshire Regt replaced by Coy of 7 Leicesters.	
July 28th	—	In the trenches. Sap blown up by Germans in A.1. and A.2 him. also Mortared at 9 am & 6 p.m. 2/Lt DAAPLES now dead. Two officers coming round trenches to inspect were wounded. LT CLARKE E.YORKS + LT WALKER 6th DORSETS.	
July 29th	—	In the trenches. Capt M STANILAND KILLED 4.15 pm Trench mortars on A.2. 5 pm. LT FOX killed in A.7. 9 pm. Several small mortars in 30 trench.	

1247 W 3299 200,000 (E) 8/14 J.B.C. & A.   Forms/C. 2118/11.

Army Form C. 2118.

WAR DIARY
or
INTELLIGENCE SUMMARY

(Erase heading not required.)

Instructions regarding War Diaries and Intelligence Summaries are contained in F. S. Regs., Part II. and the Staff Manual respectively. Title pages will be prepared in manuscript.

Hour, Date, Place	Summary of Events and Information	Remarks and references to Appendices
July 30th 1915.	3 am. Enemy attacked trenches near HOOGE held by 41st & 40th Bde. Demonstration against B4 & B8 held by 139 Bde, incl. heavy bombardment & flame projectors. Our trenches not going to trench mortars, rifle grenades & heavy rifle fire. 2.45. Bombardment by us followed by counter attack which only partially succeeded. 5th Leicester to MAPLE COPSE to support 139th Infantry Bde.	
July 31st 1915.	2 am. Enemy bombarded ZOUAVE Wood. One hundred drilled by Whizbangs. # Newton injured after being wounded + 271 SHERWELL joined 13th.	

Intte field.
4th Aug 1915.

A.W. Johnson Capt. 1/4/
1/4 Lincoln

1247 W 3299 200,000 (E) 8/14 J.B.C. & A. Forms/C. 2118/11.

138th Inf.Bde.
46th Div.

WAR DIARY

4th BATTN. THE LINCOLNSHIRE REGIMENT.

AUGUST

1915

WAR DIARY

INTELLIGENCE SUMMARY

1st Lincolnshire Regiment

August 1915

Army Form C. 2118

Instructions regarding War Diaries and Intelligence Summaries are contained in F.S. Regs., Part II. and the Staff Manual respectively. Title Pages will be prepared in manuscript.

(Erase heading not required.)

Place	Date	Hour	Summary of Events and Information	Remarks and references to Appendices
In Trenches	1st		In the Trenches. Quiet day. Attached Company 7th Lincolns left Trenches after course of instruction.	
	2nd		do Our Trenches heavily shelled with whiz bangs — Trench mortars over 50 r A 1. C.O. went sick.	
	3rd		do Lt-Col HULKE, OC 14th York & Lancaster Regt attached for instruction. 7pm Grand mortars over 50 Trench. Much damage done. Relieved by 5th Leicester Regt. Relief completed 12:30 am.	
ZILLEBEKE DUGOUTS & BARRACKS YPRES	4th		Battalion Headquarters, A & B Coys at ZILLEBEKE DUGOUTS, C & D Coys in Barracks YPRES.	
	5th		do Our artillery bombarding 3.30am to 4.30 am with reply from Germans. 250 men employed on RE fatigues N & S of ZILLEBEKE LAKE.	
	6th		do Similar bombardment commencing 2.30 am. Enemy reply by shelling YPRES. 250 men on fatigues.	
	7th		do do Artillery active on both sides. 200 men on fatigues.	
	8th		do do do (280 men)	
	9th		do The fatigue parties sent up during night returned in Trenches. 6th Division attacks & retakes trenches at HOOGE.	
	10th		Very heavy bombardment commences at 2:45 am. C & D Coys moved to ZILLEBEKE DUGOUTS. Barracks at YPRES damaged by 15 inch shells. The battalion left for trenches at 8:45 pm to relieve Lieutenants ELLIS & CLIXBY join the battalion.	
			5th Leicester Regt. Relief completes 11:30 pm.	
Trenches	11th		Quiet day. Lieut Brunsum WALES & WOOD joined the battalion.	
	12th		Short line Trenches shelled at 11:15 am. CAPTAIN HART wounded in front of A1 trench. Wiring party under fire. Corpl Seymour & Pte Martin G did good work carrying in two wounded men & later continued the wiring.	
	13th		Quiet day.	
	14th		Quiet day. Enemy heavy artillery active most of the day.	
	15th		Quiet until 5.30 pm when enemy shelled front line & supports with 4.2 inch Howitzers. A1 Trench badly damaged.	

WAR DIARY
1/4th Lincolnshire Regiment
INTELLIGENCE SUMMARY

Army Form C. 2118

AUGUST 1915.

(Erase heading not required.)

Instructions regarding War Diaries and Intelligence Summaries are contained in F.S. Regs., Part II. and the Staff Manual respectively. Title Pages will be prepared in manuscript.

Place	Date	Hour	Summary of Events and Information	Remarks and references to Appendices
TRENCHES	16th		Quiet until 5.30pm when Germans again shell A1 doing further damage. Relieved by 5th Leicester Regt. Relief completed 11.15 pm.	
"E" HUTS	17th		In rest camp. Interior economy. G.O.C. inspected camp.	
	18th		Brigadier General Kemp inspects camp. Interior economy.	
	19th		Interior economy. Digging fatigue of 150.	
	20th		Interior economy. Digging fatigue of 150 men.	
	21st		Interior economy. Enemy shell VLAMATINGHE in early morning. Relieve 5th Leicester Regt. Completed 11.15 pm.	
	22nd		Interior economy.	
Trenches	23rd		Considerable amount of shelling all morning. 2/Lieut L. ANDERSON rejoins battalion from R.E. 2/Lieuts GOOCH & WINCKLEY from 9th Lincolns posted.	
	24th		Quiet day.	
	25th		Quiet day.	
	26th		Quiet day. 2/Lieutenants SOWERBY, FRIPP, EDMONDSON & COCKS posted to batt'n from 3rd Lincoln Regt.	
	27th		Trench mortars in A1 & 50 at 5.15 am. Lieut REED killed. Artillery active all day.	
	28th		Quiet day. Relieved by 5th Leicester Regt. Relief completed 11.15 pm.	
EMBANKMENT DUGOUTS	29th		Interior economy. Working parties by day and night.	
	30th		do.	do. CAPTAIN GRAY rejoined from hospital
	31st		do.	do.

T. E. Sowken Major
Commanding 1/4 Lincoln Regt.

138th Inf.Bde.
46th Div.

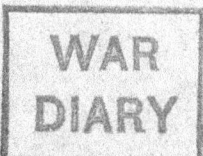

4th BATTN. THE LINCOLNSHIRE REGIMENT.

S E P T E M B E R

1 9 1 5

Army Form C. 2118

WAR DIARY
of 1/4 June 1915 [unclear]

INTELLIGENCE SUMMARY

(Erase heading not required.)

Instructions regarding War Diaries and Intelligence Summaries are contained in F.S. Regs., Part II. and the Staff Manual respectively. Title Pages will be prepared in manuscript.

Place	Date	Hour	Summary of Events and Information	Remarks and references to Appendices
EMBANKMENT & SCOUTS	Sept 1/15		Quiet day. Working parties in ARMAGH WOOD & SQUARE WOOD during day.	
TRENCHES		2:00	Quiet up to 4 pm when enemy started to bombard our trenches & mostly shelled the EMBANKMENT dugouts for 2 hours causing casualties 7 killed & 5 wounded. Lay in barrage at 8:30 am & relieved by Leicester Regt. Relief completed 12:30 am.	
TRENCHES 49, 50, A1 & 3		3:00	[unclear] at 2:15 pm heavily shelled all along the line well behind the front line & enemy air observed for 4 hours. Artillery counter support asked for & good results. 8 seigy [siege?] casualties - 2/Lt EDMONDSON wounded.	
		4:15	Bombardment over the Brigade on our left.	
		5:00	Sudden enemy bombardment over HOOGE lasting 20 minutes. As usual.	
			3rd Division gun-fired at HOOGE 4:30 am & 5:30 am and from 12-1 pm. Enemy aeroplane brought down enemy lines. Men too hungry for these days.	
		6:00	Quiet day. 82 Reinforcements arrive.	
		7:00	Quiet day. Wire put out in front of 50 trench.	
		8:00	Trenches 50 & 49 shelled at noon a considerable damage done. Relieved by 5 Leicester Regt at 10:30 pm.	
		9:00	Inspection by General Plumer & Army at 2:30 pm.	
		10:00	Lt Col Heathcote C.E. Yorkshire Light Infantry takes over the command of the Battalion	
		11:00	150 men required for working parties.	
		12:00	290 " " " "	
		13:00	Church Parade 11:30 am. Inspection by Coy Commanders followed by drill.	

1875 Wt. W593/826 1,000,000 4/15 J.B.C. & A. A.D.S.S./Forms/C. 2118.

WAR DIARY or INTELLIGENCE SUMMARY

Army Form C. 2118

Place	Date	Hour	Summary of Events and Information	Remarks and references to Appendices
Trenches	Apr 14		Inspection before Companies & in hour arose. Left for trenches at 5.30 pm to steer 1/5 Leicester R. of 2nd Leicester R. 10-10 pm. Companies occupied trenches as follows. D Coy right + A Coy. A1 + 3. C Coy A1 + 3. Our casualty (man) during relief B Coy 50. B Coy A1 + on platoon in R.R. Coy hdqtrs in Support.	
In Trenches sq 5. 20. A1. 2. 3	15th		Quiet morning. Left crawling ripped from hospital + took over duties of acting adjutant. Trenches heavily bombarded at 5.30 pm, resulting in several casualties viz 2 killed + 8 Oths + 1 NCO. Trenches not much damaged. CO hay Coy & Adjutant during the day. Capt Anstiss assumes command of D Company.	
	16		Very quiet day. Major Price Davies VC DSO (Divisional Staff) visited trenches. CO hay Coy – + Adjutant + in the trenches. Casualties 1 killed, 3 wounded.	
	17th		Our artillery bombarded German trenches opposite 49, 50 + A1, which was chased for the purpose. Bombardment from 11 AM – 11.20 AM then from 11.35 AM – 11.45 AM. It apparently took the enemy unaware as enemy retaliated by heavily bombarding Matin trenches on flanks, co-operated with rifle fire. Enemy retaliation especially at 75 French all ground immediately in rear of trenches. Right sector bombardment commenced 5 pm + finished at 6.30 pm. Casualties very slight. Quiet night. Trenches visited by CO hay Coy + Adjutant.	
	18th		Normal day throughout. Brigadier General Kemp & Hay Tarks RE visited Headquarters about 4pm. After whizzbangs car 49 + 50 trenches were shelled throwing morning caused heavy casualties viz 2 killed 11 wounded. Trenches visited by CO hay Coy + Adjutant.	
	19th		Quiet day. Brigadier General. Brigade Major, + Hay Tarks RE called at HQ at 1pm. + visited trenches with CO during afternoon. Casualties nil. Trenches visited by CO hay Coy + Adjutant.	
	20th		Quiet day. Trenches visited by CO + hay Coy. Relieved by 5th Lincs R. relief being completed at 10.10 pm. Companies proceeded as follows. A Coy + D Coy to KNUSTRAFF DUGOUTS + B Coy to RAILWAY EMBANKMENT DUGOUTS. C Coy to DEEPINE DUGOUTS. Hay Coy + HQ + B Coy. No casualties.	
Brigade Reserve	21st		Hostile arty activity on both sides. Our artillery concentrating heavy fire. Chilly morning. Parties of 2 officers + 50 men found during afternoon 2 officers + 70 men at night. No casualties.	

WAR DIARY
or
INTELLIGENCE SUMMARY

Army Form C. 2118

(Erase heading not required.)

Instructions regarding War Diaries and Intelligence Summaries are contained in F. S. Regs., Part II and the Staff Manual respectively. Title Pages will be prepared in manuscript.

Place	Date	Hour	Summary of Events and Information	Remarks and references to Appendices
Brigade Reserve.	Sept 22nd		Quiet morning. Our artillery bombarded Enemy's lines between 3+5 pm. Enemy replied by bombarding our lines & ground in rear (6-7 pm.) Working parties 2 Off 100 men during day. 2 Off 70 men at night.	
	23rd		Quiet morning. Brigadier General, Kings. + Brigade Major called at H.Q. 9.45 AM. C.O. visited KRUISTRAAT DUGOUTS 10.30 AM. Maj. Cooper + Lt Anderson proceeded on 7 days leave. Working parties. 2 Off 100 men during day. 2 Off 70 men at night.	
	24th		Bombardment intermittently throughout the day by our artillery. Enemy replied between 5 + 6 pm. Several shells dropping near RAILWAY DUGOUTS which necessitated the moving of occupants further up the line. No casualties. At 7 pm. B. Coy under Capt Hart proceeded to a position indicated by Brigade near BELLEWARDE FARM. & dug themselves in as a precaution against artillery fire, the RAILWAY DUGOUTS not being considered safe during a bombardment.	
	25th		Very heavy British artillery bombardment over Hooge commencing at 3.50 AM followed by an infantry attack by 3rd Division. Enemy shelled round the vicinity of during the afternoon. Our enemy's artillery returned with his company at 5.30 RAILWAY DUGOUTS. Capt Hart returned with his company at 5.30 pm. having had no casualties. The Battalion left the Dugouts & relieved the	
In the Trenches	26th		Quiet morning afternoon. At 7 pm. 5th Leicester Regt. in the left sector. Relief completed 9.50 pm. At 10.15 pm. heavy rifle + artillery fire in direction of SANCTUARY WOOD, lasting about ¾ of an hour. Lieut Bryman (MO) reported from Hospital. Companies took over same trenches as on 14th inst.	

Army Form C. 2118

WAR DIARY
or
INTELLIGENCE SUMMARY
(Erase heading not required.)

Instructions regarding War Diaries and Intelligence Summaries are contained in F.S. Regs., Part II. and the Staff Manual respectively. Title Pages will be prepared in manuscript.

Place	Date	Hour	Summary of Events and Information	Remarks and references to Appendices
In the Trenches 4/22 A1 + 3 R1	Sept	27	Very quiet day. Lieut Challoner joined the Battalion from base, & was temporarily attached to E. Coy. Trenches visited by C.O. + Adjt.	
		28	Very quiet day. Brig. General Kemp visited trenches at noon. Trenches visited by C/O + Adjt. All time stopped any further Cpt. Burrows & Patterson readm.	
		29	Quiet morning. Very wet round the night. Trenches visited by C.O. + Adjt. 6.30 p.m. heavy bombardment	
		30	Quiet morning. Artillery active during afternoon on our left + right. Also severe shortbanging over 4/5o. A1. A2. Casualties. 1 killed 9 wounded including 2 Lt. Sowerby. About this time a mine was exploded in right sector, apparently near 47 Trench. C.O. + Adjt visited trenches. Showery day. Trenches in a very wet condition.	

C Beauchat
B. Col.
Commanding 1/4 Lincolns

K Humbers
Capt + Adjt/Adj
1/4 Lincoln Regt

138th Inf.Bde.
46th Div.

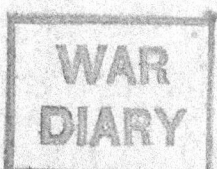

4th BATTN. THE LINCOLNSHIRE REGIMENT.

O C T O B E R

1 9 1 5

Attached:

Appendices.

Army Form C. 2118

1/4th Lincolnshire Regt
WAR DIARY
or
INTELLIGENCE SUMMARY
(Erase heading not required.)

October 1915

46 Div — 138

6.E.

Place	Date	Hour	Summary of Events and Information	Remarks and references to Appendices
In the field	Oct 1st		Quiet day. Officers of Royal Irish Rifles arrived at 11 A.M. to look over trenches. R.I.R's relieved battalion in evening; relief being completed midnight. Their M.Guns + M.Gun section did not arrive until 2 A.M. next morning, having lost their way. The Battalion returned to DICKEBUSCH HUTS when relieved.	
Dickebusch Huts	2nd		The Battalion left the Huts at 1.30 p.m. + marched to ABEELE Station arriving there at 5.30. Entrained at 5.55 + arrived FOUQUIERES near BETHUNE at 8.45 p.m. where we detrained. We then marched to BUSNETTES about 6 miles west of BETHUNE, + billeted there in barns. Only 4 men fell out during the day. The Transport set off from OUDERDOM at 2 p.m. + came by road. The machine gun limbers went by train. The Division is now attached to XI Corps. (1st Army)	
Busnettes	3rd		A fine day. Companies under company arrangements in the afternoon. C.O. + Adjt went to Brigade Headquarters at GONNEHEM at 2.30 p.m. to meet the G.O.C. The Army Commander General Sir Douglas Haig arrived during conference + spent about 2 hr at Brigade H.Q.	
"	4th		Companies under company arrangements 9–11 A.M. Route March (5 miles) in afternoon. C.O. Maj Cooper, Adjt Coy Officers + M.Gun Officer also staff officers of 5th Lincolns by motor lorry from GONNEHEM to RAILWAY CROSSING S. of VERMELLES, + walked from there to German 1st + 2nd Line to Lost round + returned at 5.30 p.m. Position visited was just N.W. of LOOS. The trenches were very much knocked about + were very chalky. Billeting party left at 4 p.m. from BUSNETTES + proceeded to HESDIGNEUL to look out for new billets.	

Army Form C. 2118

WAR DIARY
or
INTELLIGENCE SUMMARY
(Erase heading not required.)

Instructions regarding War Diaries and Intelligence Summaries are contained in F.S. Regs., Part II and the Staff Manual respectively. Title Pages will be prepared in manuscript.

Place	Date	Hour	Summary of Events and Information	Remarks and references to Appendices
BUSNETTES	Oct 6.		Battalion boarded at 8 A.M. & marched to HESDIGEUL via CHOQUES The Transport was late in starting & came on afterwards. Battalion arrived HESDIGEUL at 11.15 A.M. went into billets in the village.	
HESDIGEUL		7.	Companies under company arrangements in the morning. "A" Company undergoing instruction in bombing. Route march 8.5 miles in afternoon.	
		8.	Bombing instruction for B. C. & D Coys in morning. Route march in afternoon. The C.O. Maj Cosper, Adjt & Coy Commanders & The Gun Officer set out in a motor lorry with other officers of the Brigade at 8 A.M. for VERMELLES. The French held by the Guards division were inspected, also the ground in the front including the HOHENZOLLERN REDOUT. C.O. + Adjutant conference at Brigade H.Q. at 5.30 p.m.	
		9.	Continuation of bombing instruction. C.O. + Adjt & Divisional conference at 9 A.M. also conference at Brigade H.Q. at 6 p.m. Battalions visited trenches before breakfast at	
		10.	Companies visited most of HOHENZOLLERN REDOUT Senior N.C.O.'s P.M.O. Divine service at 10 A.M. followed by communion. visited trenches.	
		11.	Continuation of bombing instruction. At 5.30 pm C.O. Maj Cosper Adjt & company commanders attended at Div H.Q. to meet the 11th Corps commander Gen Haking.	

WAR DIARY
INTELLIGENCE SUMMARY
(Erase heading not required.)

Army Form C. 2118

Place	Date	Hour	Summary of Events and Information	Remarks and references to Appendices
HESDIGEUL	12 Oct		Companies paraded in fighting order for inspection by Coy Officers. At 3 pm the Battn joined the 5th Leicesters & marched to a field 500 yds S.E. of "SAILLY LABOURSE" via VAUDRICOURT & LABOURSE, arriving 6 pm. Here the battn had tea, collected rations for the 13th, also 6 sandbags per man & 100 extra rounds ammunition. At 7.10 the Battn moved to VERMELLES & collected bomb shovels &c, hence proceeding to the trenches opposite the HOHENZOLLERN REDOUT. Relief completed 2 am. Relieved the 2nd Coldstream Guards, in 2nd line trenches.	
	13		Our artillery bombarded HOHENZOLLERN REDOUT & trenches in rear from 12 noon to 2 pm. At 2 pm the battalion left the trenches in support to 5" Lincs & 4 Leic. * crossed over the front line trenches & went forward to the REDOUT in four lines. ½ A & B 1st line, remainder ½ A & B 2nd line, ½ C & D 3rd line, remainder of C & D fourth line. The H.Q. party including Bombers & M/Gun section followed the 4th line. Redout taken but at heavy cost. Incessant bombing machine gun & rifle fire all evening, also shelling. Gas & smoke was used to cover advance, but apparently with little damage to enemy. Maj Cooper wounded 12.50 pm by shrapnel (both arms broken). Total casualties 10 Officers - Killed 2nd Lts Anderson, Chisby, Brunnm, Halis - wounded. - Capt Hart. Capt Johnson 2nd Lt Johnson, Lt Winkley. Missing. Capt Gray, Lt Fripp & Lt Wood. and 385 other ranks K.W. & Missing.	See OPERATION ORDERS No. 14
	14		Battn withdrawn from Redout & relieved by Notts & Derby's. Battn reformed in original 2nd line trench 215 O.R. with the C.O. Adjt & 2 Lt Challenor. 2nd Lt Gooch arrived later. Shelled in trenches all afternoon. Battn relieved in 2nd line by 5th Notts & Derbys at 9.30 pm. & Battn went to LANCASHIRE trenches near VERMELLES. (Capt W.J. Johnson reported "Died of wounds" the railway line. This is behind	

Pink cards in recognition of services performed were
presented by the G.O.C. 46th Division, Maj. Gen. the Hon. E.J.
Montagu-Stuart-Wortley C.B., C.M.G., M.V.O., D.S.O., to the f
following W.Os., N.C.Os. and men of this battalion in recognition
of acts of gallantry performed in the field on the 13th.
It was stated on the cards that their conduct had been brought
to the notice of higher authority :
2385 L/Cpl G.W.Shaw.   141 Sgt. O.W.Bannister.
2849 L/Cpl W.F.Lilley.   1974 Rgt.Sgt.Maj. F.Shpherd.
 951 Sgt. J. Lickorish.   10151696 C.S.Maj. A.Peasgood.
1784 Pte F. Hibbs.   984 Sgt. S. Smith.
 390 Cpl. C.W.Jackson   2322 Sgt. C.H.Masters.

White cards were received by the following :

2367 Pte F. Gilliat.   2295 Cpl A. Vickers.

The G.O.C. 46th Div. noted that these men had performed acts of gallantry and read the report with much pleasure.

WAR DIARY or INTELLIGENCE SUMMARY

Army Form C. 2118

Place	Date	Hour	Summary of Events and Information	Remarks and references to Appendices
RESERVE TRENCHES.	Oct. 15	10/15	2 Lt Brewster Hales buried in VERMELLES CEMETERY. Battn returned to HESDIGNEUL by motor lorry at 12 noon. Draft of 39 O.R. arrived.	
HESDIGNEUL	16		Draft of 14 from No 2 Entrenching Battn arrived, also draft rejoined men 59 O.R. arrived from ROUEN. Companies paraded at 11 A.M. for purpose of collecting information about wounded & missing in recent attack.	
	17		The Corps Commander, General Haking inspected the Battn, the new draft forming up separately. Divine service 11.30 am. C O's at Coy Comdrs disposal in afternoon.	
	18	9.30 am.	C.O's parade. Coys at Coy Comdrs. disposal in afternoon.	
	19	9.30 am.	C O's parade. Battn route marches (6 miles) in afternoon.	
	20	9.30 am.	C O's parade " " " (9 ") "	
	21	9.30 am.	C O's parade " " " (7 ") "	
	22	9.30 am.	C O's parade " " " (6 ") "	
			Lecture for Officers & Senior NCO's by an Officer of the Royal Flying Corps at 6.30 p.m. Lt Ellis rejoined from Hospital.	
	23	9.30 am	C O's parade. Coys at Coy Officers disposal in afternoon. 2 O's Crabtree & Crosden joined from 3/4 Kin arms.	
	24		Divine service for Brigade at 11 A.M. After service G.O.C. presented cards for gallant conduct in the field to 10 NCO's men in the battalion.	
	25		Very wet day; company inspections & lectures.	

WAR DIARY
or
INTELLIGENCE SUMMARY
(Erase heading not required.)

Army Form C. 2118

Place	Date	Hour	Summary of Events and Information	Remarks and references to Appendices
HESDIGNEUL	26 Oct 1915	9.30–11 A.M. 3 P.M.	C.O's parade. The Battalion marched to VERQUIN & took over billets from 6th Buffs at the Brasserie. The Battn. is now in Corps Support.	
VERQUIN	27th	9 A.M. 9.30 11 A.M. 12.45 P.M. 5.20 P.M.	Coy Officers inspections. Battn inspection. H.M. the King's inspection. The Battn 250 strong took part in Divisional practice near HESDIGNEUL, forming one company of a composite Battalion, arrived back in billets.	
	28th	7.30 A.M. 8.30 9.50 A.M. 11 A.M. 1 P.M.	The Composite Company paraded at 7.30 a.m. & joined up with the remainder of the composite Battn. at 8.30, arriving at Divisional parade ground 9.50 A.M. H.M. KING GEORGE V Inspected a composite Brigade of the Division. Returned to billets 1 P.M. Wet day. The King was crushed by his horse rolling on him shortly after inspecting the composite Brigade of 46th Div.	
	29th	7 A.M. 9 A.M. 9.30 A.M. 2 P.M.	Sgt Maj's Parade for Sergts. Coy Commanders inspection. Adjts parade. Coy route march.	
	30 31st		Same as 29th. Divine Service followed by Holy Communion. Information received from C.O.'s Staff Guards that the body of Capt. C.S. Gray had been found buried. After the service the Brig. Gen. informed all present that the following members of this Battn. had been awarded "Distinguished Conduct Medals" for conspicuous bravery in the field on Oct 13th. 10.10.15. C.S.M. Rasgood A; No 390 Cpl. Jackson E.W; No 1784 Pte. Hibbs F. The Battn received 3 medals out of 9 allotted to the Division.	

.... Lieut. Col. K.O.Y.L.
Commanding 1/4th Bn. Lincolnshire Regt.

APPENDICES.

SECRET.   *War Diary*   Copy No. 2

OPERATION ORDER No. 14
by
BRIG-GENL. G. C. KEMP.
Commanding 138th Infantry Brigade.

Headquarters,
11/10/15.

Map Reference Trench Maps 1/10,000 & 1/5000.

1. The 11th Corps is to attack and capture the QUARRIES and FOSSE No. 8, in order to establish the left flank of the 1st Army and render a further advance in conjunction with the French possible.
   The line to be established is G.12.d.39 - G.12.b.82 - G.6.c.82 and 45 - G.6.a.42 - A.29.d.25 - N.W. corner of Corons de MARON - A.29.c.16 - A.28.d.49 and along AUCHY-LEZ-LA-BASSEE-VERMELLES road to our present front trench A.28.c.33.
   The task of the 12th Division is to capture the Quarries and establish the above line as far north as the track at G.5.b.68. The task of the 46th Division is to capture the HOHENZOLLERN redoubt and FOSSE No. 8 and establish the above line from the track G.5.b.68 to our front trench at A.28.c.33.
   The attack will take place on the 13th inst. The Infantry will assault at 2 p.m. Watches will be synchronized under Divisional arrangements on the morning of the 13th instant.

2. The 46th Division will attack with the 137th Brigade on Right and 138th Brigade on Left.

3. The following will be attached to the 138th Infantry Brigade for this attack :- 1st Battalion Monmouth Regiment.
   125 Grenadiers from 139th Infantry Brigade.
   2 Sections Divisional Cyclist Company.
   1/1st Field Company R.E.
   1 Battalion 139th Infantry Brigade will be at the disposal of G.O.C. 138th Infantry Brigade.

4. ARTILLERY F.O.O.
   F.O. Officers will accompany the Battalion Commanders of assaulting columns as under :-
   F.O.O. 3rd Brigade R.F.A. with 4th Leicester Regiment.
   F.O.O. 146th Brigade R.F.A. with 5th Lincoln Regiment.
   F.O.O. 36th Brigade R.F.A. will be with Brigade H.Qrs.

5. ARTILLERY ACTION.
   During the attack the Artillery will co-operate as follows :-
   (a) The Heavy Artillery bombardment is now in progress, and is being directed against the enemy's guns, machine gun emplacements, observation stations, trenches (both front line and in rear) and strong points such as the PENTAGON in A.29.c.53 and the houses in A.28.d.28.
   (b) There will be an artillery bombardment of the position to be assaulted by every available gun in the Corps commencing at 12 noon on the day of the attack. This bombardment will last two hours. From 1 to 1-50 gas and smoke will be employed, the smoke being continued to 2.0, at which hour the Infantry assault will commence. The Heavy Artillery from 1 to 1-10 will bombard the CORONS DE PEKIN, CORONS DE MARON, PENTAGON REDOUBT, and the N.E. end of the Dump, and for the remainder of the smoke and gas period will devote its attention to counter battery work and to bombarding the enemy's approaches and communication trenches and the likely positions of his reserves. During the assault the Divisional Artillery will form a barrage from about A.30.c.72 along PEKIN and CEMETERY ALLEYS to MAD ALLEY and MAD POINT, the Heavy Artillery assisting on the CEMETERY, LONE FARM and the houses near MAD POINT. This barrage will continue from 2 to 4-0, after which fire

will be lifted from MAD POINT and the houses near it to the trench A.28.c.46 - A.28.b.17, and a slower rate of fire maintained throughout the night.

- 2 -

6. The INFANTRY ATTACK.
The dividing line between the attacks delivered by the 137th and 138th Infantry Brigades will be G.4.b.60 - right edge of village E. of CORONS ALLEY - PENTAGON REDOUBT A.29.c.55. (latter to right attack).

(a) Right attack. (137th Infantry Brigade.)
The 137th Brigade from the old British front trench between G.10.b.98 and G.4.d.26 and assembly trenches in rear will assault at 2 p.m. with their left directed on the N.W. corner of the DUMP.

1st Objective. Track crossing FOSSE ALLEY at G.5.b.66 - G.5.b.39 and A.29.d.22 to PENTAGON REDOUBT at A.29.c.53 (inclusive).

2nd Objective. A.29.d.25 - 3 Cabarets - N.E. edge of CORON DE PEKIN - W. edge of CORON DE MARON - railway A.29.c.18 (exclusive).

7. Left Attack. (138th Infantry Brigade.)
The 138th Infantry Brigade from our front line trench between G.4.d.26 and G.4.a.72 and assembly trenches in rear will assault at 2-0 p.m with right directed on the N.W. corner of the DUMP.

(a) Disposition of Brigade prior to attack.
Front Line.   4th LEICESTER REGIMENT on RIGHT in Section trenches A.2 and A.3, with one Platoon in A.1.
              5th LINCOLN REGIMENT on LEFT in trenches A.4, A.5 and 1 platoon in A.6.
Support.   4th LINCOLN REGIMENT in trenches A.2s, A.3s, A.4s and A.5s.
              1st MONMOUTH REGIMENT in 3rd Line trenches.
Brigade   5th LEICESTER REGIMENT will be in Brigade
 Reserve.   Reserve disposed in 4th Line trench running from BOYAU K in G.4.c.81 to Left BOYAU in G.3.b.91, omitting portion of this trench between HAYWARDS HEATH and BARTS ALLEY. Machine Gun Section 5th Leicester Regiment will be in occupation of Machine Gun Positions in front line trenches.
              One Battalion of 139th Infantry Brigade allotted to 138th Infantry Brigade will be in RAILWAY RESERVE trenches, omitting BOMB ALLEY.

(b) Assault.
(1) 1st Objective. PENTAGON REDOUBT A.29.c.53 (exclusive) A.29.c.16 - A.28.d.65 and 45 - First of "L" of LITTLE WILLIE to our front trench at A.28.c.51.

(2) The 4th LEICESTER REGIMENT will assault on the RIGHT and the 5th LINCOLN REGIMENT on the LEFT, the line of demarcation between attacks being G.4.b.33 CORONS ALLEY, this latter (inclusive) 4th LEICESTER REGIMENT. This assault will pass straight over the HOHENZOLLERN REDOUBT without pause, and proceed without check to secure the above first objective.
The assaulting line will issue from the trenches under cover of gas and smoke (if favourable wind permits of use) at 1-50 p.m and will advance as far as our Artillery fire will permit them. Approximate distance between lines 50 yards. At 2-0 p.m the Artillery will raise and the attack spring forward.
4th LINCOLN REGIMENT will be in Support and at commencement of assault will follow one hundred ~~and fifty~~ yards in rear of last line of front line attack.
4th LINCOLN REGIMENT will clear by Bombing all trenches passed over by front line attack.

(3) The 1st Battalion MONMOUTH REGIMENT will follow in rear of 4th LINCOLN REGIMENT and will occupy the HOHENZOLLERN REDOUBT and organise it at once as a strong Supporting Point for all-round defence, connecting the Redoubt to our present front line by BIG WILLIE and the trench running through the first E in HOHENZOLLERN (Map 1/5000)

(4) Immediately the troops in front are clear of the trenches the O.C. 5th LEICESTER REGIMENT will move up his Battalion and garrison the front and support line trenches thus vacated. This Battalion, being in Brigade Reserve, must be held in a state of constant readiness to move forward in formed parties on receipt of orders from Brigade. Two Companies should therefore be kept concentrated in the Support Line. The Machine Guns of this Battalion may also be sent forward if required. Except in the event of a complete breakdown of rapid communication with the Brigade Headquarters no part of this Battalion will be moved forward without orders from the Brigade

(5) <u>Bombing Parties.</u> The 4th LEICESTER REGIMENT will send Bombing parties along
   i   Trench running North from A.29.c.16
   ii Trench running N.E. towards A.29.c.69

The 8th LINCOLN REGIMENT will send Bombing Parties along
   i   LITTLE WILLIE
   ii FOSSE TRENCH
   iii Trench running N.W. through A.28.d.63
   iv Trench running to A.28.d.49.

The 1st MONMOUTH REGIMENT will send Bombing parties along
   i   Trench through the first "E" of HOHENZOLLERN
Composition and other details concerning these Bombing Parties and issue of Bombs are given in Appendix A herewith.

(6) The 1st Corps will co-operate with long range rifle and machine gun fire on the Left flank of our attack and will send a bombing party along trench from A.28.c.81 towards LITTLE WILLIE.

(c) Further progress of the attack.
(1) 2nd Objective. Railway A.29.c.16(inclusive) A.28.d.49 - MAD POINT - Front trench at A.28.c.33.
(2) If possible both assaults will be pressed straight through to 2nd objective, which will be immediately consolidated. If the assault is checked at the first objective immediate measures will be taken to consolidate the position won and a further attack will be organized against the 2nd objective, which in its turn will be consolidated as soon as secured, in order to obtain two good strong lines of defence. The first essentials of consolidation are wire along the front and the establishment of a fire trench. Machine guns must be brought up as quickly as possible to points whence their fire will cover the front and flanks during consolidation. A smoke curtain will be established to cover the work of consolidation. Instructions are attached - Appendix "B".
(3) The inevitable confusion and inter-mixture of Units consequent on the assault render it impossible to define the frontages of Units when occupying the second objective, but as far as possible the Battalions of the first line, that is the 4th LEICESTERS and 8th LINCOLNS will make good the Railway line from Point A.29.c.16 up to, and including, the house at A.28.b.41 and the 4th LINCOLN REGIMENT will make good the remainder of the second objective.

The O.C. 4th LINCOLNS will understand that his primary object is to support the front line in securing the first objective. Additional troops will if necessary be sent from Brigade Reserve to assist in securing the left of the second objective.

8. **Machine Guns.**
(a) 4th LEICESTER REGIMENT and 5th LINCOLN REGIMENT will each retain and take forward with them during the assault three Machine Guns. Their fourth gun will be handed over to Brigade Machine Gun Officer under arrangements to be made by him, and will be in Brigade Reserve.
(b) 4th LINCOLN REGIMENT will retain and take forward two Machine Guns, the remaining two being handed over to Brigade Machine Gun Officer under arrangements to be made by him and retained in Brigade Reserve.
(c) 5th LEICESTER REGIMENT will establish their four Machine Guns in front line trenches during daylight of 15th instant 12th relieving Guns of the 2nd Brigade of Guards there at present.
(d) 1st Battalion MONMOUTH REGIMENT will take forward with them four Machine Guns and dispose them in positions for defence of HOHENZOLLERN REDOUBT.
(e) Especial care is to be taken by all Battalions to sight the Machine Guns in trenches that are being consolidated so as to bring cross fire on any probable line of counter-attack.

9. **Bombing Parties, and trench blocking parties.**
Bombing parties are to be made up as follows :-
  2 Bayonet men.
  4 Bombers carrying 15 Grenades each.
  15 Carriers, 12 of whom carry 15 Grenades each.

Each Party of Bombers will be accompanied by a trench blocking party consisting of six men carrying three picks and nine shovels. This party, together with the Carriers, will, at points indicated by Battalion Commanders, block all enemy communication trenches for a distance of not less than 50 yards, cutting a " T " at the near side. The Tool Carriers will then garrison these " Ts ".

10. **Supply of Bombs during the attack.**
Lieut. Raikes, Monmouth Regiment, will act as Brigade Bomb Officer and arrange for the supply of Bombs to the front trenches, under the supervision of the O.C. 1st Monmouth Regt. The 125 Grenadiers of the 139th Infantry Brigade will be attached to the Monmouth Regiment as Bomb Carriers. These Carriers will be dribbled forward to supply the Bombing parties whose positions will be indicated by Red Flags. These Carriers, after delivering their bombs, will join the nearest Infantry Regiment.

11. **1/1st Field Company R.E..**
One Section will be attached to 4th LEICESTER and one to the 5th LINCOLNS. These Sections will follow Battalions to assist in consolidating positions gained, and putting out wire. A Party of 20 N.C.O's and men for carrying wire will accompany each section. These carrying parties will be detailed by O.C. 5th LEICESTERS.

12. **Tools.**
All Infantry will carry one tool for every four men in the proportion of one pick to three shovels. These tools will be issued at VERMELLES.

O.C. 1st Monmouth Regiment will take up such tools as he considers necessary

- 5 -

13. **Distinguishing Flags.**
Infantry will carry 3' square screens divided diagonally into red and yellow, to mark the position of the firing line.
Bombing parties will mark their positions in captured trenches by Red Flags 10 inches square.

14. **Allotment of Communication Trenches.**
Main Communication trenches are allotted as follows :-
    (a) IN.
        137th Brigade.
        GORDON ALLEY to junction with HULLUCH ALLEY - HULLUCH ALLEY, to G.10.b.89 and thence to G.5.c.57.
        138th Brigade.
        BOMB ALLEY and LEFT BOYAU.

    (b) OUT.
        Both Brigades.
        CENTRAL BOYAU and CENTRAL TRENCH.

    (c) Evacuation of wounded.
        (1) HAYWARDS HEATH AND BARTS ALLEY (Stretcher and walking cases).
        (ii) CENTRAL BOYAU and CENTRAL TRENCH (walking cases only).

    After capture of the enemy's position, SLAG ALLEY, N.FACE and CORONS ALLEY will, as far as possible, be reserved for IN traffic and S. FACE and the trenches between the DUMP and the village for OUT traffic.

15. Troops will carry greatcoats and waterproof sheets in the attack, but not packs.
    All men in the front trenches must have their smoke helmets on before the gas cylinders are opened at 1 p.m.
    The assaulting troops will wear a smoke helmet (old pattern) and carry a tube helmet in addition. The smoke helmet will be worn on the head tucked in at the back of the neck in such a manner that it can easily be pulled down and adjusted on encountering gas.
    Every man will carry 220 rounds of ammunition (grenadiers 100 rounds) his iron ration and six empty sandbags.
    1 VERMOREL SPRAYER per Company will be carried forward and, if possible, four gallons of solution in addition.

16. Depots of grenades and engineer material and food will be formed as detailed in Appendix "C9".

17. **Prisoners of War.**
Prisoners of war will be immediately disarmed and then collected in batches of 50 to 150 and passed back by units to the road junction G.2.d.60 N.E. of VERMELLES, whence they will be forwarded under escort of the Yorkshire Hussars to Div'l Headquarters. Officers, and if possible, N.C.O's must be kept separate from their men.
    Escorts for prisoners should be on the following scale :-
        for 50 Prisoners   10 N.C.O's and men.
            100   "   15   "   "   "
            150   "   20   "   "   "
    Prisoners should be collected and sent back in as large parties as possible in order to economise escorts. Infantry escorts before returning from VERMELLES to their Battalions will report to their Brigade Headquarters, in case they may be required to carry up stores, water, etc.

18. **Medical.**
A Collecting station will be established at BARTS G.3.c.66 to which all wounded will be taken or directed if able to walk. From here wounded will be taken to an Advanced Dressing Station at the CHATEAU, VERMELLES, G.3.c.38, whence they will be evacuated by motor ambulance.

19. **Rations.**
Rations for the 13th will be issued at the halting place, this includes an extra ration of boiled bacon to be carried on the men, and eaten on night of the 13th instant.
Rations for 14th will be delivered at the QUARRY DUMP and be taken forward on night of 13th instant.
Q.M. parties will avoid going <u>into</u> the centre of the QUARRY.

20. **Communications.**
Advanced Brigade Report Centres are being established at
   (i)   At Junction of K 1 and A 2.
   (ii)   At North end of A5.
One Section of the Div'l Cyclist Company will be allotted to O.C. Brigade Signal Section for purpose of establishing service of runners between above advanced report centres and Brigade Headquarters should telephone communication break down. Battalions will be responsible for maintaining communication with advanced Brigade Report centres.

It is of the first importance that frequent and accurate reports on the progress of the attack should be sent to Brigade Headquarters. O.C. 5th Leicesters will detail two Officers, one to be at each report centre. These Officers will telephone to Brigade Headquarters details of such of the progress of the assault as they can see from front line trenches.

Each Battalion will send two resolute, intelligent and energetic men to report to Brigade Headquarters at 9 a.m on the 13th instant. These men will be required to assist in obtaining intelligence of the progress of the attack.

The O.C. Divisional Signal Company will arrange for visual signalling to be established from the South end of the DUMP to a suitable point or points in our present system of trenches, informing all concerned as to the arrangements made.

21. BRIGADE HEADQUARTERS will be in Dug-outs immediately South of point where CENTRAL ROYAU crosses Railwayline in G.T.C.65.

                                       Sd/, O. H. GODSAL. Captain.
11/10/15.   Brigade Major, 138th Inf. Bde.

Advanced Copy issued at 1 p.m. by Orderly to :-
    Copy No. 1   Brigade Major for Brigadier.
            2   O. C. 4th Lincolns.
                   5th Lincolns.
                   4th Leicesters.
                   5th Leicesters.
                   1st Monmouths.

N.B.   NO ORDERS OR SKETCHES WHICH WOULD BE USEFUL TO THE ENEMY ARE TO BE TAKEN BEYOND BATTALION HEADQUARTERS.

APPENDIX "A".

B O M B S.

Each Platoon will be issued with three bags of fifteen bombs each.

Each Bombing Party will be issued with sixteen bags of fifteen bombs each.

266 bags, each holding fifteen bombs, will be stored at VERMELLES and the same number of bombs will be in the trench bomb stores, but not in bags.

On going into trenches the following will be issued at VERMELLES
    to each platoon 3 bags i.e. 48 per Battn, Total 192.
    to 4th LINCOLN REGIMENT   64
    to 1st Monmouthshire Regiment   10

On the morning of the 13th instant, the bombs which are in boxes in trench bomb stores are to be issued by Lieutenant RAIKES (Monmouth Regiment) and put into bags which are provided at the Stores, as follows :-

    5th LINCOLNS   64 bags.
    4th LEICESTERS   32 bags.
    MONMOUTHS   46 bags.
    Bombers &39th Inf.)
    Brigade attached) 24 bags.
    to Monmouth Regt.)

All spare bombs found in trenches will be collected into the Bomb stores.

Bombs must be collected from casualties.

*******   *******   *******

APPENDIX "E".

INSTRUCTIONS FOR USE OF SMOKE.

1. The arrangements for the production of smoke from our first line trenches are being made by the Guards Division, which, on relief, will leave in the trenches such personnel and material as are required. Two men will be left in each bay with the necessary materials. Brigadier Generals Commanding 137th and 138th Infantry Brigades will arrange for orders to light up their respective fronts to be conveyed to the above men by their own Battalion Officers, as the Guards Division will leave no Officers in the Trenches.

2. The following material will probably be available for the creation of smoke curtain to cover the consolidation of the captured position -

    (i) 1000 fumite or Threlfallite hand grenades.
    (ii) 1000 lachyrmator hand gronades.
    (iii) Five 95 millemeter mortars, firing phosphor bombs.

(i) and (ii) will be issued to the Infantry (iii) to the Artillery - see (4) below.

3. Fumite and No. 1 Threlfallito hand grenades should not be used at places over which it is proposed to pass troops, as the white phosphor emitted by them is apt to set men's clothing on fire. Officers must, therefore, use their discretion, if the final objective has not been reached, in deciding whether the situation demands their use. Points against which it is thought they would be specially useful are 3 CABARETS, COROUS DE MARON and COROUS DE PEKIN.

    No. 2 Threlfallite emit a dense smoke but are not dangerous.

    The Lachrymator grenades have an intensely irritating effect on the eyes, but are otherwise harmless. They can be usefully employed prior to the assault where trenches are within throwing distance. They can also be usefully employed against men in dugouts and buildings.

4. The 95 mm. mortars fire a smoke bomb and are to be used to create a curtain of smoke while the captured position is being placed in a state of defence. The C. R. A. is providing detachments to carry forward the mortars and ammunition for them, and to make smoke curtains. Two detachments will be attached to the 137th Brigade and three to the 138th Brigade.

5. The above mentioned appliances should prove of great value in denying ground to the enemy, and so assisting us to consolidate the ground gained - every effort should, therefore, be made to push them forward behind the attack.

****

SECRET—Not to be carried forward in an Assault.

TIME TABLE OF GAS AND SMOKE.

(a)

(Minutes)		
0 to 0·50	**Gas and Smoke**	Start the gas and smoke simultaneously. At the commencement turn on two cylinders per bay at the same time, then reduce to one cylinder per bay, and finish up with two cylinders per bay.
0·50 to 0·60	**Smoke**	Turn off gas at 0·50 and thicken up smoke by using extra candles, grenades, etc.
0·60	**Assault.**	

Note:—From 0 to 0·60 hostile trenches will be kept under continuous shrapnel fire. At 0·60 artillery will lift as required.

Smoke barrages on the flanks of the assaults should be continued wherever possible after the attack has been delivered.

(b) On the whole of the front ~~where gas is not used~~, smoke is to be kept going everywhere from 0 to 0·60.

1st Army Printing Section, R.E. 552

SECRET

Divisional Squadron.
Divisional Cyclists.
C.R.A.
C.R.E.
137th. Infantry Brigade.
138th.   ,,   ,,
139th.   ,,   ,,
1st. Batt: Monmouthshire Regt.
Divisional Train.
A.D.M.S.

****

    The Division after many months of weary work in the trenches, for which they earned very high praise, is now about to engage in active operations of the greatest importance.

    It is a great honor to the Division to be selected to carry out an assault on the enemy's position, the success of which may have far-reaching results.

    The G.O.C will put the Division into the attack with the very greatest confidence, knowing well the excellent fighting spirit which pervades all ranks. He is confident that the Division will prove itself to be equal to any in His Majesty's Army.

    All ranks must remember that the word "Retire" is not included in the Divisional vocabulary: and that every yard of ground gained must be held.

    The G.O.C wishes the Division good luck and is confident that in the coming operation they will earn the commendation of the Field Marshal Commanding-in-Chief.

                              Lieut-Colonel., G.S.,
                                    46th. Division.

10/10/1915.

War Diary

46th Division.
G.C. 104.

O.C. Div'l squadron.   137th Inf. Bde.
O.C. ,, cyclists.   138th   ,,
C.R.A.   139th   ,,
C.R.E.   O.C. Div'l Train.
O.C. Signals.   A.D.M.S.
O.C. 1st Monmouths.   A.D.V.S.

The following letter received from the Corps Commander is forwarded for information and communication to all ranks :-

"G.O.C. 46th Division.

"I shall be glad if you will express to the Officers, "N.C.O's and men of 46th Division, my appreciation of the manner "in which they carried out the attack against FOSSE No. 8 on "13th inst., and I congratulate the Division on capturing the "HOHENZOLLERN REDOUBT and retaining possession of it. I believe "this is the first time that the Division has actually carried "out an attack against the enemy, and I feel confident that their "success on this occasion will lead to still greater things in "the future.

R. HAKING, Lieut-General.,
Commanding 11th Corps"

14/10/15.

15/10/15.

Lieut-Colonel.,
G.S., 46th Division.

46th Division
G.C. 102

138th Infantry Brigade.

The G.O.C., wishes to convey to the Division his deep appreciation of their most gallant conduct on the 13th instant. The attack was carried out with great bravery and dash; and it was no fault of the Infantry that the objective of the attack was not reached. The Corps Commander has desired the G O C. to convey to all ranks his admiration for the manner in which the attack was carried out.

The G.O.C deplores the loss of so many gallant officers and men, whose names will be inscribed on the rolls of honor. He is confident that every man in the Division will be ever ready to act in the same gallant manner when called upon to do so.

Sd/. S. Price-Davies, Major.
for Lieut-Col.,
A S. 46th Division.

(2)

O/C. 4/Lincs
5/Lincs
4/Leics
5/Leics

Forwarded. for communication to everyone.

W.H.Godsal Captain
Brigade Major, 138th Inf. Bde.

15/10/15

138th Inf.Bde.
46th Div.

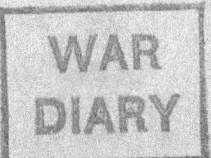

4th BATTN. THE LINCOLNSHIRE REGIMENT.

N O V E M B E R

1 9 1 5

INTELLIGENCE SUMMARY

Instructions regarding War Diaries and Intelligence Summaries are contained in F.S. Regs., Part II and the Staff Manual respectively. Title Pages will be prepared in manuscript.

(Erase heading not required.)

Place	Date	Hour	Summary of Events and Information	Remarks and references to Appendices
VERQUIN.	1/x/15		Parades in morning. Company Route marches in afternoon. Instruction of Grenadiers &c.	
"	2nd		" " " " " "	
"	3rd		" " " " " "	
"	4th		Rain all afternoon.	
"	5th		Route marches in afternoon	
VERQUIN / ROBECQ	6th		The Battalion left VERQUIN at 8.A.M. & joined the Brigade at 8.30AM. The Transport was Brigaded. Arrived near billets at ROBECQ at 12 noon. Good billets but very scattered owing to Gunners being in same area.	
	7th		Church parade at 12 noon, followed by Holy Communion.	
	8th		Company parades in morning. Company route marches in afternoon also instruction of Grenadiers & M.Gun.	
	9th		Company parades in morning Coys at Coy Comdrs disposal in afternoon also instruction of Grenadiers & M.Gun. The following Officers joined the Battalion at 1.30 p.m. Maj. H.M Gardner 2.Lt. 7.B. Webb 10 (Res) Bn The Kings Own. 2.Lt. W.G. Chambers (from W.P.) " E.F. Hindley. 11th S. Staffs " J.N. Petrie " R.F. Boxen 13th (Res) Bn Royal Warwicks " E.M Morris 9th Kincolns " S.J. Goalby " H.B. Linley " G. Fowler 9th Kincolns " W. Motton " R.N. Holmes " " H.B. Neustaria " H.C. Shaw " " F.A. Phillips. 3rd Res Bn. The Kings Own.	

INTELLIGENCE SUMMARY

(Erase heading not required.)

Instructions regarding War Diaries and Intelligence Summaries are contained in F. S. Regs., Part II. and the Staff Manual respectively. Title Pages will be prepared in manuscript.

Place	Date	Hour	Summary of Events and Information	Remarks and references to Appendices
	Nov 15th		Continued clearing up and all billets which had been left in dirty state. Co's and 2nd in Command and M.O. visited billets. Battalion relieved 6th NORTH STAFFS; in LUDHIANA LODGE 3 Coys. One Company in EUSTON CURZON, and LORETTO POST. Battn. H.Q. occupied Brigade Battle H.Q. near CURZON POSTS; dug-outs badly designed and leaky.	
	16th		Working parties of 50 men and 1 Officer 9-1, another 1-3:30pm at EUSTON under R.E. Cleaned up billets and started to improve dugout accommodation. C.O. and 2nd in Command visited CURZON and LUDHIANA in the morning. Wet.	
	17th		C.O. and 2nd in Command visited trenches occupied by 5th NORTH STAFFORDS in morning. Coy. Commdrs visited some trenches in afternoon. Sneezy Shelter Battn. H.Q. with 12 H.E. at noon: no damage. Brigadier Genl. Deetham visited HQ. in afternoon. Bombing party 150 men and 1 Officer at EUSTON 1-3:30pm under R.E. M/Gun Sec. Bomb. Officer visited Gibraltar.	

INTELLIGENCE SUMMARY

(Erase heading not required.)

Place	Date	Hour	Summary of Events and Information	Remarks and references to Appendices
	Nov 18		C.O. and 2 i/c in command visited EUSTON and LANSDOWNE POST trenches - improvements made. Battalion relieved 5th N. STAFFS in afternoon taking over about 650 yards trenches from SIGN POST LANE to BREWERY ROAD on right. A Coy on right and B on left. We also took over CHATEAU REDOUBT on left and CHURCH REDOUBT on right. 'C' Coy in reserve and in addition found Platoon in support trench about 20 x behind fire trench. 'D' Coy at MOGG'S HOLE; this is also the Dump. HQrs Paulton Villa (of D Coy) at 6.30 — Batt. H.Q. in kitchen of a shattered building 2 or 3 dugouts also adjoining. Seems in command new-fashioned trenches and redoubts and MOGG'S HOLE.	
	19th		C.O. and M.O. what round whole line in morning and visited CHATEAU & CHURCH REDOUBTS and MOGG'S HOLE. Work proceeding on front-line in wiring and breastwork and filling in sniping trench. Country flat and impossible to drain successfully; breastworks unavoidable. German were splashing and dumping last night; their trenches & waterlogged. Quiet day. No further casualties. ocr	

INTELLIGENCE SUMMARY
(Erase heading not required.)

Place	Date	Hour	Summary of Events and Information	Remarks and references to Appendices
	19th Feb		Improvements effected round Battn H.Q. Men equipped with thigh gum boots and anti-freezing grease issued. Two cases yet of frost-bitten feet. Connects CHURCH REDOUBT with Battn H.Q. by telephone.	
		20	Seen in Command & Adjt: visited our section of trenches in morning and interviewed Coy Commanders regarding work done and proposed. At 12.30 p.m. enemy put a few whizz-bang into Battn H.Q. Capt Parker [signaller] wounded. In the afternoon General improvements made at B. H.Q. the C.O. and Adjt went round all the trenches listening posts, firing trench, supports and communication trenches. Progress got work to be done — chiefly building up parapet (trenchwork) and filling in spetten trenche to ground level. Part of this had already been done in A & B line. Detailed large working parties tonight: 5000 sandbags sent up. Enemy artillery quiet today. Wire to Brigade at 2.30 p.m. Installation of pigeon post from here to South.	

INTELLIGENCE SUMMARY

(Erase heading not required.)

Hour, Date, Place	Summary of Events and Information	Remarks and references to Appendices
Nov. 21 -	The Scouts in command made tour round trenches last evening. Patrol heard working party of Germans on left of Donn Section. M/Guns in our line promptly dispersed them. German rifle brought in - machine the Scouts salvaged. This last found & the bodies with many 1915 ammunition. Some German bombs brought in also German equipment much weather-worn. Enemy put some shells on trenches in front of LUDHIANA unoccupied - which was former German line. 'Whizz-bang' fell near newly constructed dressing station and wounded Cpl. Pinchbeck, pioneer, in the hand. C.O. visited artillery observation post in afternoon tratch effect of battery shelling the MUSKRAT, a forties wound nearly opposite SUNKEN ROAD in B. Coy. front at night.	

INTELLIGENCE SUMMARY

(Erase heading not required.)

Hour, Date, Place	Summary of Events and Information	Remarks and references to Appendices
Nov. 22	Relieved by 5th North Staffords at 6.30 pm. Marched to billets in CROIX-BARBEE for the night. No casualties during relief. A few cases of trench foot occurred during tour in.	
23rd	Marched to LE TOURET via LACOUTURE about 4 miles, and took over billets for the night from 10th Worcesters. A & B Companies in LE TOURET, C and D in L'EPINETTE and CHAVATTES.	
24th	A & B Companies bathed at LESTREM (5 miles north) and part of Details. Colonel Heathcote D.S.O. went on leave. Capt Gribbin returned from leave.	
25th	C & D Companies and remainder of Details bathed at LESTREM. Major Gardner (Commanding Officers) visited Brigade HQ at 9.30 am.	

INTELLIGENCE SUMMARY

Hour, Date, Place	Summary of Events and Information	Remarks and references to Appendices

25th cont'd — Near LE TOURET on the Rue du Bois. Captain Smalley as second in command visited Battn H.Q. of 5th LEICESTERS whom we relieve in trenches tomorrow - 26th -

26th — Heavy rain at 2 am. Bright clear sun at 7am. Heavy ammunition malday.
4.45 pm Relief of 7th & 5th Leicesters by 4th Lincolns commenced.
7pm. Relief complete.
Disposition. One company in front line (relieved every 24 hours), one and a half companies in support line, half a coy in strong points viz Cat's, Dog's, Albert, Orchard, Chocolate, half a coy in Bienvillers, half a coy in reserve in the school. Half a company in reserve in the dry grey rooms at the school. Quiet night. Thirsty frost.

27th — They first in morning at 3.30pm. He enemy shelled Teetotal Corner with shrapnel H.E. Several were killed. The majority fell between Teetotal Corner & Albert Post. At 1.30 pm the support line were strafed. At 1 2 pm, Mr. Thom's intelligence officer and a guide ran into a German patrol & Aubers but got safely away.

WAR DIARY
or
INTELLIGENCE SUMMARY

(Erase heading not required.)

Hour, Date, Place	Summary of Events and Information	Remarks and references to Appendices
28th.	Very hard frost. One man killed in the trench in the morning by German sniper. At 2.30pm the Germans shelled Puriden Rows and Teetotal Corner. No casualties. Shortfort at night.	
29th.	Thaw set in during the night. Germans dis more shelling today, a number of crumps fell between Teetotal Corner & Orkneys Post. Very wet miserable night. The relief of the company in the front line trench was much delayed owing to the great difficulty in finding the path, also to the extreme muddiness.	
30th.	Fine day, a good deal warmer. There was heavy shelling on both sides today. The Germans were crumped all the route along the Rue du Bois, between Factory Corner & Teetotal Corner, most of which has been used as O.P's by the artillery. He dropped one 8" crump into our O.P near Factory Corner. They also shelled the old 4th Leicester H.Q, in which 3 of our officers were trying sleeping to sleep in, but everyone made got out safely.	

Nw Cannon
2nd Lt A/Adjt 1/4 Lincolnshire Regt

138th Inf.Bde.
46th Div.

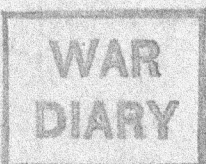

4th BATTN. THE LINCOLNSHIRE REGIMENT.

DECEMBER

1915

Instructions regarding War Diaries and Intelligence Summaries are contained in F.S. Regs., Part II. and the Staff Manual respectively. Title Pages will be prepared in manuscript.

INTELLIGENCE SUMMARY

(Erase heading not required.)

Place	Date	Hour	Summary of Events and Information	Remarks and references to Appendices
In the trenches	1.XII.15		Germans shelled TEETOTAL CORNER & batteries in rear between 10am & 12 noon. Our batteries responded with interest.	
		12.15pm	Col Jones (acting Brigadier) called. 3.30pm Major Toller & Capt Allen, 5th Leicesters, called.	
"	2.XII.15		Enemy shelled ragamuffin posts in houses along the RUE DU BOIS during the morning. 5th Leicester advance officers	
			& intelligence officer came to take over about 2.30 pm.	
		4.30 pm	Relief by 5th Leicesters commenced. 8.30pm. Relief completed.	
			The battalion moved back to KING'S BILLETS for 6 days rest.	LE SART
KING'S BILLETS	3.XII.15	5.30 am	Orders received recalling all officers. 6 am. Orders received to move units billeted at Le Sart new	
			MERVILLE at 12.15 pm. Order of march. B, A, C, D. Transport was picked up on the way, at LACOUTURE. The rifle grenaders	
			were left behind to bring their guns out of the trenches during daylight, & to move on into LE SART billets	
			the following morning. The Battalion reached their billets about 4.30 pm.	
LE SART	4.XII.15		Coy & other Coy arrangements. G.O.C. called about 11.30, & announced that we are to go to EGYPT.	
			2Lt Crabtree was evacuated to F Ambulance.	
"	5.XII.15		D Coy C of E church parade at 10.15 am. 2Lt Col Heathcote returned from leave.	
"	6.XII.15		G.O.C.'s inspection arranged for, but cancelled. G.O.C. called at 11.30am. Coys at Coy officers' disposal. Capt Burrows returned from leave.	
"	7.XII.15		Parades. 9-11.30 am Inspections, saluting, guard duties etc. 2pm. 2 hours route marching.	
"	8.XII.15		" " "	
"	9.XII.15		Brigadier General's inspection arranged for, but cancelled, owing to rain. Coys at Coy Officers' disposal.	
"	10.XII.15	9.30 am	Inspection by Brigadier General. After that, the C.O. went to ST VENANT to attend a divisional conference	
			at 11am, on the subject of wastage of clothing & equipment. 2pm. Battalion route march, accompanied by Brigade	
"	11.XII.15		band. Fatigue party for unloading coal from barge, was found by the battalion. Brelief such of 30 officers	
			and 1.28 O.R. 1st relief 8am, 2nd relief 11 am & 3rd relief 2pm.	
"	12.XII.15		Church parade (C of E) at 10 am.	
"	13.XII.15		Baths for APPB Coys, C & D Coys had normal parades in the morning, & shower route marching in the afternoon	
"	14.XII.15		" C & D Coys. APPB " " " " "	

INTELLIGENCE SUMMARY

(Erase heading not required.)

Instructions regarding War Diaries and Intelligence Summaries are contained in F.S. Regs., Part II. and the Staff Manual respectively. Title Pages will be prepared in manuscript.

Place	Date	Hour	Summary of Events and Information	Remarks and references to Appendices
LE SART BILLETS	15.XII.15			
"	16.XII.15	9-11.30 am. Coys at Coy officers disposal. 2pm. Known route marching.	
		" " " " " " " " " "	The Brigadier, 2nd in command, visited all coys, & watched their drilling	
			The CO. a/s/s Cowden Smith went off in a motor lorry at 9.15 am to reconnoitre the station at Lillers Ropeguette, to see the facilities for entraining.	
"	17.XII.15	9-11.30 am Coys at Coy Officers disposal. 2pm. Battalion route march.	
"	18.XII.15	" " " " " " " 2pm. Saluting drill for all details. The Brigadier called in the afternoon, & stayed to tea.	
"	19.XII.15	The Battalion moved to billets in THIENNES this morning. Order J march. 5th Finishers, 1st Leinsters, 11th Leinsters & 5th Leicesters followed by transport. Starting point, LE CORBIE. Time 11am. The battalion reached their billets at 1.45 pm.	
THIENNES BILLETS 20.XII.15		9-11.30 am. Coys at Coy Officers disposal. 2pm Saluting drill. Capt. Bunion went to FA.	
"	21.XII.15	" " " " " " Battalion route march arranged for but cancelled, owing to rain.	Capt. Bunion
"	22.XII.15	" " " " " " " " " " " "	RE
"	23.XII.15	106 Reinforcements arrived from the 3/4 Bn at 2.20 pm. Kit inspection held on arrival. The battalion took up an outpost line covering their billets in THIENNES. Major Gartner was in command of the sector, which extended from the NELLE MELDE canal, to the road running E.S.E. through the railway line THIENNES — HAZEBROUCK. Outposts were in position at 10.30 am. The Brigade, acting in advanced guard to the division, was supposed to be in billets in THIENNES. The division in billets W. of the CANAL DAIRE, was to resume its march N. on the 24th. The divisional cavalry was watching the flanks of the outpost line. Patrols of Uhlans had been seen in ABOESGHEM & STEENBELGUE at 4.30 pm yesterday. 2 battalion (JAEGERS & one battery) passed through HAZEBROUCK in the direction of SERCUS at 3.30 pm yesterday. The Brigadier & O. inspected the outpost line, commencing at 11.30 am. Treinfort, C. t.A. Coyp had baths.	

INTELLIGENCE SUMMARY

(Erase heading not required.)

Instructions regarding War Diaries and Intelligence Summaries are contained in F.S. Regs, Part II. and the Staff Manual respectively. Title Pages will be prepared in manuscript.

Place	Date	Hour	Summary of Events and Information	Remarks and references to Appendices
THIENNES PIPLETS	24.XII.15	9-11.30 am	Corps of Cny Officers disposal. The same outpost line that was taken up yesterday was taken up again tonight, but this was cancelled, owing to rain.	morning
"	25.XII.15		An inter-battalion soccer football was played off this afternoon. from The prize was a polished .75 shell, with a cloth Rev into it. 1st round, 4th Leicesters beat 4th Leicesters 1½ goals to 0. 5th Leicesters beat 5th Leicesters 1-0. Final 5th Leicesters beat 4th Leicesters 1-0. The cup was presented by the Brigadier. The Brigade Band played at intervals during the afternoon.	
" "	26.XII.15		Voluntary church services in the morning. Capt Brown returned from F.A. Capt Dagdon werton leave. Companies under company arrangements. The Bn. orders draft parades were inspected by In	
" "	27.XII.15		Brigadier at 10 o'clock. At 2 p.m. the battalion moved to Busquetteotation as an advance guard to a Brigade. The Brigade was represented by the infantry section, officers & seniors N.C.Os. pulled to a Brigade. The Brigade was received action for entrenchments. Reformities the facilitie	
" "	28.XII.15		Naval inspection at 9 am. At 10.45 the battalion marched to a field near movements to meet the 2nd & 5th Leicesters. Order of march D, A, B, C, field kitchen eversels accompanies the column, and dinner was eaten in the field. Brigadier General Stevens visited the battalion. The Brigadier was present, played at intervals during the meal. Sgt C.F. Skinner formis the battalion today, went on leave, in order to get arm leak.	
" "	29.XII.15		The battalion took huts in brigade operation. The brigade was supposed to have gone into close billets in THIENNE's yesterday, see 4th Leicester to have put out outposts to guard to front the country today but recurred by the enemy. They again urged posts at 9am at their huts. which the battalion marched in marched at then morning, putting through from many outposts between our outpost line at 9.45am. As noon, the advanced guard was well strong in my line over outposts were withdrawn, & the battalion took its stand in the march beside the not of the bridge. Brigade marched for about 3 miles towards SERCUS, then the battalion received orders to return to billets in a different route. We came to like through STEENBECQUE, reaching my billets about 1pm.	

INTELLIGENCE SUMMARY

(Erase heading not required.)

Instructions regarding War Diaries and Intelligence Summaries are contained in F.S. Regs., Part II. and the Staff Manual respectively. Title Pages will be prepared in manuscript.

Place	Date	Hour	Summary of Events and Information	Remarks and references to Appendices
THIENNES.	30.XII.15	9–11 am.	Coy route marching. 11.15 Inspection of transport by Brigadier a Brigade Transport officer. Route march in the afternoon of the 2nd Lincolns. Order of march A, B, C, D, m/g, men. Time 1hr. Dead slow fatigue. On reaching the 2nd Lincolns the billets the battalion fell out, switches a football match between the 2nd & 4th Lincolns, which the former won 7–2. Battalion fell in again at 3.45 & marched back again.	
"	31.XII.15	9–11.30.	Coy route coy arrangements. Open Ranks marching. Ceremonial were made out, that to be done in 2 hours. intersing the newest halt.	

Ruy Cannon Lt
a/Adjt ¼n Lincolns

1.1.16.

D. Sherlock. Lt. Col.
Comdg ¼n Lincolns

1.1.16.

1/4 Lincoln Regt
Jan
Vol IX

Army Form C. 2118

WAR DIARY
or
INTELLIGENCE SUMMARY
(Erase heading not required.)

Instructions regarding War Diaries and Intelligence Summaries are contained in F.S. Regs., Part II. and the Staff Manual respectively. Title Pages will be prepared in manuscript.

Place	Date	Hour	Summary of Events and Information	Remarks and references to Appendices
THIENNES	1/1/16	9-11.30 A.M.	Coy under Coy arrangements. 2 P.M to 4 P.M Regtl marching.	
"	2/1/16	10.30 A.M.	Church Parade.	
"	3/1/16	9 A.M-12.30 P.M.	Gulficel exercise. The entire line was inspected by the Brigadier. Orders received to entrain for Marseilles on the 5/1/16.	
"	4/1/16	10 A.M 1930 A.M	Coy under Coy arrangements.	
"	5/1/16	7 A.M	Left Thiennes proceeded by transport. Entrained at 10 A.M and left BERGUETTE at 10.20 A.M.	
"	6/1/16		In the train proceeding to Marseilles.	
MARSEILLES	7/1/16	5 P.M	Reached Marseilles, marched straight to docks + embarked at 6.30 P.M. on T.S.S. Arcuanus in company with 5th Lincs. Ammunition also an armoured car train. Lieut Worthy + Brigadier General + Staff also on board. Sailed. 3 sea rather rough.	
"	8/1/16	9 A.M.		
"	9/1/16		At sea.	
AT SEA.	10/1/16	10 A.M	Passed Malta. In afternoon Enemy submarine was reported in detail turned round and went back for an hour.	
"	11/1/16		At sea.	
"	12/1/16			
ALEXANDRIA.	13/1/16	11 A.M.	Reached Alexandria. Left Alexandria to train for SHALLUFA at 11.15 P.M.	
"	14/1/16		Halt at or near ISMALIA at NEFISHA R:-	
SHALLUFA	15/1/16	5 A.M.	In a trainload on the line ahead of us. Reached SHALLUFA at 9.30 A.M + moved over the Canal to a camp out of the latter bank of the Canal. We drew tools and afterwards pitching all the stores from the East bank of the canal to where they piled them carried by a fatigue.	
"	16/1/16	9 A.M	Church Parade for bayoneers. W. other gun more either trench digging an hour. + our camp + or on company fatigues.	
"	17/1/16	7.30-8 A.M	Signalling, W of Guns 9-11.30 A.M. By drill. 4 to 6 P.M Batt with march.	
"	18/1/16	7.30-8 A.M	Signalling drill. 9-11.30 A.M. Batt drill &c. 2 P.M. marched to GENEFFA Rest Post for bathing.	
"	19/1/16	7-7.45 A.M 5 M. Parade	7.30 to 8 A.M C'Kere signalling 9-11.30 A.M Batt drill by Batt &c. 12 K.y P.M Route marching. In the evening we heard the bugler return towards the camp. On enquiry consist of 30 o.R. each + one officer. There is also an outlying piquet of 1/2 Coy.	

Army Form C. 2118

WAR DIARY or INTELLIGENCE SUMMARY

(Erase heading not required.)

Instructions regarding War Diaries and Intelligence Summaries are contained in F. S. Regs., Part II. and the Staff Manual respectively. Title Pages will be prepared in manuscript.

Place	Date	Hour	Summary of Events and Information	Remarks and references to Appendices
SHALLUFA	20/1/16		We were Batt's in duty, the whole day was occupied in finding fatigue parties & moving camp to a position further west. We then had the 5th June on our left and the 4th on our left the Stafford Brigade.	
"	21/1/16	7-7.45 AM	S. Majors parade. 7.30 to 8 AM Officers signalling. 9-11.30 Batt. Drill. Coy drill & extended order drill &c. have to 4 P.M. route marching.	
"	22/1/16	1.25 P.M	Alarm sounded our alter. made ready to line our trenches 100 yds in front of us. O/C we had time this since 2 Coys into the 5th June in support, the Stafford Brigade in the left of them the full out. Extended parades as on the 21st/1/16	
"	23/1/16	7 A.M	Batt. paraded for rifle instruction, every man present. 10 AM Church parade for D Coy, the whole Batt. paraded further instruction during the	
"	24/1/16	7-7.30 A.M	Regt. Sergt. Majors Parade. 9 A.M - 1 P.M Practice in loading Camels. Coys not taking Camels carried on with the usual programme of training. 2-4 P.M Batt. Route march	morning
"	25/1/16	7-7.30 A.M	Regt. Sgt. Major Parade. 9 A.M - 11.30 A.M musketry and training as per programme. Batts. found outlying piquet at night. Other Parades usual in command of the intelligence Sergeant.	
"	26/1/16	6.30-7.30 A.M	Batt. out doing fatigues all day. Other officers war in command of the Piquet line. Capt Ellis in command of the intelligence Sergeant.	
"	27/1/16	7-7.45 A.M	Sergt. Majors parade and Instruction in bayonet fighting. Training, events improved, details in the ranks 9-11.30 A.M Batt's Coys drill, extended order drill, musketry &c. 5 P.M Outlying piquet	
"	28/1/16	7-7.45 A.M	Officers musketry. 8 P.M Lecture by Major Gardner.	
"	29/1/16	6.45-7.30 A.M	and task drill. Sgt. Majors Parade. 9 A.M - 5 P.M firing on the range.	
"	30/1/16	6.45-7.30 A.M	Sgt. Majors parade. 10.30 received orders to entrain by 1.15. Train left SHALLUFA 3.50 P.M and reached SIDI GABRIEL at 2.10 A.M. After untraining train and loading motor lorries the Batt. marched to SIDI BISHR	
SIDI-BISHR	30/1/16		arriving our running fatigue camp.	
"	31/1/16	7-7.40 A.M	Sgt. Majors Parade. 9 A.M - 11.30 A.M Bathing Parades various by arrangement.	

[signature] Lt. Col.
K.O.Y.L.I.

Co. 14th Lincolnshire Regt.
2.2.16

1/4 Lincoln Regt.

Feb
Vol XV

WAR DIARY
or
INTELLIGENCE SUMMARY
(Erase heading not required.)

Army Form C. 2118

Instructions regarding War Diaries and Intelligence Summaries are contained in F.S. Regs., Part II. and the Staff Manual respectively. Title Pages will be prepared in manuscript.

Place	Date	Hour	Summary of Events and Information	Remarks and references to Appendices
SD1 BISHR	1/2/16	6·45-	7·30 A.M. Sgt Majors parade. 9 A.M. – 12·30 P.M. The Battn did a practice attack. 2·30 P.M. Bathing parade under Company arrangements.	
"	2/2/16	6·45-	7·30 A.M. Sgt Majors parade 9 A.M – 1 P.M. The Battn did a practice attack. Bathing parade in the afternoon.	
"	3·2·16	6·45·	The battalion & staff, Regl Major Gardner, Corp Edw & 2nd in C & 40 O/R, entrained on S.S. MEGANTIC at noon. The remaining officers left behind, with orders to embark on S.S. MINNEWASKA on the following day.	
On board ship	4·2·16		Moved out into the stream at 9·30 a.m., anchored until 11 a.m., with the other officers on board. 2 Lt Mutton admitted to hospital at Marseilles, with Diphtheria. At 4·15 Lincoln, & 1st Monmouth on board.	
" "	5·2·16		At sea. Sighted Malta about 5 p.m.	
" "	6·2·16		At sea.	
" "	7·2·16		At sea.	
" "	8·2·16		Went into dock at MARSEILLES about noon.	
" "	9·2·16		S.S. MINNEWASKA arrived at next quay about 11 a.m., with the other officers on board. 2 Lt Mutton admitted to hospital at Marseilles. The battalion, less officers in MINNEWASKA, entrained at 6 p.m. Train left for MARSEILLES 7·15 p.m.	
Pont Remy	10·2·16		Arrived at PONT REMY Station about 7 p.m. Unloaded stores, & marched off to camp at AILLY HAUTE CLOCHER at 11·25. Arrived at camp about 2 a.m. on 12th inst. Some of the men we supposed to have had relapsing fever an contagious, we are isolated in camp. Settled down to camp. Had inspection next day. The battalion to be thoroughly disinfected in a Thresh disinfector. Kings & Church parade 11 a.m.	
AILLY	12·2·16			
AILLY	13·2·16		Officers servants were done today. In the afternoon, we were told that there had been a mistake about the relapsing fever, & the battalion moved into billets in AILLY.	
"	14·2·16		7 a.m. Physical inspection. 9-11·30 a.m. Coy drill &c. 2 p.m. Route marching. D Coy furns RSM SHEPHERD, Sgt WRIGHT & Sgt KELL, having been appointed to commissions, went home on leave 2nd Lt G. E. CRABTREE rejoined from hospital.	

Army Form C. 2118

WAR DIARY
or
INTELLIGENCE SUMMARY
(Erase heading not required.)

Instructions regarding War Diaries and Intelligence Summaries are contained in F. S. Regs., Part II. and the Staff Manual respectively. Title Pages will be prepared in manuscript.

Place	Date	Hour	Summary of Events and Information	Remarks and references to Appendices
AILLY	15.2.16		7am - 7.30am Coy Officers' inspection. 9-11.30am Coy drill, extended order drill etc. 2pm Route marching had been arranged, but was cancelled owing to rain. Lecture at 4pm on Gas by 2/Lt G.F. CHADWICK. Disinfector thoroughly tested today.	
"	16.2.16		7-7.30am Physical training. 8.15-9.15 Coy Officers' inspection. A tactical exercise (Artillery formation) has been arranged for 9.15am, but owing to heavy rain it was cancelled, and the morning's work is without incident. 2pm Route marching by Coys. 2/Lt FOWKER being transferred to the R.E. left the Battalion this morning. Draft elections throughout the day. 1pm Lecture to Officers by Major GARDNER on "Billeting & Pay of the Regiment".	
"	17.2.16		7-7.30am Physical Training. 8.45am Coy Officers' inspection. 9.15-11.30 Coys at Coy officers' disposal. 2pm Route marching under Coy arrangements. C & D Coys on 30 yards range. Major Gardner & 10 other Officers went by motor lorry to reconnoitre strong points near FORCEVILLE.	
"	18.2.16		7-7.30am Physical training. 8.45am Coy Officers' inspection. 9.15-11.30am Extended order drill and/or Coy arrangement duties, but cancelled owing to rain, as also route marching at 2pm. The CO. & 8 other Officers reconnoitred the strong points near FORCEVILLE. 5pm Received orders to move into new billets at BOIS BERGUES on Sunday Feb 20th.	
"	19.2.16		7-7.30am Physical Training 8.45am Coy Officers' Inspections. 9.15-11.30am Coys at Coy Officers' disposal. One Coy on 30 yds range.	
"	20.2.16		The battalion moved into billets at BOISBERGUES. Time of start 9am. Time of arrival in BOISBERGUES 2pm. As an experiment, the battalion marched in sections of fours instead of fours of four. This was found very useful, as it seem stopped, to a certain extent, the straggling that all necessarily occurs when a battalion turns on its march or reviews roads. Also the order of march was altered so that Halt, including coy. standing fast until the other three companies had passed.	
BOISBERGUES	21.2.16		7-7.30am Physical Training. 8.45am Coy Officers' Inspection. 9.30am Coy drill, extended order drill etc. 10.30am - 1pm Tactical exercise - Battalion in the Attack. 2.30pm Musketry. Capt ELLIS was sent to the Field Ambulance.	

Army Form C. 2118

WAR DIARY
or
INTELLIGENCE SUMMARY
(Erase heading not required.)

Instructions regarding War Diaries and Intelligence Summaries are contained in F.S. Regs., Part II. and the Staff Manual respectively. Title Pages will be prepared in manuscript.

Place	Date	Hour	Summary of Events and Information	Remarks and references to Appendices
BOISBERQUES	23.2.16.	7-7.30am	Physical Training. 8.45 am Coy Officers' Inspection. 9.30. Coy but started to fire Tactical Scheme B in trenches.	
"		7.7.30 am	Physical Training. 8.45 Coy Officers' Inspection. 9.30am. B & C Coy fired over drill the Bn at attack. 2 pm LELEU was sent for school of instruction	followers
"	24.2.16.	7-7.30am	Physical Training. 8.45am Coy Officers' Inspection. 9.15-1am Tactical Scheme. Advanced guard by an attack. 2pm Musketry. An outpost scheme was arranged for the	Bt Lt H WRIGHT
"	25.2.16	7-7.30 am	Physical Training. 8.45am Coy Officers' Inspection, but both were cancelled owing to heavy snow. Musketry for the afternoon, but returned from leave, went to school of instruction morning. Too commission in this Bn.	
"	26.2.16	7-7.30am	Physical Training. 8.45 Coy Officers' Inspection. 9.15-11.30am Coys at Coy Officers' disposal at BEAUVAL	
"	27.2.16.	9.15 am.	B Coy Route march. During the afternoon Scenaves v. Pts M Coy tickets. B Coy Route march, but this was cancelled. The Coys fired on the ranges both morning & afternoon	
"	28.2.16.	7.50 am	Coy Physical Training. 8.45 Coy Officers' Inspection. 9.15 - 12 noon Coys at Coy Officers' disposal. 2pm Musketry.	
"	29.2.16			

R.E. Shanks Major
O.C. 11th Lincoln Regt.

Cluf Tanner
Major
1/o 4th Lincolnshire Regt.

46

1/4 Lincoln Regt
Vol XVI

WAR DIARY or INTELLIGENCE SUMMARY

Army Form C. 2118

(Erase heading not required.)

Place	Date	Hour	Summary of Events and Information	Remarks and references to Appendices
BOISBERGUES	1.3.16		The battalion received orders to proceed to fresh billets in DOULLENS. Left BOISBERGUES 11 A.M., & arrived at DOULLENS at 1.10 P.M., went into close billets in the Town. Div. H.Q., 138th Bde H.Q., & the rest of the 138th Brigade were also billetted in the same town. The transport	
DOULLENS	2.3.16		7 – 7.30 a.m. Coy officers' inspection. 9.15 to 12 noon Coys at Coy officers' disposal. 2pm Route marching. The transport went for a route march under brigade arrangements. 2 P.M – 4 P.M Coys at Coy
"	3.3.16		7 – 7.30 a.m. Coy officers' inspection. 9.30 a.m – 12 noon Coys at Coy officers' disposal. 2 P.M – 4 P.M Route marching. Officers diagram.
"	4.3.16		7 – 7.30 a.m. Coy officers' inspection. 9.30 a.m. – 12 noon, Coys at Coy Officers disposal. Rifle & bayonet exercise. The C.O., 2nd Chambers & [?] shews went to reconnoitre the trenches.
"	5.3.16		2 pm. Church parade.
"	6.3.16		The battalion moved to fresh billets at HOUVIN HOUVINEUL. The whole brigade marches together, & the transport was brigaded. Left DOULLENS at 8.30 a.m. & reached HOUVIN about 1.15 p.m. Order of march, 5th Lincs, 4th Lincs, 5th Leic, 4th Leic.
HOUVIN	7.3.16		Coy officers' Inspections. interior economy.
"	8.3.16		7 am Coy officers' Inspection. 9 am Route march (Trinity) 2 pm Short school drill, training of special Cos.
"	9.3.16		The battalion moved into billets in VILLERS CHATEL. Start 10.15 a.m. Route. MAGNICOURT, AMBRINES, VILLERSSIRE-SIMON MONCHEL, AUBIGNY, MINGOVAL, VILLERS-CHATEL. Order of march C.O. A.B.D. 2nd Chambers & 2 NCO's per Coy went up to the support line at TALUS DES ZOUAVES to take over from the French.
VILLERS CHATEL	10.3.16		The battalion moved up to the support line – TALUS DES ZOUAVES. Start 3 pm. Route – CAMBLIGNEUL, CAMBLAIN L'ABBEE VILLERS AU BOIS. Relief of French completed about 10 pm.
Tuttle [Trenches]	11.3.16		Quiet. Work done – chiefly clearing up refuse left by the French. Work on communication trenches.
"	12.3.16		"

WAR DIARY
or
INTELLIGENCE SUMMARY
(Erase heading not required.)

Army Form C. 2118

Instructions regarding War Diaries and Intelligence Summaries are contained in F.S. Regs., Part II. and the Staff Manual respectively. Title Pages will be prepared in manuscript.

Place	Date	Hour	Summary of Events and Information	Remarks and references to Appendices
In the Trenches	13.3.16		Quiet. Work as before.	
"	14.3.16		Quiet " " A French aeroplane was brought down by the Germans. Enemy shelled communication trenches at intervals.	
"	15.3.16		Relieved 5th Leicesters in trenches (left section) Relief completed without incident at 6.25pm. Front line parapet very low, such bullet proof at the top.	
"	16.3.16		Quiet. 11.30pm warning was given that a mine was expected to go up at the front of the salient (held by B Coy). Everyone except sentries & listening posts were withdrawn, no retrenchment dug behind its salient. 24 Highlanders were killed while the mine was being dug. The mine went up at 6.15 afternoon 20th, Capt Scorer joined the battalion. 2/Lts S.S. Stephenson & monte Kettles.	
"	17.3.16		Quiet. Capt LHC Hart & 2/Lt W Mitton rejoined. Enemy sent several trench mortars over, returned a small bombardment during the night, but we are now relieved.	
"	18.3.16			
"	19.3.16		Quiet except for several more trench mortars. Lt RN Hutchinson & Enemy air craft very busy.	
"	20.3.16		Enemy sent 28 trench mortar over during the afternoon. We replied with artillery & stokes mortars. Observation	
"	21.3.16		Quiet. Relieved by 5th Leicesters. Relief completed 11pm. The Battalion then moved back into huts at CAMBLAIN L'ABBEÉ	
CAMBLAIN L'ABBEÉ	22.3.16		Day spent in cleaning up.	
"	23.3.16		9-11:30am. Coys at Coy Officers disposal. 2pm. Route Marching. Capt. C.R. Scorer & 2 Anoth.	
"	24.3.16		9-11:30am. Coys at Coy Officers disposal. 6.30pm. Lecture to Officers and Senior N.C.Os. 2/Lt G.H. Morris rejoined.	
"	25.3.16		9am. Coy Officers inspection. 9.30am & 11:30am Route Marching. 6.30pm Lecture to Officers and sergeants.	
"	26.3.16		Church Parade. C. of E. 11:15am. Wesleyan and United Board 10.45am.	
"	27.3.16		Inspection Coys. Proceeded to trenches to relieve 5 Leicesters. Relief completed 12.35am.	
In the Trenches	28.3.16		Quiet. A Trench mortars sent over during early afternoon. Answer silenced by RA rifle grenades. Cpl Jones Acting. (B&C colls)	
"	29.3.16		during the morning. Fair day.	
"	30.3.16		Very quiet. Bde Major called during morning. Fair day.	
"	31.3.16		Very quiet again. Enemy aircraft very busy. Fair day.	
"			Quiet again. Enemy and our Gunners active between 3 & 4:45pm. We replies with heavy retaliation mortar enemy emplacements from our two sets. 2/Lt A.F. Stephenson wounded on duty in trench & gallery on 4	

1.4.16

Lt Col Kemp Infantry
Commanding 1/4th Leicester Regt B.E.F.

46

1/4 Lincoln Regt
Vol XVII

Army Form C. 2118

WAR DIARY
or
INTELLIGENCE SUMMARY
(Erase heading not required.)

Instructions regarding War Diaries and Intelligence Summaries are contained in F.S. Regs., Part II. and the Staff Manual respectively. Title Pages will be prepared in manuscript.

138/46

Place	Date	Hour	Summary of Events and Information	Remarks and references to Appendices
In the Trenches	1.4.16		Quiet except for enemy trench mortars in afternoon. Allied aeroplane brought down behind our lines about 1 mile N. of Souchez.	
"	2.4.16		Quiet. Large draft (173 men) arrived. Capt. E. Burrows proceeded to 3rd Army Infantry School. German aeroplane brought down at 10.15am allied in front line by 5th Leicesters. Relief completed. 9/Lt J.M. Stead rejoined from leave.	
"	3.4.16		Quiet. Major R.M. Gardner proceeded on leave. Lt. R.M. Holmes rejoined from leave.	
"	4.4.16		Quiet. Work done - repairing trenches.	
"	5.4.16		New draft inspected by C.O. G.O.C. called.	
"	6.4.16		Quiet. Army Commander called.	
"	7.4.16		Work - draining & repairing trenches. Capt. Cushing proceeded on leave. 9/Lt. S.O. Simpson joined from Base.	
"	8.4.16		Quiet. 9/Lt. W.G. Chambers to hospital. Work - draining and repairing trenches. Relieved 5th Leicesters in left sector. Relief completed 8 p.m.	
"	9.4.16		Quiet. 9/Lt. H. L. Shaw rejoined.	
"	10.4.16		Quiet. 2/Lt. E. G. Elliott rejoined from Brig. School of Instruction.	
"	11.4.16		Quiet day.	
"	12.4.16		Considerable activity by enemy trench mortars in afternoon between 2.10 pm & 4.30pm. About 25 yds of front line trench blown in.	
"	13.4.16		Quiet day.	
"	14.4.16		Some enemy fire & aeroplane activity in front of our lines. One man was killed & two who went to rescue him were gassed by fumes. Relieved by 5th Leicesters. Relief completed.	
CAMBLAIN L'ABBEE	15.4.16		Day spent in cleaning up. Bathing during afternoon.	
"	16.4.16		C.O. inspected battalion by Coys in morning. Church Parade 12.30 p.m. Bathing during day. Lt. Col. G. C. Heathcote proceeded to St. Pol to attend "Artillery Course".	
"	17.4.16		Coys at Coy officers disposal. General inspection, smoke helmet drill, bombing & instruction in sandbag revetment & wiring. Capt. E. J. Cricklay rejoined from leave.	
"	18.4.16		Inspection by G.O.C. during morning who congratulated Officers & men on excellent appearance of battalion. He was very pleased to see how well the men were turned out & also the cleanliness of their clothing, arms and equipment. Relieved 5th Leicesters in trenches at night. Relief completed.	
In the Trenches	19.4.16		The R.E. exploded a mine April No 15 C.T. and also a small camouflet against the big listening post on the Right. Q.91. These were all exploded at 10.30 P.M. At the same time a bombardment of their trenches was carried out by the Stokes civil light also an artillery bombardment. T.M. Batteries of the Brigade machine guns fired long range fire on the enemy's support & communication trench. There was no enemy machine guns fired for 50 seconds after the mine went up and their guns about 3 minutes afterwards. Their artillery was however protected by our heavy guns taken by the same retaliation.	

1875 Wt. W593/826 1,000,000 4/15 J.B.C. & A. A.D.S.S./Forms/C. 2118.

WAR DIARY
INTELLIGENCE SUMMARY

Army Form C. 2118

Place	Date	Hour	Summary of Events and Information	Remarks and references to Appendices
In the Trenches	20.4.16		The enemy blew a mine very nearly under our front line trench at 6.30 P.M. yesterday. The Crater is just on the left of the new mine Thursday where 2nd Lt WRIGHT and 15 O.R. were buried 8 O.R. or more dug out by the explosion. The enemy immediately started to shell all our lines and also the valley behind. He sent a great many shells on the ERSATZ Avenue practically outside the Batt'n H.Q. and on the grid. Rally across the valley. The mine itself in a miraculous fashion of our front trenches (Q90) and the shelling also did a good deal of damage. The near lip of the mine is held: at 10.20 P.M. the enemy blew a camouflet on our redoubt right. This also hurled round a good deal of Mansfeld but no casualties were incurred. No action followed.	
" " "	21.4.16		Working party (100 men from 6th LEICESTERSHIRE Regt & 160 from D Coy) continued work on the crater until dawn. The enemy were quite throughout the day. Lt CANNON went down to Hospital "sick". Quiet evening. Some bombing between our "Stand down" in the morning at 10A.M the 13th LANCASHIRE FUSILIERS commenced to relieve the Battalion. Relief complete 12.58. On relief companies proceeded to a rest dugout and was again billeted in the avenues by the 11th CHESHIRE Regt.	
" " "	22.4.16		executed the Route at VILLERS-AU-BOIS & emerged on to AVERDOINGT.	
AVERDOINGT	23.4.16		Battalion arrived from the trenches at the place at 8 A.M. The Battalion rested for the remainder of the day.	
"	24.4.16		Day spent in cleaning up of the Battalion.	
"	25.4.16	7.30 a.m.	Medical inspection. Coy Commanders at Bn Offices dinner throughout the day for cleaning up.	
"	26.4.16		In the afternoon the C.O. inspected the Battalion by companies.	
"	27.4.16	9 A.M.	Medical inspection. 11th Brigade battalion companies at the Divisional Baths at TINQUES.	
		7 A.M.	March Out. C.S Major 9thKSLI was to Tunnel Medal lecture & demonstration at LIGNY ST FLOCHEL.	
		2.30 P.M	All Offices 1st SOMERSET L.I.J sent the Battalion to take on establishment 3 Coy scale	
		6.45 a.m	R.S.M. Parade. 7 A.M. Medical Inspection 840 Coy Officers instruction 9 a.m – 12 noon Company at.	
			Lt C N Berg of 1st SOMERSET L.I.J ached the Battalion. hoisting of awds, smoke helmet parade 9 C. training of bombers	
"	28.4.16	2 P.M.	Rots marching under Coy arrangement.	
MAROEUIL	29.4.16		Drill and special parade. Battle of building staff French advance. That the Battalion marched to new area (inside N. of ARRAS) by bus, remainder marched a distance of 14 miles, was in very hot, and were tired of dust. Enroute Lunch Enchaphill has made all the difference to eschew thery have taken over easy frontage of 5 in Division from 6A SHERWOOD FORESTERS inadequately present by 1 bus took over ANZIN ½ D at ANZIN, ½ D at ROELINCOURT. A very difficult H Q. H 7 B Companies at MAROEUIL, C Coy at ANZIN, ½ D at ANZIN, ½ D at ROELINCOURT.	
"	30.4.16		relief only made a visible because else corporation visit 6th SHERWOOD FORESTERS 2.30 P.M. Riding class many parts at which	
"	1.5.16		The Battalion officers arrived in the mess. LT E.N. MARRIS, Lt. J.H GARDNER took over command of the Battalion. Colonel HEATHCOTE at arrived & they remained with Maj. H.CHATEL for C.O. Conference	

C.H Bent Lt Col. 1st Roy L
1st Batt. Linc. Regt

1875 W.593/825 1,000,000 4/15 J.B.C. & A. A.D.S.S./Forms/C. 2118.

Army Form C. 2118

1/4 Lincoln Regt
Vol 5

WAR DIARY or INTELLIGENCE SUMMARY
(Erase heading not required.)

Instructions regarding War Diaries and Intelligence Summaries are contained in F.S. Regs., Part II. and the Staff Manual respectively. Title Pages will be prepared in manuscript.

Place	Date	Hour	Summary of Events and Information	Remarks and references to Appendices
MAROEUIL	2.5.16		Work of previous day continued. 2.30 P.M. Riding class continued. LT E.N. MARRIS proceeded on leave. One casualty (slightly) midnight 2-3/5/16. Mining fatigues continued.	
"	3.5.16		Two casualties (wounded). 2.30 P.M. Riding class.	
"	4.5.16		" " 2.30 P.M. Riding class.	
"	5.5.16		" " 2.30 P.M. Riding class. 9 P.M. Lecture to officers by Captain BINNS "5th LINES on the STAR".	
"	6.5.16		Mining fatigues continued. Colonel Heathcote returned from 3rd Army School at AVESNES. CHATEAU and resumed command of the Battalion. 2.30 P.M. Riding class.	
"	7.5.16		Mining fatigues continued. 2.30 P.M. Riding class. Colonel Heathcote gave farewell dinner before taking up appointment as Brigadier of the 7th Infantry Brigade. Officers present:- Major H.M. GARDNER, Lt Adjutant C.H. BOND, R.M.O. Hon Major SIMPSON, Captain HART, Captain GRIMALDI, Captain BURROWS, Captain MAPLES, Lt HOLMES, Lt CROWDEN, Lt CANNON M.O., 2nd Lt H.L. SHAW.	
"	8.5.16		Mining fatigues continued. Colonel Heathcote proceeded to Mont St Eloi to take up appointment as Brigadier General of the 7th Infantry Brigade. Major H. GARDNER assumed command of the Battalion. Lt CROWDEN proceeded on leave. Relief of the Battalion by 8 P.M. The RIFLE BRIGADE commenced. 9 P.M. A, B & B" R.B. Relieved. Maroeuil to the men No 2 & 3 Platoons Coy R.B. arrived at ANZIN to take over. 2/Lt Elliott conducted billeting party to SUS ST LEGER to prepare for Battalion.	
"	9.5.16		The Relief of A Coy by B" & A" The RIFLE BRIGADE and C, D Coy by B" R.B. took over. At 4/tgne, D Coy B" R.B. arriving ANZIN at 12 noon to take over morning 1/5/C [?] relieved. En Bn The Battalion moved to fresh billets at SUS ST LEGER in the following order – Coy Rifts marching body marched 11.45 am noon Captain BURROWS & half C Coy 11.30 am AVESNES-LE-COMTE, Grand Rullicourt, arriving SUS.ST. LEGER about 12.30 P.M. No transport 2.45 P.M. Half C Coy arriving SUS ST LEGER about 5 P.M. Lt E.N. MARRIS returned from leave. 2/Lt Chambers came from base.	
SUS ST LEGER	10.5.16		Company of Coy officers lectures. Musketry & Bombing etc.	
"	11.5.16		7 AM Coy parade. 6 p.m. 2.30 P.M. Coy Officers Conference. 7-7.30 am [?]	
"	12.5.16		Ordinary parades. 11.45 am 1.15 p.m. Special training.	

WAR DIARY
or
INTELLIGENCE SUMMARY

(Erase heading not required.)

Army Form C. 2118

Instructions regarding War Diaries and Intelligence Summaries are contained in F.S. Regs., Part II. and the Staff Manual respectively. Title Pages will be prepared in manuscript.

Place	Date	Hour	Summary of Events and Information	Remarks and references to Appendices
SUS-ST-LEGER	12.5.16		7 a.m. Sick parade. A,B,9 D. Cy each detailed 100 men also N.C.O's & work under R.E. in LUCHEUX WOOD 9 a.m. to 12 noon & 1 pm to 4.30 pm felling trees, making hurdles & fascines. C.Cy's parade were as on the 11th inst. Batting under Battalion arrangements. 2nd Lt. SHAW proceeded on leave	from the 11th inst.
"	13.5.16		7 a.m. Sick parade. Wood fatigue continued by AB 9 C. D Cy Carried out range practice. All officers and about 4 N.C.O's per Cy attended a lecture by Major Campbell on "The Bayonet" at LUCHEUX Cinema at 11.30 am.	
"	14.5.16		Church parade at 11.45. Wesleyan & R.C. at 8.45 am. CAPT W.D. PERRY R.A.M.C. joined for duty vice LT. J. CANNON proceeding to England (Terrn. Engrs.) LT. G.R. SHERWELL rejoined.	
"	15.5.16		Companies at O.C. Cos disposal for drill, bombing, musketry, bayonet fighting 9-12 noon.	
"	16.5.16		300 men continued fatigue in LUCHEUX WOOD. B Cy on the range, bombing practice. Snipers class & bombers Cy under Sgt. Gregory. Bayonet fighting class under Lt. G.H. MARRIS. CAPT BURROWS left battalion to proceed on instrn. course at ROUEN. LT. E.N. MARRIS took over command of C Cy from CAPT BURROWS. Inoculation proceeded with. The following officers joined for duty from the 4/7th Middlesex Regt. LT. L.D.E. FYFFE. D Cy, 2LT S.C. MEREDITH. A Cy, 2LT R.T. THOMSON B Cy. 2LT A.V. COULSON A Cy, 2LT C.A. GOWERS, C Cy, (LT. G.H. MARRIS transferred from C to B Cy)	
"	17.5.16		8 am. Battalion paraded full strength & work over both fatigues in LUCHEUX WOOD. Regimental Canteen opened. Inoculation proceeded with. The following officers joined from the 4/7th MIDDLESEX REGT. 2LT W.S. BATES, D Cy. 2LT R. ELLIOTT. C Cy. LT E.N. MARRIS awarded Military Cross 15th Inst. and Military Medals to 3388 Sgt. J. BAGGLEY & 2935 L/Cpl B.J. JENKS. LT PHILLIPS proceed on leave	
"	18.5.16		Companies at O.C's disposal for bombing, bayonet fighting etc. Sniping and bayonet fighting Classes continued. LT E.N. MARRIS transferred from C to A Cy. LT R.N. HOLMES from D to C Cy. LT. G.R. SHERWELL from A to C (Command) D Cy provisionally. CAPT E.J. GRINLING left the battalion for duty with the 138th BRIGADE STAFF. Battalion played 4th LEICESTERS at football at LESOUICH	Result LEIC. 9 goals LINCS. 1

Army Form C. 2118

WAR DIARY
or
INTELLIGENCE SUMMARY
(Erase heading not required.)

Instructions regarding War Diaries and Intelligence Summaries are contained in F. S. Regs., Part II. and the Staff Manual respectively. Title Pages will be prepared in manuscript.

Place	Date	Hour	Summary of Events and Information	Remarks and references to Appendices
SUS-ST LÉGER	19.5.16		6.30 a.m. Adjutant Parade. 9-12 noon Coy at O.C.'s disposal. Bathing parade for B Coy. Lewis gunners, 2nd Lt Chambers, Sgt Waite & 9 men proceed to HUMBERCAMP. Bathing for HQ, Lewis, Transport, Orderly half. 2nd Lt Chambers, Sgt Waite & 9 men proceeded to HUMBERCAMP. Coys at O.C.'s disposal at 5.30 p.m. the Battalion paraded the stationary train en route for HUMBERCAMP area.	Range to Snipes
"	20.5.16		WARLUZEL, COUTURELLE, arriving in billets about 8.30 p.m.	
HUMBERCAMP	21.5.16		Church parade at 10.30 a.m. 500 men to Bruyure alley fatigue at BIENVILLERS at 8.30 a.m. under R.E. Lt E.N. HARRIS returned on leave. 2nd Lt SHAW returned from leave.	2nd Lt C.E. RICE
"	22.5.16		Coys under Battalion arrangements during the afternoon. 500 men proceeded to BIENVILLERS at 8.30 a.m. to continue fatigue under R.E. Lt E.N. HARRIS & another No adjutant no returns to billets. joined for duty from the 4/7 th M(iddx) Regt and posted to D Company. LEWIS GUNNERS and transport better. The Battalion Coys at O.C.'s disposal during the afternoon, 66 men per company detailed at 8.30 a.m. moved to fresh billets in husments during the afternoon.	2nd Lt C.E. RICE
"	23.5.16		behind FONQUEVILLERS. Coys and generals parade a section of trench behind FONQUEVILLERS.	
"	24.5.16		Coys at O.C.'s disposal during the morning. Rain fell very heavily all afternoon and B & D Coys were forced to leave their huts & return to their old billets. 50 men per Company detailed at 8.30 a.m. to continue the work of the previous night.	
"	25.5.16		50 men despatched clearing the morning to continue last night work. 12 men detailed for officer cleaning under the orders of the Town Major. The rest of the Battalion at Coy officers disposal. 3.30 p.m. Entertainment by the "Whiz Bangs".	
"	26.5.16		150 men despatched to continue the work on the section of trench behind FONQUEVILLERS. 30 mm detailed for refuse cleaning. 3.30 p.m. The C. in C. attended by the Army Commander, Divisional Commander and Brigade Commander inspected the Battalion - 800 Coy (sfat) 300 men on fatigues drawn up in quite extended order leaving ord & other details with their companies. The absence of the Battalion was 340. The men looked well and were very steady in the ranks. Captain MAPLES proceeded on leave. 2nd Lt PHILLIPS returned from leave. Major (A) STIPSON R.A.M.C. joined for duty vice Captain W.J. PERRY proceeding to 3rd NORTH MIDLAND R.A.M.C.	
"	27.5.16		6.30 a.m. 50 men and an officer and 4 file rank detailed for work at WARLINCOURT at excavating gravel. 8.45 a.m. 30 men and 3 NCO's detailed for village cleaning. 50 men detailed to continue work of the previous day behind FONQUEVILLERS and a further 50 men detailed to continue the work at 8.30 a.m.	
"	28.5.16		8 a.m. Same fatigue as yesterday. 9 a.m. A & B Companies under detailed for work under O.C. No 3 Railway Company at LA BAZEQUE. 10.30 a.m. Church parade for all officers and men of LP rank and 5 officers and men of 63 rank. Church parade did not take place. 6 men detailed as ... and 7th men to work at BIENVILLERS under R.A.	

Army Form C. 2118

WAR DIARY
or
INTELLIGENCE SUMMARY
(Erase heading not required.)

Instructions regarding War Diaries and Intelligence Summaries are contained in F. S. Regs., Part II. and the Staff Manual respectively. Title Pages will be prepared in manuscript.

Place	Date	Hour	Summary of Events and Information	Remarks and references to Appendices
HUMBERCAMP	29.5.16		Same fatigues as yesterday, but with slight alteration in the time and will be following alterations 7th One officer 70 men for work under SIGNAL COMPANY. LT. C. N. BOND proceeded on leave.	
"	30.5.16		Same fatigues as yesterday. LT. P.W.J. CANNON injured and transfer to "C" Company	
"	31.5.16		Same fatigues as yesterday. LT E.N. MARRIS returned from leave. Captain SCORER injured and transferred command of "D" Company. LT. G. R. SHERWELL rejoined "A" Company for duty.	
	3.6.16		T. Sheriff Lieut. for Adjt. 1/4th Lincolns	T. Mullin Lt Col. Commanding 1/4th Lincolns

1/4th Batt. Lincs Regt.

OR. 34.

To H.Q.
 3rd Echelon

Herewith War Diary of above unit for month of June 1916.

G. J. Barrell Lt. Col.
Cmdg. 1/4th Lincs Regt.

14.7.16.

Owing to recent operations & casualties amongst officers, this Diary has been delayed.

WAR DIARY or INTELLIGENCE SUMMARY

Army Form C. 2118

1/4 Lincoln Reg
Vol 19

46

Place	Date	Hour	Summary of Events and Information	Remarks and references to Appendices
HUMBERCAMP	June 1/16		Fatigues continued. Battalion bathed. Routes given arrangements. One officer per Company under Captain	HART
"	2/6/16		recommended a bench at FONQUEVILLERS. Lt. COETZEE R.A.M.C.	
"	3/6/16		Fatigues continued. Major STIGSON proceeded to 3rd NORTH MIDLAND R.A.M.C.	
"	4/6/16		Fatigues continued. Church Parade for all not actually on fatigue. 2nd Lt BOPLEY from leave.	
"	5/6/16		10 a.m. Church Parade for all not actually on fatigue.	
"			The Battalion relieved the 6th NOTTS & DERBY in line near SAILLY-AU-BOIS – HUMBERCAMP relay square. Bn Hqrs from STATIONERY dugouts, LEEFING farm, ST AMAND, SOUASTRE to detention. Bn moved dust to 2/4 HA1 R C Coy 7.50 p.m. D Coy 8.01 p.m. Route ST AMAND, SOUASTRE, FONQUEVILLERS. A guide at FORT DICK, C Coy 7.50 p.m. D Coy 8.01 p.m. C, D Coy & Pte JA. Qu. attains at FONQUEVILLERS. A guide at FORT DICK, E25 a.37, C, D Coy + Pte JA. Qu. attains at FONQUEVILLERS. A guide at FORT DICK, CHATEAU was a junction E25 a.37, C, D Coy Coy + Pte JA. Qu. attains at NCO and one guide to proceed to the new JUNCTION KEEP and THE BLUFF. Each Company details one officer and NCO and one guide to proceed to the new junction 3 to take over from the NOTTS & DERBY. Captain MAYLES returned from leave. 2nd Lt BOPLEY proceeded on leave crews arriving 3 a.m. to take over from the NOTTS & DERBY. Captain MAYLES returned from leave. 2nd Lt BOPLEY proceeded on leave	
FONQUEVILLERS	6/6/16		Fatigue parties during the day from Town Major. Without during night in front of Trench 48 (a lift System of Groundwire) in position. Front Line to be dug towards GOMMECOURT. Fatigue parties from the Battalion supplied during the day in carrying GAS cylinders, ammunition etc to the front line. 2nd Lt C.F. SKINNER rejoined from Base. 2nd Lt W.S. BATES returned from leave. Lt Colonel G.J. BARREL reported	
"	7/6/16		Fatigues. Town Major. 9.30 P.M. Digging Parties, 240 strong, under Captain HOLMES & 2nd HARRIS commenced digging from 3/4 Battalion on new line in command. 9.30 P.M. Digging Parties, 240 strong, under Captain SCORER at the same line from 3/4 Battalion On new line in command. Winding party under Captain SCORER at the same line. new tracks from Trench 48 towards the German Lines, and a distance of about 250 yards. Winding party under mostly coverings carried the tracks under arrangement. Lt Colonel H.M. GARDENER arrived, assumed command of the Battalion. Fatigue parties found during the day. The Battalion received a rations	
"	8/6/16		Lt Colonel G.J. BARREL took over the command of the Battalion. Fatigue parties found during the day. The Battalion received a rations from the G.O.C. on very congratulations upon the work done during the night of 7–8. 9.20 p.m. was on the sun. Trench manning. The wiring	
"	9/6/16		parties outside FONQUEVILLERS Continuing. 2nd Lt MITTON arrived from leave. 2nd Lt MONTGOMERY joined 2nd Lt ELLIOTT proceeded on leave. 2nd Bond returned from leave. 2nd Lt MONTGOMERY joined the Batt.n for duty from the Base. Wiring, digging new trench continued at 9.20 p.m. Wires covering the work, parties with a Lewis gun. 2nd Lt H. SHAW, 4 1 Lewis Gunner were killed. 2nd Lt SHAW had kept this Diary up to today. Digging party a Lewis gun. 2nd Lt H. SHAW, 4 1 Lewis Gunner were killed. 2nd Lt SHAW had kept this Diary up to today. Digging party Casualties 1 man wounded.	
"	10/6/16		Capt L. HART proceeded to 3rd Army School at Auxi-le-Chateau. Capt SCORER looks out during ad 2nd in Command. 2nd Lt R. ELLIOTT proceeded on leave GIVENCHY. Wiring continued in front of BUCK trench. Casualties 2 men wounded. Also work carried on communication and support trenches.	
"	11/6/16		2nd Lt SHAW buried in English Cemetery in Cemetery lane at noon: The C.O. & 2nd in Command and other officers of the Batt.n present at the ceremony. CAPT ELLIS rejoined for duty from Base &s posted to D Coy. Work on new communication and cord trenches continued. B Coy lost 2 men wounded near Church by H.E. Wiring party completed new line in front of Bush trench.	

WAR DIARY
or
INTELLIGENCE SUMMARY
(Erase heading not required.)

Army Form C. 2118

Place	Date	Hour	Summary of Events and Information	Remarks and references to Appendices
FONQUEVILLERS	12.6.16		Work on communication and support trenches continued in the evening and rest maybe. No casualties.	
"	13.6.16		Work continued evening and night	
"	14.6.16		—do— All time put forward 1 hour at 11.0 pm. 2nd Lt STEPHENSON proceeded on leave.	
"	15.6.16		—do— 2nd Lt BADLEY returned from leave. 2nd Lt CALEY joined for duty from base and posted to B Coy.	
"	16.6.16		Fatigues, digging & unloading parties continued. Detachment of 2 officers & 56 men per Coy together with details detailed for special duty as smoke bombers.	
"	17.6.16		Fatigues etc continued. Smoke bombers carry on separately in regard to training & work.	
"	18.6.16		—"— in morning. Battalion relieved by 6th Sherwood Foresters. Relief commenced 11.30 pm and was complete by 12.25 am. Smoke Bomb detachment proceeded to Bienvillers Sunday. 2nd Lt MITTON and men relieved them. Remainder of C & D Coy remained in Fonquevillers in hut. Remainder of A + B Coys proceeded to the huts in HUMBERCAMP.	2nd Lt CALEY Capt.
HUMBERCAMP	19.6.16		100 men supplied for fatigue under R.E. 85 in morning. 130 men supplied for fixing in cable trenches 3 miles. 2nd Lt DOBBY joined for duty from leave and posted to C Coy. 2nd Lt ELLIOT & 2nd Lt returned from leave. Capt ELLIS proceeded to BIENVILLERS to take over command of Smoke Bomb Detachment	
"	20.6.16		The fatigues supplied. Specialists training continued.	
"	21.6.16		No fatigues. Parade of hr during morning for drill, wire avoidance etc. Parade 3/4 hr during evening. Baths used during morning. Cricket played.	
"	22.6.16		Parade 1½ hrs during morning. Cpls & R/Cpls under R.S.M. for 1 hour for drive & training. H.B.E. parade under the Adjutant. Evening at 8.15 pm. 200 men supplied for fixing in cables trenches behind FONQUEVILLERS. Party returned about 2.30 am. 2nd Lt SIMPSON sent to Field Ambulance	
"	23.6.16		Parade in morning. Specialist training continued from 11.0 am to 12.0 am. Afternoon parades stopped by heavy rain.	
"	24.6.16		No fatigues. 2nd Lt STEPHENSON returned from leave. 2nd Lt STEPHENSON sent to I/O Ambulance. 9.0 pm No fatigues supplied. the C.O. held a conference with all Officers and a few senior NCO's by Coy at	
"	25.6.16		Capt HOMEL, 52 OR returned from Bienvillers. G.O.C. 46th Bri inspected Batt at Humbercamp at 11.0 am on parade. Batn dress up the following 2 full ranks. 20 men paraded 7.0 am. 4 are carried to Sarnadon by the making of dug-outs etc. like R.E. Fatigue party. 5.0 pm. Church parades: R.C. 8.30 am at HUMBERCAMP CHURCH. Wesleyan W.B. & combined with S.W. Lincs. Returned S.W. Lincs. on parade ground at 11.0 am. C of E in conjunction with S.W. Lincs, on parade ground at 11.0 am Party of 2nd Lt CALEY & 80 OR proceeded to FONQUEVILLERS for special duty with trench Morter Battery. Party left at 3.0 pm. Later in evening LT SHERWELL proceeded to FONQUEVILLERS to take over command of this detachment. Officers on return 35 OR each. 2nd Lts QUANTRAIL & GELIOT joined for duty from base and posted to A & B Coys respectively	

1875 Wt. W593/826 1,000,000 4/15 J.B.C. & A. A.D.S.S./Forms/C. 2118.

"A" Form. Army Form C. 2121.
MESSAGES AND SIGNALS.

Secret

TO 4 Lincolns

Sender's Number: SC 531
Day of Month: 30
AAA

Zero time will be 7-30 am 1st July

From: 138 IB
Time: 4-45 pm

SC 135 IB

WAR DIARY or INTELLIGENCE SUMMARY

Army Form C. 2118

Place	Date	Hour	Summary of Events and Information	Remarks and references to Appendices
Hulluch	26.6.16		Fatigue supplied at night for finishing cable trench behind Tourquennes. Party 150 strong + 3 officers.	Paraded 8.15pm and returned 2.0 am. This parade in morning.
"	27.6.16		Battalion parade at 11.30am to 12.30. Bombing dresses police cooks sanitary men + 4 grooms returned to Camp for duty in trenches. Hemi detachment paraded 2.0 pm proceeded to Tourquennes to finish cable trench of the Humbercamp to trenches opposite Bayencourt. This work was joined by an headquarters parade at 9.0 pm. Batt'n moved from Humbercamp to trenches opposite GOMMECOURT at 9.0 pm + 7.0 pm. 2 Coys at 9.0 pm Batn strength including HQrs Det about 250 O.Ranks frontage taken over 1200 yds. 2 Coys between 4.0 pm + 7.0 pm. 2 Coys at 9.0 pm Batn 2 Platoons - 2 officers & the 4th division were loaned my Bde for manning trenches. Relief complete 1.50 am. 2 officers & from 4th Division. 2nd & 5th Lee. Diggs + Wigan joined for duty from Case. reported to B.A+D Coys respectively.	trenches taken over
Fonquevillers	28.6.16		Heavy shelling by our artillery; feeble retaliation on the part of the enemy. Patrols sent out by 4 Coys to examine enemy's wire at 11.0 pm. Returned with no casualties at 12.15 & 12.30 pm. Enemy wire found intact with exception of 2 gaps made by our artillery.	
"	29.6.16		Day quiet except continuation of bombardment of enemy trenches by our artillery. At 11.0 pm artillery put barrage over enemys trenches opposite flag referred to above. At same time raiding party left our trenches. Our party consisted of 3+ O.Ranks under Lt Col Bond, 2nd Lt Elliott + 2nd Lt Queen Smith. At 11.15 our party reached enemys wire + were discovered by 2 German listening posts. At 11.30 pm fire was opened on them both from trenches and from enemy listening posts. Enemy ahead in force + attempts to remove our party failed. Men stopped by rifle fire + bombs. 2/Lt Bond was wounded in neck and died on the way to the dressing station. 1 man was killed wounds by a bomb. Enemy went up Red Lights. 12.30 pm When signal to return was given from our trenches all our party returned. The only casualties being the 2 mentioned. No enemy prisoners were taken.	
"	30.6.16		Day quiet. Very few signs of enemy. At 10.45 pm enemy mean except 2 men put Lewis gun (.15 mm) proceeded to dig a false trench in front of our own wire. So much snow as possible was made of the digging. The trench dug was very shallow but the parapet was made very obvious party returned at 1.30 am. No casualties. This false trench was dug to attract enemys fire next day.	

C.P. Powell Lt Col,

Comdg 4/5 Batt Lines Regt

4th 8 Battalion Regt

4 LEICS RGT
4 LINCOLN RGT

Ref. Op. order 37 para 2.

1. When relieved by 4 Linc Rgt on the evening of 27th inst, O.C. 4 Leics Rgt will arrange to hand over to O.C. 4 Linc Rgt two platoons for his use for holding the line of trenches.
   These 2 platoons will be at the disposal of O.C. 4 Linc Rgt until further orders. They will not bring a Lewis Gun ammunition belonging to 4 Leics with them. All details of the transfer to be arranged by C O's concerned. This party will be relieved by 4 Lincoln Rgt for 28th & after.

2. No further orders of relief of 4 Leics by 4 Linc will be issued. All details of relief will be settled between Battns. concerned. The 4 Lincoln will not move the bivouac until dusk.
   26.6.16.

   C H Jordan
   Capt Bde
   M.G.R.

"A" Form.   Army Form C. 2121.
MESSAGES AND SIGNALS.   No. of Message

Urgent
DR

TO   4. LINCOLN.

Sender's Number Day of Month In reply to Number
LSM 6/8   25   AAA

4th Lincoln will take over trench line
South of Gommecourt Road on night
of 27/28th. aaa Transport will
move by "C" and "D" tracks
into Fonquevillers aaa all movements
to take place after dark from
Humbercamps. aaa details will
be forwarded later.

Please report by returning
D.R. what will be your approximate
strength of officers and O.R. for going
into the trenches. 138. 1. B.

From
Place
Time   6.30 pm

Confidential

O.C. 4th Lincolns.

I am surprised to see by your report today that my message C.B.M. 693 of 26th was not complied with. This urgent message was received by you at 5.30 p.m. on 26th some 3½ or 4 hours before dark yet no steps appear to have been taken to reconnoitre the trench by daylight or to comply with the suggestion that small parties should proceed by daylight & commence work as soon as light began to fail. Such neglect to comply with the ordinary precautions to ensure the performance of an urgent duty is difficult to understand & points to a lack of comprehension of the importance of our present preparations which is most regrettable.

It also indicates an indifference to the welfare & wellbeing of the men; for it must have been foreseen that should the work not have been completed last night the men would have lost their rest & been unnecessarily exposed to the weather for no result.

It is hoped that no occasion will present itself in the future which will necessitate further comment of this description.

J Clumby
Maj fed
Coy 138 2/ka

27.6.16.

OPERATION ORDER No 29

By Lt. Col. G. J. Barrell, Commanding 1/4th Battn. Leics Regt
In the Field   20.9.1916

1. The Lewis Detachment and the remnant of the Battalion at HUMBERCAMPS will move to take over trenches S. of GOMMECOURT ROAD to S. end of trench 39a from 4th. Leicesters. Route. ST AMAND, SOUASTRE, to destination.

2. The Lewis Detachment will be attached, 2 guns and teams per Coy. and will march up as a detachment starting HUMBERCAMPS 8 p.m. T.O. Officer will arrange regarding limbers. Signallers will parade at 6.15 p.m. and march up separately.

3. Coy. Commanders with one guide per Coy. will reconnoitre their portions of line tomorrow afternoon and will send guides to meet their two Lewis Gun teams at X roads E.27 C.89 at 8 p.m. They will then place their Coy. guns in position by daylight. The T.O. Officer will advise Coy. Commanders regarding emplacements.

4. The remnant of "A" & "B" Coys. will parade at pond near Church ready to march off at 9 p.m. The remnant of H.Q, C & D Coys. in that order outside Orderly Room ready to march off at 9.10 p.m. These two parties will move independently of each other under senior officer present.

5. 4th. Leicester guides for each Coy. will meet these parties at X roads E.27 C.89 at 11 p.m.

6. Disposition of line.
   A. Coy. 39—40 trenches
   C "   40—41
   B "   42 & 2.43
   D "   1/2.43 — GOMMECOURT ROAD.

   Coy. Commanders will make certain that they are in touch with Coys. on their flanks.

7. Ration & water parties 1 N.C.O. & 4 men per Coy. will be detailed in advance and will report to Battn. H.Q at THE BLUFF at times to be notified later. Tea, ration and Bacon Sandwiches will come up on night of the 27th. and will be issued to Coys. Coys. will ration all details including Signallers, who are attached to them.

8. Coys. will carry their own pack carriers and men will take up 200 rounds S.A.A. to be issued tomorrow. Coy. records to be put in charge of Coy. Q.M.Sgts. and surplus stores (blues &c.) to be ready for collection by transport at Coy. messes at 5 p.m. 2/Lt. W.G. Chambers will arrange to collect brass discs.

9. Transport will move as arranged.

10. Waterbottles are to be filled before Coys. move off and Coy. Commanders will see that this water is kept in reserve.

11. Completion of relief to be reported to Battn. H.Q.

12. Billets are to be left clean.

Issued by Orderly at   p.m.
Copy No. 1. Adjutant S.O.
         2. "A" Coy.
         3. "B" "
         4. "C" "
         5. "D" "
         6. Lewis Det.   14. Lt. T.O.W.
         7. Transport Off. 15. Lt. C. Porter
         8. T.O. Officer

C.H. Bond, Lt. & Adjt.
1/4th Battn. Leics Regt.

4 pm Start the mounted   Coolies leave at 6.0 pm.   Cycle to Artillery
    24 Valises   1 limber   Cross Road
    64 Shovels }   1   "   at 11.0 p.m.
    80 Picks   }   1   "   to meet procession
       Orderly Cart   1   "   of pack mules.
       Clothing   }
       Implements }
       Officers Mess Kit

WAR DIARY or INTELLIGENCE SUMMARY

Army Form C. 2118

H+Q Dy 1/4 Lincoln Rgt
Oct 17

Place	Date 1916	Hour	Summary of Events and Information	Remarks and references to Appendices
Fonquevillers	1st July	7.30 am	attack on GOMMECOURT, 1st wave 7.15" No2 & D Coys. 2 Lt Jelliott killed, 2 Lt L.B.S. Wounds, we were relieved at night by 1-1/4th Bn. 9 2nd Lieuts (London Scottish) & Kensingtons. We proceeded to HANNESCAMP Trenches 13.6m.c. on return to RAND in support. 1 Car. B.pt. Blew.	2 Lt L.B.S. Wounds, 2 Lt Skinner Shell Shock
HANNESCAMP	2nd do	8.10 am	3 men A Coy killed & 4 hit in LEICESTER Sec A Coy in reserve in village	
	3rd do	2. 0pm	A Coy moved to centre of firing line	
	4th "		Rest in trenches	
	5th "	9.0pm	2 Lt Badley & fatigue Pty 5 (carrying boots) returns from BIENVILLERS Reinforcement of 43 men & 5 NCO arrived	
	6th	—	Capt Ellis & another Officer's men returns to FONQUEVILLERS	
	7th "	8 pm	Ball' relieved B St LEICESTERS & both went Trenches 71-77 at BIENVILLERS	
	7/8	night	D Coy & Lewis Guns in support	
	8th	11 am	Lewis Guns relieved of 5 LEICESTERS & moved into BIENVILLERS	
BIENVILLERS	8/9/	night	working parties out (full strength) carrying guns & ammunition	
	9th	9.30/1	do do	
	10th	—	do do	cleaning up Battalion in appearance Coy Comdrs reports from their Coys
	11th		The following Officers joined the Batt". Major T.R. Sen. 2 Lt Geo. Strelley, 2 Lt. H. Scott, 2 Lt J. Portey Loop. Lieut arrived to R & damage into entr'ment 2 Lt J. Peacock 2nd R.I. Lamps	
	—	11 am	30 men from A.B.C.D B"s & 32 Lewis & Lincoln N 26 Bombers were tested	
LACOUCHE	12th	9.30 am	Battn relieved by 4th MDSX & proceeded to LACOUCHE by Platoons	
	13th	11.30 am	Battn forward & relieved for 1 day next 8 days refit & cleaning up of billets, clothes, removing mud etc	
	14th	2 pm	Lewis Gunnery Tactics by Capt Thadeo Raff	
BERLES	14th	6 pm	A Coy Billet area Trenches 90-92 from RFG 63 Bgde. B.D. B"s both now Trenches 93-103 from 6 SS Staff	
	—9 pm	137 B.D.E. 16. & on RAVINE in support	
	aug 14/15.	2 am	Our artillery bombard the enemy who did not reply to any extent at 3.5 Hrs 1 Casl. Officers & Men	
	15.	10-1 pm	Genl Thorpe, Brigadier & Lieut Willsons inspect our trenches	
	19/6	night	Capt Ellis proceeded to Field Ambulance	
	16 1st	night	No Patrols sent out to enemy's Our artillery bombarded their many gun positions—German reserves attacker 7.30 Gun Shells ~18 shower

1875 Wt. W 593/826 1,000,000 4/15 J.B.C. & A. A.D.S.S./Forms/C 2118. Work on cleaning trenches continues B Coy making dug-outs

WAR DIARY
INTELLIGENCE SUMMARY
(Erase heading not required.)

Army Form C. 2118

Instructions regarding War Diaries and Intelligence Summaries are contained in F.S. Regs., Part II. and the Staff Manual respectively. Title Pages will be prepared in manuscript.

Place	Date	Hour	Summary of Events and Information	Remarks and references to Appendices
Pselu	17	11 P.M.	A Co. went up to B3 O.R. to examine enemy wire, report very strong, work done 50 more yards (this one support line)	
Pomies	18	3 P.M.	Steaming up with Co's Engineers. The Bluff was relieved by 5 Kings & reported to Pomies.	
	19	—	The Batt. was engaged in cleaning up. Three Co's, 3 Officers arrived 3/L. Statler. Weather fine. Batt. on defence flying as follows — B.2, 3, 6, & at H.Q. One battery shelled and [illegible] shower falling as follows — 2.3 [illegible] transport &c passed Pomies to Lewis guns returned to their Co's. Basting Bn. 4 hu died the party 2nd Badly new boring offr & 21 P.Bleve 3 came up at 5.0 p.m.	
	20	12 N. 12 P.M.	Expiry offrs Capt. Off Emery started drilling Somme-Thiaulne road at 4.15. no damage weather fine. A.B. on fatigue, also part B. Co. Brellis lumb [illegible] refused & drilling 5 mins march 6 p.m. Camp huts only 5 to take P. Co. train on after [illegible] was A/73 [illegible]. Recon's parts lesson at 2-3 in morning fatiguing the Co. Paid on afternoon. Touch relieved at 5.30 p.m.	
	21	1 P.M.	Lt. Thompson left for Short Course. Battn Purple, Post 10 O'clock Inspection by Bn. 2nd 4 Coys. & 57 men arrived for parade at 2-3. instr. for [illegible].	
	22		3-4.15 N.Co's trained 5 Capt. on poetry operation. Copy gave lecture to [illegible] & Div. & [illegible] & hour & platoon.	
Bselu	23		Batt. returned 5 Pomies to Bselu. R.1. Coy or A. Left. 6, D. Centre C. Right. 15, B 5.30 D 5.45. HQ Co. 6 miles & 1 platoon to HQ. Euvers & Road Complete refused at 3.4.5 p.m. no person on duty sent [illegible] & Co to transport	
	24		— 12 whiles supplying off [illegible] in & part with [illegible] for intradd[?]	
	25		C Co. sends BCo. an support suppy of Lyons Patrol. Lewis Emma Cleary ammunition 1s 1st & [illegible] from 10.15 to touchpost from 11-1 AM. Patrols in experience & reports approaching. B 6 emlaling[?]. A 6 had a patrol of 1 officer Pair of 9 N Co. of 9 men armouring 3 hop & supported. D 6. N Co. 9 men under R.E. Came and used [illegible] no enemy reactor any [illegible] from one out but 9.9 N Co. 9/10 men [illegible] mapping Tuesday not	
	26		D6 officially. N Co'n [illegible] some enemy active D 6. on [illegible]. Weather very misty and [illegible] very warm in the day night 2nd 4/2 A.6. Battn of 1 officer & 30 other ranks arrived 4.0 & transport arrived D.6. (M) 3 men B (M) 1 man in transport. also Commanding. Ben'd [illegible] Monchy & 6 fatigue & 30 men [illegible] [illegible] a man Comps mon [illegible] 5 land at 3.30 a. 26. D. D. [illegible] 3 Officer & 3 O.R.	
	27		[illegible] strays from all units [illegible] 1 AM. Enemy very quiet [illegible] from conversation D.6 aired boiling pressure [illegible] 11 p.m — 1 AM. Enemy very quiet day. No again of enemy [illegible] on our front. 2 p.m. M.C to F.A sand 5 ammunition [illegible] S spare shelters [illegible] 10.3 + Earing acft. 5 and [illegible]	
	28		Very quiet day. No again of enemy [illegible] on our [illegible]. Capt Warner leaving Boulogne & 4 [illegible] from S.W. Ridge & Gros [illegible]	

WAR DIARY
or
INTELLIGENCE SUMMARY
(Erase heading not required.)

Army Form C. 2118

Place	Date 1916	Hour	Summary of Events and Information	Remarks and references to Appendices
In the trenches Bailer	July 29		Very misty morning, very warm later in day. Shows N.E. & S. very light. Enemy very quiet. Snipers & Gunners apparently have altered their tune to remarkable degree. 2 Lt Elkes proceed to Sandy returning with car. Officers & 6 men worked on wiring T.9,11,92 support line. 12 cwts of T front wire erected in afternoon 94. Remainder of support section carried on with the support fire bays. Lads were read at jumbled est. D.6 all fund, regrades improved T.9.0. Big no. of T.103. completed bomb recess etc in NOODLES AVE. C.6. crews 9.0 gants of T.96. with trench mor. other work in gallery 4 m 986 wounded from enemy rifle	
	30		Last night 29/30. Our Lewis Gunners swept parapet at intervals from 10–10.40 from 11.20 – midnight. Enemy fired two rifles at the gallop at same enemy non-chalantly also on schedule an outburst 20 aimed bing travel was sent @ 1.30 today. Gerry E. as we watched it. Stores also afternoon & forwards and filled up. BIENVILLERS. Bath were relieves of previous. Lewis Gunners fly covers relieves first. Draft of 80 men carried. S.O.S. radio Tunaba. (1 man wounded)	
BIENVILLERS	31		B.6. in duty. Breakfast 7.45. for man on night fatigues under 6 non-commiss. 1 NCO & 6 men detailed book on the precise lights to the enemy's snaphook of enemy 3 wheels to hard when attempt was forced out best also thrown. Lamps note in billets by 9.10 m. ration on fatigues any. R. & S. call 9 p m. Lights out 9.30 pm. D.R.O. 1807 29/7/16. "Precise of machine" in 2 will be discontinued. Route of wastage for August fixed at Officers = 3/7. All men who who are receipts uniform. Parties cutting down trees on footballers cross. CRO 2x9 at 11 AM tomorrow for investigation.	

G. Rowell Lieut Col.
Commanding 1/4 ....

V. H....
2nd Lt H Ayres
.....

"C" Form (Duplicate).
MESSAGES AND SIGNALS.

Army Form C. 2123.
(In books of 50's in duplicate.)

No. of Message..........

Charges to Pay. £ s. d.

Office Stamp.

Service Instructions.

Handed in at........................Office..............m. Received..............m.

TO O.C. A Coy

| Sender's Number | Day of Month 2.7.16 | In reply to Number | AAA |

A Coy will move to the Bluff
Junction Keep & Fort Dick as
occupied by them the last time
the Battⁿ was in Longpont lines.
Own route to be taken. O.C Coy
to report arrival. Batt HQrs
will be notified later.
2nd Lt Macduff who is
at the Bluff should be
informed. Arrangements to
be made with him to
move to Fort Dick Bluff etc.

FROM
PLACE & TIME

2nd Lieut
A Coy

"C" Form (Original).
MESSAGES AND SIGNALS.

Army Form C. 2123.
(In books of 50's in duplicate.)

No. of Message..................

Prefix....... Code....... Words.......	Received	Sent, or sent out	Office Stamp.
£ s. d.	From..................	At.............m.	
Charges to collect	By..................	To..................	
Service Instructions.		By..................	

Handed in at.................. Office.........m. Received.........m.

TO

*Sender's Number	Day of Month	In reply to Number	A A A

lie at H.Qtrs tonight.

All Lewis Guns Teams will remain in the trenches for 24 hours. Lewis Gun Officer will remain also at present Batn HQtrs.

Coys will make arrangements to supply guides + NCOs to remain in trenches till tomorrow.

Remainder of Smoke Details will move separately to their billets at Fouquex. + there await their Coy. Officers.

Coys of Smoke Details attached to Coys will rejoin their own Coys tonight after arrival in billets.

FROM
PLACE & TIME

*This line should be erased if not required.
Wt. 432—M437 500,000 Pads. H W V 5 16 Forms C. 2123.

"C" Form (Duplicate).
MESSAGES AND SIGNALS.

Army Form C. 2123.
(In books of 50's in duplicate.)
No. of Message ....

Charges to Pay. £ s. d.

Office Stamp.

Service Instructions.

Handed in at............... Office.......... m. Received.......... m.

TO Orders for Move

Sender's Number | Day of Month | In reply to Number | AAA

Batt. will move into billets in Forquevillers tonight after relief. A & C Coys will be relieved by London Scottish and London Regt. Coys. On the Kemmel from one Batt will arrange guides themselves with Coy Commanders of incoming Battalions. All trench stores including Spades & Shovels very lights etc will be handed over to incoming Coys. Regt stores such as waterskins very pistols, periscopes will be returned by Coys as early as possible to H.Qrs. 1 N.C.O. & 2 men per Coy have been taken from remainder of Smoker Details. These will act as guides and will

FROM

PLACE & TIME

Operation Order No 30 by Lt. Col. G.J. Barrell, Cmdg.,
1/4th. Battn. Lincs Regiment.
In the Field.
2.7.16.

Copy No.

1. The Batty will relieve the 8th. East Lancs tonight in the trenches in front of HANNESCAMPS.

2. Batty will be distributed as follows :-
   a. Front line Right Coy. B. Coy. will hold trenches 68 to 73 inclusive with 3 platoons in front line & 1 platoon in support in LILLE STREET.
   b. Front line. Left Coy. C. Coy will hold trenches 74 to 77 inclusive with 3 platoons in front line and 1 platoon in support line in LONGY STREET.
   c. Support Coy. D. Coy. 3 platoons in dugouts just off LEFT AVENUE and 1 platoon in village.
   d. Reserve Coy. A. Coy. in dugouts in the village.
      Headquarters in HANNESCAMP.
      H.Q. Bombers in dugouts at village entrance to LULU LANE.

3. MARCH. 1 Guide per platoon from East Lancs will be at the Gendarmerie tonight at 9. p.m.
   Order of March and times for Coys. to arrive at Gendarmerie.
   C. Coy. 9 p.m. B. Coy. 9.10 pm. D. Coy 9.20 pm. A. Coy. 9.30 pm.
   Coys. will proceed by platoons at 100 yds interval.

4. ADVANCE PARTY. Coy. Commdrs. and Coy. S.M's and 2 guides per Coy. will arrive at Batty H.Q. in HANNESCAMP at 6.30 pm. to take over stores, reconnoitre trenches etc.
   H.Q. Capt. Scorer & C. H.Q. guides to take over Hdqrs.
   Signallers with all kit & equipment will proceed with this party to take over telephone Stations.

5. HEADQR. BOMBERS will be returned from Coys. and will be under the charge of Lt. M.H. Woods. For the march they will follow A. Coy. H.Q. Bombers are to report to Sgt. Brittain at the Brasserie at 9. pm tonight.
   Lt. M.H. Woods will proceed with the advance party and will take 1 H.Q. Bomber from D. Coy. with him as guide. He will arrange for a guide from East Lancs. to be with the other guides at the Gendarmerie at 9 pm tonight.

6. LEWIS GUNS. L.G. Officer with 1 N.C.O. from detachment to proceed with advance party.
   2 L.G. limbers will be at the Brasserie at 10.45 pm. and will there report to L.O. Sgt. These limbers on being loaded will proceed with limbers to HANNESCAMP. The L.G. officer will arrange for 2 guides to be at the Brasserie from East Lancs at 10.30 pm to guide party.

7. TRANSPORT. Officers mess kit. 2 servants per Coy. should be detailed off to be in charge of officers mess kit. B, C & D. Coys. mess kit is to be brought to H.Q. by 8.45 pm. and to report to Orderly Room. A Coy's. mess kit will remain at junction keep under charge of 2 servants. A limber will proceed direct to junction keep, load A. Coy's. mess kit and any Coy. stores to be carried: it will then proceed direct to H.Q. & report to Pte. F. Chambers, load Coy. & H.Q. mess kit & any other stores to be carried. It will then proceed to HANNESCAMP and dump load at Batt H.Q. where servants will see that mess kits are properly dealt with.
   If necessary this limber will make a second journey to the Brasserie. After dealing with mess kits & stores, it will take back to the Q.M. Stores empty water tins of Lt. Sherwell's party. Lt. Sherwell will arrange for a guide to be at H.Q. to report to Pte. Chambers at 8.30 pm. to show Pte. Chambers the position of the empty tins.

8. RATIONS & WATER. Rations will be brought via BIENVILLERS to barricade on HANNESCAMP, BIENVILLERS Road (400 yds. outside HANNESCAMP). Ration & water limbers cannot leave BIENVILLERS before 11.30 p.m. Watercarts are to proceed to dump in HANNESCAMP to unload.
   R.S. Maj. will be in charge of rations & water. Fatigue parties shown on separate list.

9. Lieut. Sherwell's party will rejoin their Coys. Arrangements to be made between O.C. Coys. with Lt. Sherwell.
   Coys. will arrange to draw Very pistols & wire cutters from Batt. H.Q. before leaving for HANNESCAMP.

10. CARRYING PARTIES. A. Coy. to provide 2 full ranks & 30 O.R. who will report to L.O. Officer at Batt. H.Q. HANNESCAMP at 11.30 p.m. for carrying to front & support lines.
    A. Coy. will also provide 1 full rank, 1 L/Cpl. & 30 men to report to R.S.M. at Batt. H.Q. in HANNESCAMP at 11.15 pm for carrying rations to front line.
    D. Coy. will parade their platoon billetted in village at 11.15 p.m. at Batt. H.Q. They will report there to R.S.M. for the carrying of rations from limbers to HANNESCAMP. In addition D Coy will parade 1 full rank & 12 men to carry rations to their 3 platoons in dugouts of LEFT AVENUE.
    Re. Rations, Coy. S.M. should see that rations are correctly distributed to avoid confusion later.
    H.Q. Rations will be drawn by party of 1 L/Cpl. & 12 men of the Bombers who will report to R.S.M. at 11.15 pm.

J.A. Phillips
2/Lt. & A/Adjt.
1/4 Batt. the Lincolnshire Regt.

Operation Order No. 31. by Lt. Col. G.J. Barrell cmdg.
1/4th Batt'n Lincolnshire Regiment
In the field.   6.7.16.

1. **RELIEF.** The Battalion will be relieved by the 5th Leicesters on the night of the 7th inst. On relief the Batt'n will move into billets in BIENVILLERS. Relief will commence about 8 p.m.

2. **ORDER OF RELIEF.** Coys. will be relieved in the following order and by the Coys. of the 5th Leics. noted against each:

4TH LINCS.	5TH. LEICS.	Trenches taken over.
D.	D.	Support
A.	B.	71 - 75
B.	A.	68 - 70
C.	C.	76 - 77

3. **GUIDES.** Coys. will each detail one guide per platoon to report to Batt'n H.Q at 7 p.m. Signallers will detail one guide to report to Batt'n H.Q at 6.45 p.m. The Leicesters will arrive by platoons & Coys. will arrange that as soon as a platoon is relieved it marches away & proceeds to destination.

4. **UP & DOWN TRENCHES.** While the relief is continuing, up traffic will use LULU LANE and down traffic LEFT AVENUE.

5. **LEWIS GUNS.** will not be relieved till 11 a.m. 8th inst. Further orders will be issued later.

6. **Coy in support to 4th Leicesters.** D. Coy will on the night of the 7/8th occupy trenches in support of 4th Leicesters. On relief, therefore, they will proceed direct to support trenches. The Coy. will return to billets in BIENVILLERS after stand down in the morning.

7. **ADVANCE PARTY.** 2/Lt. W.G. Chambers together with 1 N.C.O & 1 guide per platoon from each Coy. & 2 H.Q. guides & 1 guide from bombers will report at Batt'n H.Q at 9.30 a.m. to proceed to BIENVILLERS to arrange billets for the battalion. This party will return as soon as possible. D. Coy. will detail 1 officer, the C.S.M. and 1 N.C.O. per platoon to report to Batt'n H.Q at 10. a.m. to proceed to reconnoitre the support trenches they will have to occupy.

8. **H.Q. BOMBERS.** will proceed on relief under Lt. Wood to their billets in BIENVILLERS.

9. **SIGNALLERS.** will proceed after relief to billets under Signalling Sergt. The Signallers will also detail one man to accompany Advance party under 2/Lt. Chambers.

10. **REPORTING.** Coys. will report by runner to Batt'n H.Q as soon as they have been relieved and D. Coy. will in addition report to Batt'n H.Q as soon as they have taken up their position in support trench.

11. **TRANSPORT.** The transport of the 5th Leicesters will be available for us to take back stores etc., to BIENVILLERS. Coys. may send their mess tent to BIENVILLERS during the day if they wish. All mess tents to go by transport will be sent to R.S.M. by 9 p.m. Box periscopes, Very pistols will be carried by Coys. to BIENVILLERS. All water tins & dixies are to be returned to R.S.M. by 8 p.m. The latter is important as otherwise water & cooking arrangements will be thrown out. Coys. will render a report to Batt'n H.Q by 8 pm that this has been done.

12. **RATIONS.** Rations, 2 water carts & the Coy. cookers will arrive at BIENVILLERS at 6.15 p.m. and will be met by party mentioned in next para. The 1 N.C.O per Coy. and Pte Coy. Cooks will report to Batt'n H.Q at 5.30 pm & will proceed to BIENVILLERS & meet transport at Church at 6.15 pm. The N.C.O per Coy. will take over rations & the cooks will, after installing cookers, arrange to have hot tea ready by 9.15 p.m when the Batt'n will probably begin to arrive. The 2 watercarts will remain until the limbers from HANNESCAMP arrive with empty tins, when the tins will be filled. Coys. will have 30 tins allotted to them, & H.Q. 20. If there are any tins there are in the Q.M's stores ready filled. The transport will bring up any tins there are in the Q.M's stores ready filled.

13. **VALISES.** Valises for officers will be brought up by transport and will be delivered to the various billets. The N.C.O per Coy will be responsible that this

                                                        [signature]
                                                   2/Lt. & A/Adjt.
                                                   1/4th Lincs Regt.

WAR DIARY OF INTELLIGENCE SUMMARY

Army Form C. 2118

1/4 Leicester Regt

Vol 21

16.E

Place	Date 1916	Hour	Summary of Events and Information	Remarks and references to Appendices
BIENVILLERS	3 Aug		This fracas was very quiet. Enemy artillery work being the order of the day. Showing my men interest shelled BIENVILLERS for 13 hrs. from 9 a.m. to 10 a.m. little material damage resulting. Two casualties in the battalion. CO2 moved into trenches at BERLES relieving the 5th Lines of Leicesters commenced 3.30 p.m. Everything satisfactory	
TRENCHES	4	3.30 a.m.	At 3.30 a.m. this morning the enemy endeavoured to raid part of our centre coy. The enemy shelled our front line and support forwards of minutes close to our line bringing their him a barrage. A number of bombs & other interesting articles. He failed in our Lewis gun fire having a coy of his own behind. We have 2 men wounded & 2 killed by the bombardment. After this everything was very quiet	
	5		Quiet day. 2Lt R Jessop evacuated to F.A. with trench fever.	
	5/6	11 p.m.	Our artillery into bombarded the German line, fire in a raid of prisoners of the 1/5 Leicesters. The raid was not successful owing to the Bosches being enemy. We had 3 men wounded. 2 Lt Death killed in make of the enemy trench on his return.	
	6	6.30 p.m.	Capt Lovett was wounded in the head by a sniper. Evacuated to C.C.S. & on mother following joins another. Army School at 9.30 p.m. Capt Holmes took over B Coy. Lieut Sherwell became O.C. D Coy	
	7		Quiet day	
	8/9		The operation in charge of the I.T. endorsement reported that at least 2 Germans were going to make an attack on our line and the enemy by to make all day. The enemy shelled about 4.30 a.m. Sundry lachrymatory by proves. Good machine gun activity on hill on both sides	

Army Form C. 2118

WAR DIARY
or
INTELLIGENCE SUMMARY
(Erase heading not required.)

Instructions regarding War Diaries and Intelligence Summaries are contained in F.S. Regs., Part II. and the Staff Manual respectively. Title Pages will be prepared in manuscript.

Place	Date 1916	Hour	Summary of Events and Information	Remarks and references to Appendices
TRENCHES	Aug 13		We were relieved this afternoon by the 8th S. Lives. & proceeded to POMMIER R. through the trenches as usual.	
POMMIER	14		During our stay in POMMIER everything & everyone looked happier. On the 14th inst. 2/Lt. BADLEY returns from 6 b S.B. & was appointed bombing officer for the Bn.	
		2 P.M.	The Battalion were inspected by the Brigadier General	
TRENCHES	15		We relieved the BERLES trenches this afternoon relieving the 5 Lines. Capt PERRY took over Battalion medical duties during the temporary absence of Lt COETZEE	
	16		Very quiet. The G.O.C. & Brigadier visited our sector this morning.	
	17		Quiet. Heavy storm continues	
	18	1.40 P.M.	A small German patrol of about 3 men or 4 men went up the communication trench to our line. They were promptly engaged upon examination & was found to be a N.C.O. & 2 men of the ___ reg. He stated that he had not been up to this sector before & apparently decided to return at 5 A.M.	
	19		Very quiet. Enemy have now & again dropped enemy & at about 9.30 P.M. they opened fire on our trenches & sent over a few ___	
	20		Very quiet.	
	21		We were relieved this afternoon by the 5 Lines & proceeded to BIENVILLERS where Capt MYERS, Capt CLARKE & 2/Lt BARRETT joined us from ___	

WAR DIARY or INTELLIGENCE SUMMARY

Army Form C. 2118

(Erase heading not required.)

Place	Date	Hour	Summary of Events and Information	Remarks and references to Appendices
BIENVILLERS	22 Aug 1915		Major YOOL 7/S. Staffs took over command of the battalion from to day vice Major Barrell. A draft of 80 men arrived from the Base.	
	23/26		During this time nothing of note occurred. Lt. COETZEE rejoins us as M.O. taking over from Lt. Off. SPERRY.	
	27		We relieved the 5' Lines' BERLES. moving by companies. 2 Lt BADLEY appointed as TRANSPORT OFFICER in place of 2 Lt BATES.	
TRENCHES	28		Nothing of importance to report. The weather has been unsettled & stormy.	
	29		Quiet day. Thunderstorm in afternoon with much rain.	
	30		2 Lt B. H. CHALLONER & 2 Lt A. W. M. ROBERTSON arrive and join Coys.	
	30	10 P.M.	The enemy's very favourable to the R.E. in middle of No attack upon the emplacements they they worked smartly. No warning signals were heard save from the enemy lines & their outrageous bombardment was feeble	
			1 wounded during enemy's bombardment	13
	31	9–	Enemy artillery very active, incuring shrapnel & heavy shells into POMMIER. We also answered able to our support from series in matters & emplacements. Casualties 1 man killed	
		10 A.M.		

References to TRENCHES W.55a.3.2 to W.23.8.9 (Ofthorne) on HYWOOD) MAP USED 57c S.E (part 1).

Ralph Crawford, Lt. Col.
Commanding 1/4th Bn. LINCOLNSHIRE REGT.

[signed] Adjutant
1/4th Bn. LINCOLNSHIRE REGT.

WAR DIARY or INTELLIGENCE SUMMARY

Army Form C. 2118

(Erase heading not required.)

Instructions regarding War Diaries and Intelligence Summaries are contained in F.S. Regs., Part II. and the Staff Manual respectively. Title Pages will be prepared in manuscript.

Vol 22

Place	Date	Hour	Summary of Events and Information	Remarks and references to Appendices
TRENCHES (BERLES)	1916 Sept 1		The day has been very quiet indeed. A place in the German wire having been discovered we had a strong party out to lie in wait for enemy working parties and patrols, but unfortunately none were seen or heard.	maps S.S.E. (over 8)
	2	10.30 pm 2.30 am	We were relieved in the afternoon by the 5th Lancashires and proceeded to billets in POMMIER	
POMMIER	3 to 5		Uneventful, only ordinary routine work being carried out	
	6		We were inspected at LABAZEQUE by the G.O.C. who was accompanied by his staff. He was pleased with the general turn out and smartness of the men. Major East joined us from the Base.	
	7		Uneventful	
TRENCHES (BERLES)	8		The battalion left POMMIER in the afternoon to relieve the 5th Lancashires in the BERLES trenches. The 5th Lancashires left behind two parties, each in charge of an armoured tube (Bangalore Torpedo), which they carried into 'no mans land' and placed in the wire prior to 2 a.m.	17.E

WAR DIARY of INTELLIGENCE SUMMARY

(Erase heading not required.)

Army Form C. 2118

Instructions regarding War Diaries and Intelligence Summaries are contained in F. S. Regs., Part II. and the Staff Manual respectively. Title Pages will be prepared in manuscript.

Place	Date 1916 Sept.	Hour	Summary of Events and Information	Remarks and references to Appendices
TRENCHES (SER4 E3)	9		When the fuze countering the torpedoes were fired. The enemy at once opened up a bombardment, which lasted for about an hour, but there was no damage was done to our trenches.	Trench map 51. S.E. 3r4 (pt G3)
		11.30 a.m.	The Brigadier arrived at Battalion H.Q. and spent several hours Company our trenches accompanied by the C.O.	
		9.30 p.m.	2/Lt. F.J. Clarke joined from the Base.	
	10.		Very little happened during the day. At night (and also on the two nights following) gas cylinders were carried up to our front line and placed in position.	
	11		The enemy's artillery has been busy during the day, his fire being mostly directed at the support line and communication trenches. Our artillery did not reply to any extent as we had no desire to start a duel, in which case any gas by trench mean have been his view disastrous result to our own men.	
	12	10 a.m	The Brigadier visited the trenches.	
	13		The day has been exceedingly quiet.	

WAR DIARY
INTELLIGENCE SUMMARY

Army Form C. 2118

3

(Erase heading not required.)

Place	Date 1916 FEB.	Hour	Summary of Events and Information	Remarks and references to Appendices
TRENCHES (Berles)	14	4.45 p.m.	We were relieved by the 5th Lincolns and proceeded to billets in BIENVILLERS.	Trench map 51.S.E. 3rd (Pontoit)
BIENVILLERS	15		During the Battalion's stay in BIENVILLERS only ordinary routine work has been carried out. 'A' Company has been practising to carry out a raid on the enemy trenches some night during the next few.	map 51.C & 57.D
	16			
	19			
	18		Lieut. J. W. Harrison joined us from the Base.	
	20	2.30 p.m.	Battalion left BIENVILLERS to relieve the 5th Lincolns in the trenches.	
			2/Lts F. Dow and T.E.B. Kidd joined us from the Base.	
TRENCHES (Berles)	21/22		Both days have been exceedingly quiet.	
	23		The G.O.C. - Major General H. Thwaites - toured our trenches accompanied by our C.O.	
	24		The Brigadier toured the trenches.	
	25	8 p.m.	The enemy sent over an assortment of trench mortar and fits	
		9.40 p.m.	shells, and we replied with our Stokes guns and a few rounds from our howitzer. We suffered no casualties and practically no damage to our trench.	
	26		We were relieved by the 5th Lincolns and proceeded to billets in POMMIER.	

Army Form C. 2118

WAR DIARY
INTELLIGENCE SUMMARY
(Erase heading not required.)

Instructions regarding War Diaries and Intelligence Summaries are contained in F.S. Regs., Part II. and the Staff Manual respectively. Title Pages will be prepared in manuscript.

4

Place	Date	Hour	Summary of Events and Information	Remarks and references to Appendices
POMMIER	1916 Sept 27 28 29		2/Lt J.R. Neame joined from the Base	Maps 51.C.♭57.
			2/Lts J. Summerbell, E.W. Barker and C. Trupper joined from the Base, and Captain F.B. Clarke went to Field Ambulance sick.	
	30		Battalion Sports were held at POMMIER during the afternoon, and proved very successful. Lt. Col. Sandall, 5th Lincoln Regt., who is acting Brigadier during Brigadier General S.C. Kemp's absence on leave, was present and distributed the prizes.	

S.C. Kemp(?)
2nd Lt
2 i/c off.

[signature]
Commanding 1/4th Bn. Lincoln Regt.

1875 Wt. W593/826 1,000,000 4/15 J.B.C. & A. A.D.S.S./Forms/C. 2118.

138th Inf Bde.

Ref: my conversation with the B.G.C.
Will you kindly inform me what batteries will be available, and the approximate number of rounds that may be considered as a maximum, which will be available.

[signature] Lieut. Col.
Commanding 4th Bn Lincolnshire Regt.

15-9-16

BM.8/5

II

4th Lincolnshire Regt.

Batteries available A.231, D 232 (1 Sect.)
                     A.232, D 230 (1 Sect.)
                     B 232.

No of rounds cannot be stated at present.

16-9-16 [signature] [signature] Holdsworth
                      Capt. B.M.
                      138 I.B.

Bombardment. Phase I.

Unit	Time	Task	Ammunition	Remarks
2. 2" Trench Mortars	3.0 pm – 5.0 pm	Wire cutting about E.5.c.70.75		Secondary attack
2. 2" Trench Mortars	3.0 pm – 5.0 pm	Wire cutting about W.29.d. S.2		Secondary attack
4. 2" Trench Mortars	3.0 pm – 5.0 pm	Wire cutting at { E.5.a. 10.60 E.5.a. 10.75		Raiding Points
2. 18 pdr Bats	3.0 pm – 5.0 pm	Bombard with H.E. fire trench from E.5.a. 65.85 to W.29.c. 50.90. Support him between three points and Enfilade O. Trenches in this area.		Covering fire for T.M's
1. 10 pdr Bat	4.30 pm – 5.0 pm	Complete wire cutting with shrapnel at points E.5.a. 10.60 and E.5.a. 10.75		
198 T M Bat	3.0 pm – 5 pm	Bombard fire and support lines S of E.5.a. 10.00 and N.of W.29.c. 25.40		
2 Sects 4.5" Hows	3.0 pm – 5 pm	Register upoints :- E.5.a. 13.60 (small salient) E.5.a. 14.17 (small salient) E.5.a. 10.6c (cross trench) E.5.a. 30.80 (cross trench) E.5.a. 30.50 (top of C trench) W.29.c. 24.34 (top of C trench) and other suitable points for harassing unregistered points.		
6" How	3.0 pm – 5 pm	Bombard Houses about E.5.a. 5.5. Register in points indicated for 4.5" Hows		If available

Phase II

Arm	Time	Task	Ammunition	Remarks
6" Hows	9.18 pm – 9.40 pm	Bombard points as in Phase I		as in Phase I
2 Hows 4.5" Hows	9.35 pm – 9.40 pm	Bombard points as in Phase I		
3. 18 pdr Bat.	9.35 pm – 9.45 pm	Bombard area described in Phase I	H.E.	
4. 2" T. Mortars	9.35 pm – 9.40 pm	Continue wire cutting at raising points, should reports of wire cutting & traps not be satisfactory.		

Phase III

2 Hows 4.5" Hows	9.40 pm – –	Lift from fire trench between points E ?a 15.00 and W.29.c 20.00 and search beyond enemy's line ditto		
3. 18 pdr Bats	9.45 pm –	and enfilade with shrapnel C. trenches behind support line.		
8. 1" T. Mortars	9.45 pm –	Bombard any enemy M.G. supposed C. trenches also any known M.G. emplacements outside rubbish area		
M.G. M G Coy	9-9.45 pm –	Bring machine gun communication front in MONCHY with occasional bursts		
150" T.M. Bn	9-9.45 pm –	as in Phase I		

Ballot Maps
and of trenches of

When to get out in front of wire before
    bombardment.
5 mins bombardment commencing at ?
    with 18 pdrs & 4.5" on blocking pts.
after 5 mins 18pdrs to lift.
(bombardment asked from N Salis Reentrant
                    to S. pt of Salient)

afternoon 6" on M G emplacements. 2 pts of entry
              100 yds   3   +1 near tip of
? 12" will fire on 'Monchy Ch.   Salient.

WAR DIARY / INTELLIGENCE SUMMARY

Army Form C. 2118

4th J. Winchester

16th Division

Place	Date 1916 Oct.	Hour	Summary of Events and Information	Remarks and references to Appendices
POMMIER.	1	10 a.m.	The Battalion left POMMIER and proceeded to LA CAUCHIE.	Maps: 51:F:57:D
LA CAUCHIE	2	3 p.m.	The Battalion left LA CAUCHIE and to relieve the 5th Lincolns in the trenches E.9.	Maps: 51:S.S.E 3rd (Part 9) 57:D:N:E 1 & 2 (part 4)
			BERLES.	
TRENCHES	3/4		Very quiet.	
	5		During the afternoon our artillery and trench mortars turned some were engaged on cutting two gaps in the enemy wire ready for 'A' Company to carry out the raid. They had previously been pronounced. The Company was divided into two parties (Right and Left) and had work in position in our front line trench. N.B. Young (9/1) by 9.20 p.m. At 9.30 p.m. two patrols under 2/Lt. Couzon and 2/Lt. HALLIDAY respectively, went out and subsequently reported that there was a good gap opposite the right point and that a couple gap on the left had not quite been established. The reports were considered satisfactory and the programme was ordered to be carried out. The left party on arrival to effect a path through the wire. The right party succeeded in entering the enemy trench, shot two men and bombed a dug-out in which were believed to be seven more. Unfortunately the party were between two blocks	

WAR DIARY or INTELLIGENCE SUMMARY

Army Form C. 2118

4th Lincolns 46 Div

Place	Date	Hour	Summary of Events and Information	Remarks and references to Appendices
Fonquevillers (Bellac)	Oct 5		in the trench only 15 yards apart and as the time they were allowed to spend in the trench had elapsed, they returned in good order having only suffered one casualty (one man being scratched on one finger by a splinter). The left party did not work so smoothly and were made to find the tape leading to the gap in the enemy wire and were ordered to return 12 minutes after the time they should have exited the German trench. 2/Lt DIBB suffered a slight wound in the head and was the only casualty in the party.	
	6 7 8		Both days very quiet.	
Bienvillers	9 10		We were relieved in the afternoon by the 5th Lincolns and proceeded to billets in Bienvillers. Routine work. Enemy shelled S.E. part of village with 5.9" commencing 6.0 pm on the 10th and continued till 11.0 AM next morning. Shells came over at the rate of 1 per 5 minutes. Enemy was evidently searching for batteries. The R.A. took 2 men killed and 7 wounded. The G.O.C. inspected and addressed the Raiding Party, he complimented them upon their work and on the spirit shown by them on the night of the raid, and hoped that when they were called upon to do bigger things that they would do just as well. He personally thanked 2nd Lieut COULSON and 2nd Lt HALLIDAY for the work in laying the tape to the Boch parapet. 2/Lieut MEREDITH S.C. and 2nd Lt FYFFE to Field Ambulance. Capt LUDOLF R.A.M.C. relieved Capt PERRY as Regt. M.O.	
	11 12		2/Lt Bates to Field Ambulance; day uneventful.	

WAR DIARY
or
INTELLIGENCE SUMMARY
(Erase heading not required.)

Army Form C. 2118

4 L Warwicks 48 Div 3

Place	Date 1916	Hour	Summary of Events and Information	Remarks and references to Appendices
TRENCHES (BERLES)	14		The G.O.C. inspected the Transport & expressed his satisfaction. Battalion left BIENVILLERS to relieve the 5th Warwicks in the trenches. 2/Lt F.G. Baker joined us from the Base.	
	15		The Brigadier inspected the trenches. The enemy unusually quiet both day and by night.	
	16		Unusual inactivity of enemy continues.	
	17		The Brigadier visited the trenches	
	18		Our 5" French Mortars were cutting gaps in enemy wire from 2 P.M. to 5 P.M. The 5th Warwicks intending to raid the enemy trench S.E. of the new gaps, our infantry went out to deceive the enemy. Another diversion was carried out North of the raiding point by a Bangalore Tube. This was in the hands of 2/Lt Greek L/Cpl Griffin & Pte Jones. The C.O.'s dispatches great coolness by whom it was found that the Tube he had had in fact been lost & L/Cpl Greek struck three matches before he was able to light the fuse. The Raid was carried out between 8.30 P.M. & 9 P.M. During this time the enemy bombarded the whole of our sector, doing a little damage to our trenches & killing three men. The Brigadier General arrived at Battalion Headquarters at 6.45 P.M. & remained there until the Raiding Party had all returned.	

WAR DIARY or INTELLIGENCE SUMMARY

Army Form C. 2118

1st Lincoln 46th Inf Bde

Place	Date	Hour	Summary of Events and Information	Remarks and references to Appendices
Trenches (BERLES)	19th		Quiet day. The whole Battalion engaged in repairing trenches, numerous land-slides having occurred owing to the heavy rain.	
	20th	5 P.M.	Relieved by the 5th Leicesters & proceeded to billets at LA CAUCHIE.	
	21.		Routine work.	
	22.	3 P.M.	The Battalion left LA CAUCHIE for POMMIER. Lt Col Innes, commanding, presented cards received by the Divisional for gallant conduct in the field to five NCOs & men, to wit: 2/Lt R.C. Hope, Sgt G. Graham, Sgt A. T. Bennett, A/Cpl B. Nightingale, Pte E.A. Edwards and L.E. Bunn.	
POMMIER	23°		Arthur P.M. 2/Lt R.C. Hope proceeded to Field Amb. 2/Lt G.A. Hope, 2/Lt C.W. Clark, A.V. Cockram proceeded to Field Amb. 2/Lt F.S.M. Savage Armstrong & S.O. Hay are on the command of the 72nd Div 2/Lt R.W.G.A. Grant was proceeded to England on leave for few days. Major G.P. Peto Moncrief to Field Amb. The Battalion left POMMIER & relieved the 5th LINCOLNS in the BEALES trenches.	
	24			
Trenches (BERLES)	25	4 pm	Quiet day. The Battalion engaged in pumping water out of trenches & clearing some of same that had slipped down owing the previous few days owing to constant rain. The French Sentry which is situated near the BERLES-MONCHY road was into Nos.1174 on the names of some of the French soldiers on the ours were made estimated. 2/Lt Ramsey & Taffe	
	26th		reported the names of the fallen heroes.	

Army Form C. 2118

WAR DIARY
or
INTELLIGENCE SUMMARY
(Erase heading not required.)

4th Lincolns 46th Div

Instructions regarding War Diaries and Intelligence Summaries are contained in F. S. Regs., Part II. and the Staff Manual respectively. Title Pages will be prepared in manuscript.

Place	Date	Hour	Summary of Events and Information	Remarks and references to Appendices
Humbh. Oct 27. (BERLES)			In the early part of the morning Gen Coplands were relieved on our Right Sect.	
	28.	10 a.m.	At 11.30 a.m. the Brigadier, accompanied by the Brigadier of the 20th Division, inspected our trenches & the 10th expressed himself pleased with state of same & the employees very favourably compared with the trenches he had recently come back of FLERS. Officers of 2nd Ruthevs visited our trenches & took particulars of same & the readiness for taking over on 30th inst.	
	29.	9 a.m.	The enemy fired about a dozen shells into the Pomme - one other that a shell containing fifteen mm - Kft/Lt G. Nightingale & Pte ? Wharton were killed	
	30.	3 p.m.	our men properly occupied & the rear slightly wounded Relieved by the 2nd Bedfordshire Regt & marched to Humbh—cans POMMIER.	
MONDICOURT		5.30 pm	Relieved by the 20th Kings Shropshire Regiment and marched to Humbh on MONDICOURT VIA LA BAZEQUE. Lt-Col. F.S.N. SAVAGE - ARMSTRONG. D.S.O. was attached to 2nd BEDFORDS and Major R.M. EARL took over the command of 4th LINCOLNS. Major G. R. SILLS returned from field ambulance. 2/Lt J. E. Peacock returned from Army Ambulance.	

Army Form C. 2118

4th Lincolns 46 Div

WAR DIARY
or
INTELLIGENCE SUMMARY
(Erase heading not required.)

Instructions regarding War Diaries and Intelligence Summaries are contained in F. S. Regs., Part II. and the Staff Manual respectively. Title Pages will be prepared in manuscript.

Place	Date	Hour	Summary of Events and Information	Remarks and references to Appendices
MONDICOURT	Feb 3/16		The Battalion arrived in MONDICOURT. 2/Lt E.W. BARKER proceeded to First Army Musketry [School]	

Th Harrison
2/Lt Sgt Offr

A S Cull Lieut-Col.
Commdg. 1/4th Bn. Lincolnshire Regt.

OPERATION ORDER No.1

Capt. ?.Harris
Comdr A Coy 1/4th Bn. Lincolnshire Regt.   ?-?-??

Ref: Map 57d - N.E. - FONQUEVILLERS)   1/10,000.
     51c - S.E. - SANSART   )

....

1.- Object   To kill Germans, obtain prisoners and bring back
                       useful objects.

2.- Composition   H.Q.   2 Signallers
    of Parties   i   O.C. Raid, C.S.M., 2 runners & 1 drummer.

                 ii   A Party (Right storming party)
                      2nd Lieut COULSON in Command: Sgt. ?oistein 2nd-in-
                                                                command.

                      A1 - Blocking party.
                           Sgt. Lilley, 2 Bombers, 7 Riflemen.
                      A2 - Trench clearing party.
                           2nd Lt. COULSON, Sgt. Vincent, 2 Bombers 8 Riflemen.
                      A2a - C.T. blocking party.
                           Sgt. Marshall, 2 Bombers, 5 Riflemen.
                      A3 - Prisoner conducting party.
                           Cpl. Fryer, 5 Riflemen 4 R.B.?.

                      ....

                 iii   B Party (Left storming party)
                      2nd Lt. GIBB in command - 2nd Lt. HALLIDAY 2nd-in-
                                                                command.

                      B1 - Blocking party.
                           Sgt. Palmer 2 Bombers, 7 Riflemen.
                      B2 - Trench clearing party.
                           2nd Lt. GIBB, Sgt. Raison, Cpl. Reid, 2 Bombers
                                         12 Riflemen 1 Drummer.
                      B3 - Prisoner conducting party.
                           2nd Lt. HALLIDAY, Cpl. Braybrook, 5 Riflemen
                                                                4 R.B.?.

                      ....

                 iv C   C Party - (Right covering party)
                           2nd Lt. F.J.CLARKE in Command.
                           L/Cpl. Carter, No.? L.G. team & 6 R.?.?

                      ....

                 v   D Party (Left covering party)
                      2/Lt Temple in Command
                           Cpl. ?alson, Cpl. Benwith, No.1 L.G. team & 6 R.?

                      ....

3.- Reserve   1.Off., 25 O.R. provided by B Coy 4th Lincolns.
    party

- 2 -

4. Parades   A & C Parties will parade in Jintrench 93
              B & D Parties will parade in J.S. NEWARK ST. with all
              4   inspections finished and ready to move off by 8.45 pm.

5 - Points of   A & C parties - Trench 93 : Bays 2,3 & 4.
    assembly   B & D   "   -   "   91 : "   12,13 & 14.
                          These parties will be in position by 9.20 pm.

6 - Dress   Clean fatigue, one Gas Helmet. All ranks will
                 remove identification marks and papers etc.

                 Riflemen : Rifles with bayonets fixed (bayonets will be
                            darkened) - 50 rounds S.A.A., 4 Mills Bombs in
                            pockets, Wire cutters as available.
                 Bombers : 12 Mills Bombs in waistcoats, knob-kerry,
                            wire-cutters (hand).

                 Flash Lamps will be carried by all Officers & senior
                 N.C.O.s.
                      A & B parties will carry 5 Trench ladders per party.
                      C & D parties wear full trench equipment.

7 - Operations   At 7.0 pm   - 2nd Lt. COULSON & 5 O.R. will leave
    Zero   T.90 Bay 2 to reconnoitre Right Gap.
    = 9.0 pm   2nd Lt. HALLIDAY & 5 O.R. will leave
    11.30 pm   Zero-25   T.91 Bay 14 to reconnoitre Left Gap.
                                Both parties will lay tapes and straighten them on return journey:
                                They will return by 9.30 p.m. and report
                                to O.C. Raid.
                      At   p.m. - Both A & B parties will form up outside
                                our wire in waves.
                                C & D parties will take up a position slightly
                                to right and left flanks respectively of
                                A & B.
                 Zero   At   p.m. - Both raiding parties will advance on
                                their respective gaps: (if Bangalore tubes
                                are necessary they will be fired now)

                      O.C. Raid, C.S.M., 2 runners, drummer, will advance
                 with A party and will follow progress of attack on
                 German parapet.
                      A5 & B5 will remain at German parapet opposite their
                 respective gaps.
                      C & D parties will take up positions in NOMANS LAND
                 on Right and Left flanks respectively.

8 - Countersign A countersign will be arranged before leaving for
                 front line.

9 - Watches   All watches will be synchronised at 6.0 p.m.

10 - Signallers   2 Signallers will run out cable in rear of A party
                 and will take up a position as close to German parapet
                 and right gap as possible.

-3-

11 - Silence   Absolute SILENCE will be maintained between time of
               leaving and time of returning to the RAVINE.

12 - Reserve   Dress : Full trench order
     Party   Parade in Upper part of New Street, ready to move to
               positions in T.91, Bays 13 - 15 at 11.10 pm
                                    11.0pm

13 - Reports   Reports up to 11.0pm will be sent to T.91 Bay 14.
               During progress of raid - on parapet near.
                                              Party A.C.

                                  (signed) E.N.MARRIS, Capt.
                                            O.C. A Coy.
22-9-16.   1/4th Bn. Lincolnshire Regiment.

SECRET.   Copy No. 3.

OPERATION ORDER No. 46,
by
Major G. A. Yool,
Commanding 1/4th Bn. Lincolnshire Regiment.

4th October, 1916.

Ref. Maps :- 57.D N.E. FONQUEVILLERS.)   1
            51.C S.W. RANSART.   ) 10,000

Operation order No.45 dated 23/9/16 is cancelled, and the following substituted :-

1. Intention.   I intend to carry out a raid in the German front trench at points N.5.a.11.58 and N.5.a.13.77 on the night of the 5th October, 1916.

2. Object.   To kill and capture Germans, and to bring back useful objects.

3. Artillery   The wire will be cut at the two raiding points
   Co-operation   and also at points N.5.c.70.75 and N.5.c.60.83.
                    Points of junction of fire and support trenches with communication trenches and Machine Gun emplacements will be bombarded with Heavy Artillery.
                    A general bombardment of the sector will be carried out.

4. Division   The raid will be carried out by two parties
   into Parties.   named Right Party and Left Party.
                    Each party will furnish a patrol for preliminary reconnaissance, strength 1 Officer and 3 Privates, which will examine and report on gaps, and lay tapes.

5. Composition.   Commander - Captain E. N. MARRIS.

     (i)   Commander, 1 W.O., 2 Runners, 2 Signallers, and
                                                          1 Drummer.
     (ii) 'A' (Right) Party.
           Blocking party - (a) 1 N.C.O. 9 Ptes.
              - do -   - (b) 1 N.C.O. 7 Ptes.
           Attacking party - 1 Off. 1 N.C.O. 10 Ptes.
           Prisoner conducting party - 1 N.C.O. 5 Ptes 4 S.Bs.
           Covering party - 1 Off. 1 Cpl. 6 Ptes with 1 L. Gun
                                                      and team (5).
           Total Strength :- 2 Off. 6 N.C.Os. 46 Ptes.

     (iii) 'B' (Left) Party
           Blocking party -   1 N.C.O 9 Ptes.
           Attacking party - 1 Off. 2 N.C.Os. 14 Ptes.and
                                                        1 Drummer.
           Prisoner conducting party - 1 Off. 1 N.C.O. 5 Ptes.
                                                      and 4 S.Bs.
           Covering party - 1 Off. 1 Cpl. 6 Ptes with 1 L. Gun
                                                      and team (5).
           Total strength :- 3 Off. 5 N.C.Os. 44 Ptes.

     TOTAL STRENGTH :- 6 Officers, 1 W.O., 10 N.C.Os. 95 Ptes.

Reserve party :- 1 Officer and 25 Other Ranks of 'D' Coy.

- 2 -

6. Assembly Points
   Right Party :- Trench 90, Bays 2, 3 and 4.
   Left Party :- Trench 91, Bays 12, 13 and 14.

7. Preliminary.
   Time Table :-
   2-0 p.m - Wire cutting by 2" Trench Mortars commences.
   3-30 p.m - 2" Trench Mortars cease firing, 18 pdr Batteries clean up gaps.
   4-30 p.m - 2" Trench Mortars again take up wire cutting, with the 18 pdrs co-operating.
   2-0 to) - The 38th S.B., R.H.A., will engage
   6-0 p.m) Machine Gun emplacements at E.5.a.11.17, at E.5.a.12.31 and E.5.a.24.84.
   The 9.45" Heavy Trench Mortar Battery will also bombard the WHITE HOUSE at E.5.a.72.70.
   Time at which fire will begin will be notified later. The necessary trenches will be cleared whilst this mortar is firing.

   Night. ZERO ~~9-0~~ 11.30 p.m.
   7-0 p.m - Reconnaissance starts.
   8-30 p.m - Reconnaissance completed.
   11.10 ~~9-0~~ p.m - Raiding Party commences to cross parapet, and forms up outside wire.
   Zero -3 - "Feint" bombardment of trenches opposite Right Battalion sub-sector begins.
   Zero - Barrage is formed round raiding area, and bombardment of whole sector continues.
   Zero + 5 - Raiding parties advance (if use of Bangalore torpedoes is necessary, the Raiding party will advance immediately on its explosion).

8. Return
   The Raiding Party will not remain more than 20 minutes in the trenches. Signal - a bugle call blown from German lines.
   The Artillery will be notified when they have returned.
   Bunches of three white rockets will be fired from Support Line at Zero + 25 p.m, and at 5 minute intervals as a guide.

9. Papers.
   No papers or identification marks will be carried. Parties will be inspected before leaving the trenches.

10. Bayonets.
    Bayonets will be darkened.

11. Identification.
    Steel helmets with sandbag covering will be worn.

12. Medical.
    An Advanced Regimental Aid Post will be established at S.B.8 and S.B.9.

13. Countersign.
    To be issued later.

14. Watches.
    All watches to be synchronized at 6-0 p.m. Os.C. Trench Mortar Battery and Machine Gun Co., will obtain correct time from O.C. 1/4th Lincs Regt.

15. 138th Trench Mortar Battery.
    The Stokes Gun will co-operate from Zero -3 till bombardment ends, against suitable targets South of point E.5.a.15.30 and North of point W.29.c.25.40.

- 3 -

16. 138th Machine Gun Coy.	The Machine Gun Company will co-operate from Zero -3 till bombardment ceases, by traversing main communication points in and around MONCHY, and known Machine Gun emplacements (including Machine Gun positions near Quarry) with occasional bursts.
17. Lewis Guns.	Will sweep the German parapet North of point W.29.c.25.40 with short bursts from Zero till ordered to stop.
18. Garrison in Trenches.	'B' Company will furnish necessary garrison for trenches 93 to 98 during operations.
19. Reports.	Reports to be sent to Trench 91 Bay 14.

(Signed) F. A. PHILLIPS, 2/Lieut,
and Adjt.
1/4th Bn. Lincolnshire Regiment.

Issued at 3 p.m by Orderly to :-

Copy No. 1 138th Inf Bde.
2 Retained.
3 War Diary.
4 O.C. RAMC.
5 O.C. 'D' Coy.
6 O.C. 'B' Coy.

7 O.C. 'C' Coy.
8 Centre Group, R.A.
9 5th Leics Regt.
10 6th South Staffords.
11 138th M. Gun Co.
12 138th T.M. Btty.
13 4th Leics Regt.
14 5th Lincolnshire Rgt.

Copy No 2

Operation Order No 52 by Lieut-Col. G. A. Yool, Commanding 1/4th
Battalion Lincolnshire Regiment.
In the field 1. 11. 16.

Map Ref. LENS 11.

1. <u>Move</u>. The Battalion will move to billets in MAISON PONTHIEU tomorrow.

2. <u>March</u>. Battalion will parade ready to march off at 7. 25 am in column of route on the AUXI-LE-CHATEAU - DOULLENS ROAD with the head of the column 600 yards N. W. of the junction of this Road with the MEZEROLLES - REMAISNIL ROAD.
Order of Parade:
Signallers, B. C. D. & A. Coys, Transport.
Dugout Platoon will march as the 5th platoon of B Coy.
Route; via AUXI-LE-CHATEAU.
Battalion will join remainder of Brigade at WAVANS.

3. <u>Lewis Guns</u>: will be in rear of Coys. The transport Officer will arrange for mules to be sent one to each Coy at 6. 45 am for pulling the Handcarts.

4. <u>Billeting Party</u>. 2/Lt. C. Temple and C.S.M. Joyce have proceeded this afternoon to billet Battalion.
Cpl. Bilton and 3 Hd. Qr. Guides will leave at 6. 30 am and report to 2/Lt. Temple at MAISON PONTHIEU.

5. <u>Stores</u>: will be sent to Q. M. Stores as follows:-
Blankets at   6. 15 am
Officers Valises   6. 15 am
Other Stores   6. 15 am
Officers mess kits will be sent to Battalion Hd. Qrs by 6. 45 am.
Coy storemen will report to Quartermaster at 6. 30 am

6. <u>Transport</u>: will be ready loaded by 7. 0 am.

7. <u>Sick Men</u>. Arrangements will be notified later.

8. <u>On arrival at billets</u> Coys will report numbers of men who fell out on the march.

9. <u>Orderly Room</u>: will close at MEZEROLLES at 7. 0 am and open at destination, on arrival.

10. <u>Detail for tomorrow</u>:
Coy on duty B Coy.
Breakfast   6. 45 am
Sick Parade   6. 15 am
Dinners will be cooked on the march.

F. Phillips
2/Lt. & Adjt.
1/4th Battalion Lincolnshire Regiment.

Copy No 1 Retained
      ✓2 Office Copy
       3 A Coy
       4 B Coy
       5 C Coy
       6 D Coy
       7 Transport Officer
       8 Quartermaster.
       9 War Diary
      10 R. S. M.

Copy No. 2

Operation Order No 48 by Lieut-Col. G. A. Yool, Commanding
1/4th Battalion Lincolnshire Regiment.

In the Field 21. 10. 16.

Map Ref. France Sheet 51 C.

1. <u>Move.</u> The Battalion will move into billets at POMMIER tomorrow
             (22nd inst).

2. <u>March.</u> Battalion will pass Road Junction V 18 a 57 by Coys, as
              follows:-

              Signallers and Hd. Qr. Guides   3. 0 pm
              D Coy   3.10 pm
              A Coy   3.20 pm
              C Coy   3.30 pm
              B Coy and remaining Hd. Qr. details   3.40 pm
              Blankets will be carried on the man.

3. <u>Advance Party.</u>
             1 Sgt, 4 Men and 1 Officers servant per Coy, together
             with the R.S.M. and 1 Officers servant for Hd. Qrs. will
             parade at Road Junction V 18 a 57 at 1. 30 pm under
             Battalion Billeting Officer. *B Coy will send only 1 Sgt 2 men & 1 officers servant*

4. <u>Lewis Guns</u> and Ammunition will be taken by Coys on the Handcarts.

5. <u>Stores.</u> Officers mess kit will be dumped at Hd. Qrs. by 2. 30 pm.
              All other stores will be stacked in the empty hut in
              B Coys lines or in the orchard by D Coys lines as is
              more convenient, by 2. 15 pm
                 Coy on duty will detail loading party of 1 NCO
              and 8 Men to report at O. Room at 2. 0 pm.

6. <u>Transport:</u> will arrive by 2. 15 pm. Cookers will move with limbers.

7. <u>Rear Party:</u> Battalion Orderly Officer and Sanitary Cpl will report
                to Town Major at 3. 30 pm to hand over billets.

8. <u>O. Room:</u> will close at LA CAUCHIE at 3. 0 pm and open at POMMIER
             at 3. 30 pm.

                                            [signature]
                                            2/Lt. & Adjt.
                                            1/4th Battalion Lincs. Regt.

Copy No. 1 Retained.
        2 Office Copy
        3 Hd. Qrs. 138th Brigade.
        4 A Coy.
        5 B Coy.
        6 C Coy.
        7 D Coy.
        8. Transport Officer & Q.M.
        9 War Diary.

Copy No. 2

Operation Order No 49 by Lieut-Col. F. S. N. Savage Armstrong D.S.O
Commanding 1/4th Battalion Lincolnshire Regiment.
In the Field 24. 10. 16.

Map Ref. France 51 C.

1. Move. Battalion will relieve 5th Lincolns tomorrow.

2. Distribution.

    Right Coy C   Left Coy B
    Centre Coy A   Support Coy D

3. March. Route via VALLEY ROAD to BERLES and NOBS WALK.
March will be by platoons at 3 minutes interval and will
pass the Cemetery(W 25 d 35)POMMIER at following times:-

Advance Party	2. 45 pm
Lewis Gunners	4. 15 pm
Signallers and Hd. Qr. Guides	4. 20 pm
C Coy (1st platoon)	4. 25 pm
A Coy do	4. 40 pm
B Coy do	4. 55 pm
D Coy do	5. 10 pm

Advance party will consist of
   1 Officer, C.S.M. & 1 Guide per Coy.
   R.S.M. for Hd. Qrs.
and will rendezvous at the Cemetery.
NOBS WALK will be clear of all down traffic between 5. 0 pm
and 6. 0 pm.

4. Transport.
a) Baggage for LA BAZEQUE will be stacked at Billet 106 by
1. 30 pm.
D Coy will send 1 NCO and 4 Men as loading party.
b) Baggage for Officers Mess Cart will be stacked at Billet
106 at 2. 30 pm. 2 Servants per Coy will be sent with it
who will proceed with it and unload at BERLES.
c) Shoemakers and Tailors Kits, Orderly Room Gear, Cooks
dixies etc and Canteen will load by 4. 15 pm.

5. R.E. Loading Fatigue. O.C. 'D' Coy will detail 1 NCO and 6 Men
for loading R. E. Stores for Ravine at Bienvillers. To
report to R. E. Dump at 6. 0 pm.

2/Lt. & Adjt.
1/4th Bn. Lincs. Regt.

Copy No. 1 Retained
      2 Office Copy
      3 Hd. Qrs. 138th Brigade.
      4 A Coy
      5 B Coy
      6 C Coy.
      7 D Coy
      8 Transport Officer & Q.M.
      9. War Diary
    10 5th Lincolns.

Battalion Orders by Lieut-Col. F. S. N. Savage Armstrong,
Commanding 1/4th Battalion Lincolnshire Regiment.
In the Field 24.10.16.

1. Detail.

Coy on duty	C Coy.
Bn. Orderly Officer	2/Lt. G. L. Barritt.
Next for duty	2/Lt. R. T. Thomson.
Bn. Orderly Sgt.	2813 L/Sgt. Read J. W.
Next for duty	3224 L/Sgt. Hawkins E.
Tailors Shop	B Coy.
Shoemakers Shop	C Coy.
Baths	C Coy.

2. Parades. Coys under Company Commanders.

3. Move. The Battalion will relieve the 5th Lincolns tomorrow according to operation orders issued separately.

4. Fatigues. 'D' Coy will arrange to relieve the Brigade Hd. Qr. Guard and the Road Control Guard at 3. 0 pm tomorrow. These guards will remain on until relieved by incoming Battalion on the 26th. Rations for the 26th will be handed them by D Coy tomorrow.
Fatigue party for the Town Major will not be required tomorrow.

5. Appointment. 2/Lt. C. Temple takes over duties of Battalion Billeting Officer from date.

6. Fires. Fires will not be lighted in deep dug-outs, except in stoves provided with proper chimneys.

7. Guard Mounting. Guard mounting and Retreat will in future be at 4. 0 pm.

2/Lt & Adjt.
1/4th Bn. Lincs. Regt.

ORDERS FOR WIRING FATIGUE

1.) Fatigue will be in charge of Capt R. D. Ellis.

2.) Parties will be made up as follows:-

No.	Coy.	Offs.	O. Ranks.	
1	A	1	35	
2	D	1	35	
3	B	1	35	
4	C	1	35	
5	D	1	35	
6	A	1	35	
7	B	1	35	
8	C	-	19)	
			16)	Under Signalling Officer.
9	A	1	32	
	Hd. Qr. Guides		3	
10	D	1	33	
	Hd. Qr. Guides		2	
11	Carrying Party			
	A. C. & D Coys each 5.O.Rs.		15)	
	Hd.Qr. Signallers 1 Sgt &		11)	
	Pioneers		5)	Under Signalling Sgt.
	Hd.Qr. Guides		3)	

Coys can call on Hd. Qt. Details other than above.

3.) Parties will parade at the POMMIER end of the BIENVILLERS Road, and will march to R.E. Dump, Bienvillers and report to O.C. fatigue.

4.) Dress: Lighting Fighting Order.

5.) Wire Cutters will be taken. Wiring gloves to be issued to Coys at the rate of 11 per wiring party. These gloves will be returned to O.Room immediately after parties have returned.

6.) Times of parade will be notified by 1. 0 pm.

7.) In the event of Coys not being able to turn out the full number of men given in para. 2, they will arrange to decrease parties proportionately. All shortages to be reported to the Adjutant as soon as possible.

24. 10. 16.

Sd. F A Phillips 2/Lt. & Adjt.
1/4th. Lincs. Regt.

Copy No

Operation Order No 50 by Lieut-Col. F. S. N. Savage Armstrong, D.S.O.
Commanding 1/4th Battalion-Lincolnshire Regiment.
In the Field 29.10.16.

1. The Battalion will be relieved by the 2nd Bedfordshire Regiment tomorrow.
Coys will be relieved by following Coys of the Bedfords:

(Right) C Coy by   Coy.
(Centre) A Coy by   Coy.
(Left) B Coy by   Coy.   will be notified later.
(Support) D Coy by   Coy.

2. Route & Times. Relieving Battalion will arrive (by platoons at minutes interval) approximately as follows:-

Right Coy (1st platoon) at   pm)
Centre Coy   do   do   pm) via NAKED STREET

Left Coy   do   do   pm)
Support Coy   do   do   pm) via NOBS WALK
Times will be notified later.

Coys will arrange for guides as follows:-

Will be notified later:

3. March. On relief Coys will move by platoons to Billets in POMMIER by following routes:
Centre & Right Coys   via   NAKED STREET
Left & Support Coys   via   NOBS WALK.
Coys will report their arrival to Bn. Hd. Qrs. at POMMIER.
Teas will then be provided from Cookers.

4. 2nd Relief. At about 5.0 pm the 20th Kings Liverpool Regiment will arrive to relieve Battalion at POMMIER.
Coys will each send 1 guide per platoon to Bn. Hd. Qrs. at 4.50 pm. Relief to be reported to Bn. Hd. Qrs.

5. March. On relief Coys will form up in column of route on POMMIER-HUMBERCAMP ROAD in following order:-
Hd. Qr. Guides and Signallers.
C Coy.
D Coy.
A Coy.
B Coy.
Battalion will then march to billets in MONDICOURT via LA BAZEQUE. All details other than above and those given below will march with their Coys.
Following transport will accompany Battalion:-
1 Watercart.
Cookers with cooks.
Medical Cart with Medical Orderly.
On the march cooks will arrange to prepare hot tea or soup to be in readiness to issue to Coys on arrival at destination.

6. Billeting Party. Composition:- 2/Lt. C. Temple in charge.
1 NCO & 2 Men per Coy.
CSM Joyce for HD.QRS.
Parade at Orderly Room at 5.0 pm today to proceed to Transport Lines.
The party will proceed to MONDICOURT early tomorrow morning and will meet Battalion etc at MONDICOURT near ARRAS ROAD.

7. Lewis Guns. Relieving Battalion's Lewis Gunners will arrive this evening. This Battalion's Lewis Gunners will remain in trenches till tomorrow. Guns will be dumped at O. Room tonight. S.A.A. will be stacked in Bath House. Limbers will be at BERLES at 1.0 pm tomorrow, and Lewis Gunners will load them. Limbers will then proceed to POMMIER. The Guns will then be loaded on to Handcarts.

8. **Transport & Stores.** Lewis Gun S. A. A. will be dumped at Pommier tonight by transport. Remaining stores will be taken to LA BAZEQUE tonight.

O. C. 'D' Coy will detail Sgt Doe & 3 Men to proceed with limbers as guard over dump.

Remaining stores on Battalion charge will be taken by Coys to Pommier, or placed in limber at Berles as is convenient. Limber and Officers Mess Cart will be at Berles at 1. 0 pm. 2 servants per Coy and 2 for Hd. Qrs will accompany mess cart. These will be marched under the Provost Sgt.

Cookers will be at Pommier at 1. 0 pm and have tea ready by 3.45 pm

Battalion Water Carts will meet the Battalion at the junction of the La Bazeque-Saulty Road and the main Arras Road.

To move Q.M. Stores, Officers Valises, Blankets etc., one Motor Lorry will be available at 9. 0 am and can make two or more journeys as required but must be returned to the Supply Column by 4. 0 pm.

A Divisional Dump has been formed at No 2 Billet, LARBRET, where surplus stores and kit can be sent for storage.

9. **Cooks.** Will leave immediately after dinner tomorrow for Pommier.

10. **Sick Men.** A Horse ambulance will be at Pommier at 4. 0 pm tomorrow to take men who cannot possibly march. Those who are doubtful will be sent to La Bazeque tonight and will leave there at 4.30 pm tomorrow under senior NCO or Private.

11. **Details joining Battalion.** The following will join Battalion tomorrow:-
    a) Brigade Bomb School at Pommier.
    b) Dug-out Party at Pommier.
    c) Trench Wardens at Ravine.

12. **Rations:** have been arranged for.

13. **O. Room.** Will close in the Ravine at 1. 0 pm and re-open at Mondicourt at 10. 0 pm.

F. Philip
2/Lt. & Adjt.
1/4th Bn. Lincolnshire Regiment.

Copy No.

Operation Order No 51 by Major R. M. Earl Commanding 1/4th
Battalion Lincolnshire Regiment.
———————————
In the field 31. 10. 16

Map Ref. LENS 11.

1. Move. Battalion will move into MEZEROLLES tomorrow.

2. March. Battalion will parade in column of route on the main
ARRAS ROAD near the S. W. Railway Crossing at 7. 50 am
in the following order:-

Hd. Qr. Guides, Signallers, A. B. C. D. Coys, Dugout
Party, Transport.
Lewis Guns on Handcarts in rear of Coys.
Dress: full marching order: leather jerkins to be carried
under waterproof sheets.
Route: via DOULLENS.
 The Field Ambulance and R. E. Coy will be marching
behind Battalion from L'ESPERANCE.
Capt R. D. Ellis will after Battalion has paraded, proceed
to L'ESPERANCE to prevent the F. A. and R. E. Coy from
leaving before Battalion arrives.

3. Billeting Party. 2/Lt. C. Temple and C.S.M. Joyce proceeded this
afternoon to billet Battalion. Hd. Qr. Guides except
the C. Os. Orderly will leave ahead of the Battalion to
act as guides on Battalion's arrival at destination.

4. Stores: will be sent to Q.M. Stores as follows:-
Blankets at   6. 30 am.
Officers Valises   7. 0 am
Coy Mess Kit   7. 30 am
Other Stores   6. 30 am
all Coy storemen will report at Q.M. Stores at 7. 0 am.
Hd. Qr. mess kit will be collected by mess cart at 7. 0am

5. On arrival in billets, coys will report numbers of men who fell
out on the march.

6. Orderly Room: closes at MONDICOURT at 7. 30 am and opens at
MEZEROLLES on arrival of Battalion.

7. Detail for tomorrow.
Breakfasts   6. 0 am
Sick Parade   6. 30 am
Dinners will be cooked on the march.

8. Sick Men. Arrangements will be notified later.

 2/Lt. & Adjt.
1/4th Bn. Lincolnshire Regiment.

Copy No 1 Retained
        2 Office Copy
        3 A Coy
        4 B Coy
        5 C Coy
        6 D Coy
        Transport Officer & Q.M.
        8 War Diary
        9 R. S. M.

VIIth Corps GS 1113
46th Division 2084/G.

46th Division.

The Corps Commander has read with much interest the account of the raid delivered by the 4th Battalion, Lincoln Regiment, on the night of the 4th/5th October. He congratulates the unit on the care and forethought expended on the preparations and the officers and men on the manner in which they carried out the raid.

It was unfortuante, though unavoidable, that greater results as regards loss inflicted on enemy were not obtained, and the result seems to suggest that in the present circumstances, more latitude should be given to the Officer conducting the raid as to his objective and moment for withdrawing.

7th October, 1916.
(sgd) F.Lyon, B.G., G.S.,
VIIth Corps.

***   ***   ***

138th Infantry Brigade.

The G.O.C has much pleasure in forwarding this letter of the Corps Commander.

As regards para 2, he considers that more latitude should in future be given as to timing return of raiding parties

G. Thorpe
Lieut-Colonel,
8th October, 1916.   General Staff, 46th Division.

Copies to 137th Infantry Brigade) For
        139th   ,,   ,,) information.

SECRET.   G.724.

Report on Raid carried out by 4th Lincolns on night 5th/6th October.

1. The objective of the raid was the enemy's trenches between E.5.a.11.58 and E.5.a.13.77.

2. The outlined plan was as follows :-

   Two gaps were to be cut in the enemy's wire at E.5.a.11.58 and E.5.a.13.77. Raiding parties were to enter at these two places, place blocks on their outer flanks and then work inwards.
   To distract attention from the objective, two other gaps were to be cut in the enemy's wire at E.5.c.70.75 and E.5.c.60.83. The bombardment of these gaps was timed to start 3 minutes before the bombardment on the actual objective. This bombardment succeeded in drawing the enemy's attention off the objective.

3. The artillery programme was as follows :-

Afternoon 5th.   1 pm. to 2.30 pm.   Wire cutting by trench mortars.
                 2.30 pm.   "   "   " B.232 battery.
                 3.30 pm.   "   "   " trench mortars.
                 5 pm.   9.45" H.T.M. to bombard WHITE HOUSE, E.5.a.72.70.
                 2 pm. to 6 pm.   38th S.B. R.G.A. to engage certain machine gun emplacements.

Night 5th/6th.   Bombardment of false front to commence 11.27 (3 minutes before zero) lifting at 11.32.
                 Bombardment of front of attack to commence at 11.30 pm. (zero) and lift at 11.35 pm.
                 Box barrage around front of attack to be kept up till "all clear" is reported by O.C., 4th Lincoln Regiment.

4. Wire cutting was carried out on the afternoon of the 5th October, 8, 2" trench mortars and one battery 18 pr: being employed. All four gaps were satisfactoryily cut except the northern one on the front of attack. This solitary failure was due to one trench mortar being knocked out by the enemy's shell fire.

5. Reports of Brigade Commander and of O.C., 4th Lincoln Regiment are attached.

                                             Thorpe
                                             Lieut-Colonel,
                                     General Staff, 46th Division.

7th October, 1916.

Report on Operations on 5th October, 1916

by 138th Inf. Bde.

1. **Action on the front of 5th Leicester Regt:-**

    Two gaps were well cut in the enemy wire during the afternoon by T.M.B.

    About 7.15 p.m. the enemy put a heavy rifle grenade into the bay of the trench where two ammonal tubes were being put together and connected with an electrical lighter. Two officers who were doing this work were wounded and two sappers killed; the ammonal tubes and electrical apparatus were damaged.

    Other sappers with tubes were sent up from POMMIER but after reaching the front trench at 11.15 p.m. were too late to put out the tubes.

    The 'feint' bombardment started at - 3. The enemy almost at once threw up white flares and parachute lights and opened a considerable rifle and M.G. fire. His artillery opened on our support and front lines at about zero, but did no damage. His heavy T.M. continued firing on this sector for about half-an-hour but did no damage.

    The enemy ceased firing when our artillery stopped (12 midnight).
    The 'feint' bombardment appears to have served its purpose.

2. Report on operations by O.C., 4th Lincolnshire Regiment is attached.

3. The Brigade M.G. Company fired 8,500 rounds.
    X.46.T.M.B.   ,,   618   ,,
    138th Bde. T.M.B.   ,,   393   ,,

                                sd/ T.E. Sandall.
                                        Lt-Colonel,
    6.10.16.   Commanding 138th Infantry Brigade.

1/4th Lincolnshire Regiment.

Report of Operations carried out on the 5th Oct: 1916.

A raid took place last night on the German trenches.

The parties were in position in our front line trench by 9.20 p.m. Two patrols consisting of 1 Officer and 3 men each were despatched at 9.30 p.m. to reconnoitre the enemy wire at the two raiding points, and at 10.45 p.m. 2/Lt: COULSON reported by runner, that at the right point there was a good gap, that a torpedo would not be required, and that he had laid a tape from the enemy parapet, through the gap to our own trench. At 11 p.m. 2/Lt: HALLIDAY returned and reported that there was a partial gap opposite the left point, that, in his opinion, an entry could be made with a not unreasonable amount of handcutting, and that his tape was too short to reach our trench. I considered the reports sufficiently satisfactory, and ordered the programme to be carried out, the left party only to take a Bangalore Torpedo.

Right Party. At zero - 20 this party commenced to leave our trench and were all lying down close in front of our wire by zero - 10. At zero + 5 they advanced, and took five minutes to reach the enemy's trench. The various parties had kept well together and there was no confusion: An entry was made by means of ladders, the trench being well constructed, estimated depth 12 feet, and width at bottom 4 feet. The grids were more strongly made than our own pattern, the lower 6 ft of trench revetted with stout timber and the upper part unrevetted. There was a shaft quite close to the point of entry (in the parados) descending to a considerable depth, and a light was visible at the bottom. A man in the mouth of the shaft shouted "Who the hell are you?" and fired on the party: he was shot and fell down the shaft where another man was seen and he too was shot and fell. The shaft was then bombed and it was estimated that about 7 men were in it.

The blocking party working to the right and the attacking party working to the left were both stopped by blocks, the former finding the trench completely blown in, and the latter being confronted by a block which had been constructed previous to the bombardment. The total distance between the two blocks was only about 15 yards, and ladders would have been required to scale either of them. The raid Commander did not consider himself justified in proceeding beyond this block as the time was then zero + 24, so he sounded the recall on a bugle, which was heard in our fire trench.

No flank attack was made against the party but a very large number of bombs were thrown from the German support trench, all of which fell short and were of a remarkably inferior quality.

The party withdrew in an orderly manner and returned to our trench without loss at a walking pace.

The only casualty in this party was one man very slightly wounded in one finger by a splinter.

Left Party. This party did not work as smoothly as the other.
A long time was taken in finding the end of the tape, during which period the men remained behind each other instead of shaking out as soon as our wire was passed, with the result that the gap was blocked, and it was zero + 4 before the last man cleared the trench.

At zero + 15 a runner reported to me that the tape had not been found and at zero + 17 I ordered the party to return, the rear man being by then only just clear of the gap. The return was carried out in an orderly manner, and was completed by zero + 24 with the exception of one officer and two men of the covering party, who remained out for another ten minutes. 2/Lt: DIBB suffered a slight wound in the head from a splinter and was the only casualty of the party.

During the

2.

During the raid the enemy retaliation was chiefly directed against the Brigade Right Sector, the plan of wire cutting and bombarding a "dummy objective" being completely satisfactory from the point of view of the raiding party. The enemy, however, got two direct hits in our fire trench between the starting points of the two parties.

The co-operating artillery performed the task allotted to it in a capable and satisfactory manner, and proved amply sufficient.

The 9.45" T.M.B. failed to render any valuable assistance in the afternoon bombardment, owing to the hopeless unreliability of its ammunition.

The wire-cutting of the right gap by 2" mortars and 18 pr: shrapnel was a complete success and was at the exact place indicated in orders. At the left gap the cutting was less successful owing to a defect in one of the 2" mortars.

There was no machine gun fire at all brought to bear on the attacking party when in the German lines, on 'No Man's Land' or on our line during the raid, which, in my opinion, was due to the most efficient handling of the 138th M.G. Company aided by 4 guns of the 137th M.G. Company, which (guns of the) co-operated against the QUARRY.

The assistance of the 138th T.M.B. was also of great value in keeping down fire, and the Battalion Lewis Guns proved similarly useful.

I consider that the size of the raiding party might have been reduced with advantage. The value of careful rehearsal was fully demonstrated. The details arranged by O.C. Raid were carefully brought out and worked satisfactorily, and the conduct of all ranks was excellent. The telephone wire was cut before communication could be established but this accident proved to be of no consequence. The time allowed in the trench was insufficient. The O.C. Raid might have been allowed more latitude in deciding when to retire.

Much amusement was afforded by our friends the enemy, when, at exactly zero + 120, they delivered a heavy bombing attack against the raided point, a report of which operation is not to hand.

                        sd/ C.A. YOOL,
                            Major,
Commanding 1/4th Bn. Lincolnshire Regt:

Army Form C. 2118

4th Lincolns Vol 24

19c

WAR DIARY or INTELLIGENCE SUMMARY
(Erase heading not required.)

Place	Date	Hour	Summary of Events and Information	Remarks and references to Appendices
MEZROLLES	Mar 1st/16	7.30 a.m.	The Battalion marched from MONDICOURT to billets in MEZROLLES via DOULLENS. Lieut-Col. G.A. YOOL returned from leave & took over the command of the battalion vice MAJOR R.M. EARL. 2/Lt L.D.E. FYFFE proceeded to Field Ambulance.	
MAISON PONTHIEU	2nd	7.30 a.m.	The Battalion marched from MEZROLLES & moved to billets in MAISON PONTHIEU via AUXI-LE-CHATEAU.	
APENVILLERS	3rd	9.15 a.m.	The Battalion marched from MAISON PONTHIEU & moved to billets in APENVILLERS via HIERMONT. 2/Lt C.E. RICE rejoined from Field Ambulance. Kernel equipment came to during the morning – fallen & followed the afternoon.	
	4th			
	5th	9 p.m.	Other parts or ground immediately South of APENVILLERS - followed by a route march of about 3½ miles. 2/Lt F.J. PEACOCK rejoined from Field Ambulance.	
	6th		Rain quite interfered with certain 2 platoon drill, bayonet fighting & bomb throwing during the morning – company lectures on active during the afternoon, on the evening, Officers & Platoon Sergeants marched on Company training.	

Army Form C. 2118

WAR DIARY
or
INTELLIGENCE SUMMARY
(Erase heading not required.)

4th Lincolns

Instructions regarding War Diaries and Intelligence Summaries are contained in F.S. Regs., Part II. and the Staff Manual respectively. Title Pages will be prepared in manuscript.

Place	Date	Hour	Summary of Events and Information	Remarks and references to Appendices
AGENVILLERS	Nov 7th		Heavy rain again. Enterprised with training during the forenoon - in the afternoon the battalion marched about 6 miles under Company arrangements.	
	"8"		Handling of arms, close order drill & open order work during the morning - Fielding in the afternoon on the 6 mile zone captured position & various trenches - in the evening 2 Platoons per Company marched on Company training roleplayed as instructors. MAJOR B. R. SILLS proceeded to Field Ambulance.	
	"9"		Coy. extended line of attack 2½ mile followed by Company attack & advance on the front - work march during the afternoon.	
	"10"		Handling of arms, bayonet fighting, extended order work in the forenoon - Church in the field - work march & extent & billets via Sr RIQUIER and MILLANCOURT during the afternoon.	
NEUILLY L'HOPITAL	"11"		General training & Battalion drill in the forenoon - drill on the field - marched to billets in NEUILLY L'HOPITAL during the afternoon.	

Army Form C. 2118

4th Lincolns

WAR DIARY
or
INTELLIGENCE SUMMARY
(Erase heading not required.)

Instructions regarding War Diaries and Intelligence Summaries are contained in F.S. Regs., Part II. and the Staff Manual respectively. Title Pages will be prepared in manuscript.

Place	Date	Hour	Summary of Events and Information	Remarks and references to Appendices
NEUILLY L'HOPITAL	Nov. 12"	9-15am	Church Parade. Relieved by Ratcliffe Buff. 2/L? B.H. CHALLONER proceeded to 2/2nd Ambulance.	
	" 13		Ratcliffe drill, Platoon work in extended order, Arty Coy practised Night Operation.	
	" 14		Ratcliffe Bn.H.Q. platoon by extended order work.	
	" 15		Ratcliffe drill followed by extended order work, C?D. Coy practised Night Operation.	
	" 16		Lectures in Autumn work, followed by practical work in same. Ratcliffe Night Operation commenced at 6-30 p.m.	

2/Lt P. Belton.
Sergt J. H. Carter.
Pt. T.A. Clapham
Cpl. E.H. Peet.
Pte B.R. Roys.

Military Medals were awarded to:-

Serjt. W. Smith.
C.S. Major A.B. Howson.
Sgt. W. Inman.
Sgt. W.F. Lilley.
Pte. J.H. Slater.
Cpl. P.S. Wells

Army Form C. 2118

WAR DIARY
or
INTELLIGENCE SUMMARY
(Erase heading not required.)

A.H. Lancasters

Place	Date	Hour	Summary of Events and Information	Remarks and references to Appendices
NEUILLY L'HOPITAL	Nov. 17		Battalion training in the "attack". 2/Lt. H.B. CHALLONER returned from Field Ambulance.	
	"18		Battalion Skill & Gunnery training	
		5.30pm.	Lecture by the Divisional Commander to all Officers on "The attack".	
	"19		Interior economy, physical drill, platoon parade. Lectures by Heut. Col. WEBER. D.S.O. at S˙ RIQUIER on "Operations on the SOMME."	
	20"		Brigade Field Operation.	
	21"		Battalion training in "The attack". March by company teams & platoons by night.	
BEAUMETZ	22ⁿᵈ Jan.		The Battalion moved into billets in BEAUMETZ. via S˙ RIQUIER, COULONVILLERS & MOULIN DE CRAMONT.	
BONNIERES	23ʳᵈ Jan.		The Battalion moved into billets in BONNIERES via MAIZICOURT & WAVANS.	
	24"		Interior economy	

Army Form C. 2118

4 Lincolns

WAR DIARY
or
INTELLIGENCE SUMMARY
(Erase heading not required.)

Instructions regarding War Diaries and Intelligence Summaries are contained in F.S. Regs., Part II and the Staff Manual respectively. Title Pages will be prepared in manuscript.

Place	Date	Hour	Summary of Events and Information	Remarks and references to Appendices
HALLOY	Nov. 25/16	9.15 am.	The Battalion moved into Hutts in HALLOY via BOUQUEMAISON and LUCHEUX. - Rain during the whole of this march. 2/Lt R. ELLIOTT proceeded to ENGLAND.	
	26		Parties in Hutts. Lieut-Col. G.A. YOOL proceeded to a Commanding Officers' Conference at AUXI LE CHATEAU. Major R.M. EARL took over the Command of the Battalion.	
	27		Company training in the morning. Rev^t. match during the afternoon. 2/Lt. J. ROCKEY appointed Bⁿ. Lewis Gun Officer vice 2/Lt R. ELLIOTT who proceeded to ENGLAND on 25-inst. Q.M.S. J.W. UPEX appointed Q.M. with the Honorary Rank of LIEUT. See Oct. 15th 1916.	
	28		Parties training during the forenoon. Bathes, interior economy & play in the afternoon.	
	29		Company training during the forenoon. Route march in the afternoon. 2/Lt. G.L. BARRITT proceeded to HESDIN to join the R.F.C. as an Observer.	

Army Form C. 2118

WAR DIARY
or
INTELLIGENCE SUMMARY 4th Lincolns
(Erase heading not required.)

Instructions regarding War Diaries and Intelligence Summaries are contained in F.S. Regs., Part II. and the Staff Manual respectively. Title Pages will be prepared in manuscript.

Place	Date	Hour	Summary of Events and Information	Remarks and references to Appendices
HALLOY	Nov. 9		Company training during morning - Route march and Cross Country Run of about 6½ miles in the afternoon. 2/Lts F.J. CLARKE and H.K. CALEY proceeded to CANAPLES to join the 7th South Lancashire Regt.	

E.F.G. Hanson 2/Lt.
4th Lincolns. Int. Off.

J.W.Burd
Major O.C. 4th Lincolns

Copy 1

Operation Order No. 55 by Lieut - Col. G. A. Yool, Commanding 1/4th
Bn. Lincolnshire Regiment.
                                    In the field 21. 11. 16.

Ref. Map ABBEVILLE 1/100000 - 14.
     LENS 11 Ed. 1.

1. <u>Move</u>.   Bn. will move into billets in BEAUMETZ tomorrow.

2. <u>March</u>.   Bn. will parade ready to march off at 9. 0 am in column
                of route on the ST. RIQUIER Road with the head of the
                column at the Cross Roads 200 yards East of the Church.

                Order of Parade: Signallers, D. A. B. C. Coys, Transport
                Route: via ST. RIQUIER: COULONVILLERS & MOULIN DE
                GRAMONT.
                Battalion will march with 200 yards distance between
                Coys.

3. <u>Lewis Guns</u> in rear of Coys on carts pulled by pack animals, which
                will be sent to Coys by 8. 15 am.

4. <u>Billeting Party</u>. 1 NCO per Coy, on Coy bicycle will leave O. Room
                at 7. 0am under 2/Lt. B. H. Challenor for whom 1 Hd. Qr.
                bicycle will be available. Cpl Bilton will proceed for
                Hd. Qrs.

5. <u>Advance Party</u>.   1 man per platoon and 1 Hd. Qr. Signaller will
                parade at the O. Room at 7. 15 am under Sgt. to be
                detailed by O. C. 'D' Coy. This party will on arrival
                at BEAUMETZ make themselves acquainted with their
                respective platoons billets and will be at the entrance
                to BEAUMETZ at 12. 30 pm to meet Battalion.

6. <u>Stores</u>.   Following will be sent to Q. M. Stores at times stated:-

                Blankets (neatly rolled in bundles of ten) at 6. 45 am.
                Officers valises   7. 0 am.
                Other Stores   6. 45 am.
                Officers mess gear will be collected by the Mess Cart
                at 8. 0 am.
                Coy Storemen will report to the Quartermaster at 7. 15 am.

7. <u>Transport</u> will be ready loaded by 8.30am.

8. On arrival at billets Coys will report at once numbers of men who
                fell out on the march, giving reasons for their falling out.

9. <u>Orderly Room</u>: will close at NEUILLY L'HOPITAL at 8. 30 am and open
                at destination on arrival.

10. <u>Detail for tomorrow</u>:   Coy on duty   : A Coy
                          Breakfasts   7. 0 am.
                          Sick Parade   6.30 am.
                          Dinners will be cooked on the march.

                                        Lieut & Adjt.,
                                     1/4th Bn. Lincolnshire Regt.

Copy No. 1 Retained
        2 Office Copy
        3 A Coy
        4 B Coy
        5 C Coy
        6 D Coy
        7 Transport Officer
        8 Quartermaster
        9 War Diary.

Copy No. 2

Operation Order No. 56 by Lieut- Col. G. A. Yool, Commanding 1/4th Bn.
Lincolnshire Regiment.

Ref. Map LENS 11. 1/100000   In the field 24. 11. 16.

1. Move.   The Battalion will move into billets at HALLOY tomorrow
                   (25th inst)

2. Parade.   Battalion(less two platoons A Coy and Echelon B Transport)
                   will parade ready to march off at 9. 15 am in column of
                   route facing S. E. on Main Road with the head of column
                   at the Church BONNIERES.
                   Order of Parade: Signallers, B.C.D.A.Coy(less 2 platoons)
                                    Echelon A Transport.

3. March.   Bn. will march in Brigade from Cross Roads 1500 yards West
                   of MON LEBLOND.
                   Route: MON LEBLOND: BOUQUEMAISON: Road Junction 600 yards
                          N. of CALIMONTS FM: LUCHEUX: Road Junction 425 yards
                          S. W. of LUCHEUX CHURCH: L'ESPERANCE.
                   There will be a halt for fifty minutes when the head of
                   the column reaches a point ¼ mile West of the LUCHEUX-
                   LE SOUICH Road.

4. Lewis Guns: As for yesterdays march.

5. Billeting Party. Proceed this afternoon to billet Battalion.

6. Advance Party. 1 man per platoon and 1 Hd.Qr. Signaller under 1 NCO
                   to be detailed by O.C. 'B' Coy will parade at Q.M. Stores
                   at 7. 45 am to proceed to HALLOY and to report there to
                   2/Lt. CHALLENOR.

7. Transport.   Echelon A will move with Battalion and will be ready loaded
                   by 8. 45 am. Echelon B will be at Brigade starting point
                   at 9. 15 am.

8. Baggage Guard. A Coy will detail two platoons as Brigade Baggage Guard
                   these two platoons under Capt. MYERS will pass Church
                   at 8. 55 am and proceed to MON LEBLOND and report to
                   Brigade Transport Officer.

9. Stores.   Will be sent to Q. M. Stores as follows:-
                   Blankets and Officers Valises   7. 30 am
                   Officers Mess Gear   7. 45 am
                   Other Stores   7. 30 am

10. Dinners.   Will be had at the fifty minute halt between BOUQUEMAISON
                   and LUCHEUX.

11. Reports.   Usual reports in regard to men falling out will be sent in
                   to O. Room on arrival at destination.

12. O. Room will close at BONNIERES at 8. 45 am and open at destination
    on arrival.

13. Detail for tomorrow.   Coy on duty   D Coy
                                   Next for duty   A Coy
                                   Sick Parade   7. 30 am
                                   Breakfasts   7. 0 am

Copy No. 1 Retained
        2 Office Copy   Sd. F. A. Phillips, Lieut & Adjt.,
        3 A Coy   1/4th Bn. Lincs. Regt.
        4 B Coy
        5 C Coy
        6 D Coy
        7 Q.M.
        8 Transport Officer
        9 War Diary.

Copy No.

OPERATION ORDER No. 57
by
Lieut- Col. G. A. YOOL, Commanding
1/4th Bn The Lincolnshire Regiment.

Ref. Map - LENS 11.   In the field 5. 12. 16.
1/100,000.

1. Move. The Battalion will move into Billets in BIENVILLERS tomorrow.

2. Parade. Bn. will parade ready to march off at 12. 15pm in column of route on the HALLOY-HURTEBISE Fm. Road and facing W.S.W. with the head of the column 600 yards from Road Junction West of 'H' in HALLOY.
Order of parade:- B.C.D.A. Coys.

3. March. Route via PAS, HENU & SOUASTRE.
From PAS to SOUASTRE, Bn. will march by Coys at 200 yards distance: from SOUASTRE to BIENVILLERS by Platoons at 100 yards distance.

4. Lewis Guns will be on Handcarts in rear of Coys. Pack animals will be sent to Coys by 11. 30 am.

5. Billeting Party. 1 NCO per Coy on Coy bicycle, together with Cpl Bilton for Hd. Qrs., will report to 2/Lt. B. H. CHALLENOR at O. Room at 7. 30 am.

6. Advance Party. 1 man per platoon and 1 Hd. Qr Signaller will parade at 9. 0am at O. Room under the R.S.M. This party will report to 2/Lt. Challenor on arrival at BIENVILLERS and will arrange to be outside Brigade Hd. Qrs at BIENVILLERS at 3. 30 pm to meet the Battalion.

7. Stores etc. Will be sent to O. Room as follows:-
Blankets at   7. 30 am
Officers Valises, Coy mess boxes and Orderly Room Gear at   9. 30 am
Other Stores at   7. 30 am
Coy Storemen will report to the Q. M. at 7. 0 am.

8. Transport. Will move under arrangements of the Transport Officer with the exception of the following which will parade with the Battalion:-
Coy Cookers, 2 Watercarts, Messcart & Medical Cart.

9. Arrival in Billets:- on arrival in Billets Coys will at once report numbers of men who fell out on the march, if any.

10. O. Room:- Will close in HALLOY at 11. 45 am and open at destination on arrival.

11. Detail for tomorrow:-
Breakfasts   7. 0 am
Sick Parade   8.30 am
Dinners   10.45 am

Sd. F. A. Phillips. Lieut & Adjt.,
1/4th Battalion Lincolnshire Regiment.

Copy No. 1 Retained
2 Office Copy
3 War Diary
4 138th Inf. Bde
5 A Coy
6 B Coy
7 C Coy
8 D Coy
9 Transport Officer
10 Quartermaster.

Copy No.

Operation Order No 58 by Lieut-Col. G. A. Yool, Commanding 1/4th
Battalion Lincolnshire Regiment.
In the field 10.12.16.

Ref. Map FONQUEVILLERS 1/10,000.

1. **Move:** Battalion will relieve the 5th Lincolns in 'Y' Sector trenches tomorrow (11th inst).

2. **Distribution in Trenches.** C. D. & B. Coys will be in the line in that order from right to left.
A Coy will be in reserve in dugouts in FONQUEVILLERS.

3. **March:** Starting Point: Road Junction BIENVILLERS E 8 b 90.85.

	To pass starting point.	Route.
B Coy (1st platoon)	9. 45 am	via HANNESCAMP & CHISWICK AVENUE
D Coy do	10. 5 am	do do
C Coy do	9. 45 am	via FONQUEVILLERS & CRAWL BOYS (LANE.
A Coy do	10. 5 am	to FONQUEVILLERS.
Hd. Qrs.	10. 25 am	to FONQUEVILLERS.

Coys will march by platoons at 5 minutes interval.
After relief outgoing platoons of 5th Lincolns will leave under orders of O.C. 5th Lincolns.
Crawl Boys Lane will be closed to down traffic between 10. 20 am and 11. 10 am and CHISWICK AVENUE between 10. 15 am and 11. 15 am.

4. **Advance Party:** C.S.Ms. and 1 Runner per Coy together with the R.S.M. and Cpl Bilton will pass starting point at 8. 30 am.

5. **Signallers** will pass starting point at 8. 15 am.

6. **Lewis Guns.** Lewis Gunners with guns will proceed to trenches tonight and will pass starting point as follows:-
C & A Coys at 5. 0 pm
D & B Coys at 5.10 pm
Guns will be taken into the line or kept at FONQUEVILLERS as the case may be to enable the 5th Lincolns to take away their guns tonight.
2 new guns will be taken by A Coy and kept with their own guns.
O. C. 5th Lincolns will arrange for a guide from each of their teams in the line to meet Lewis Gunners, as follows:-
Right Coy at Bn. Hd. Qrs at 5. 30 pm
Centre & Left Coy at Cross Roads HANNESCAMP at 5. 30 pm.
The Transport Officer will arrange for one limber for C & A Coys guns and S.A.A. and one limber for D & B Coys .
The Lewis Gunners will draw their breakfasts tomorrow morning from the 5th Lincolns to whom necessary rations will be issued by the Q. M. Remainder of the days rations will be sent up with Coys rations:

7. **Cookers & Rations:** will be sent up tonight as soon after dusk as possible. B Coys Cooker and rations will proceed to HANNESCAMP where the cooker will be stationed. Remaining cookers and rations will proceed to FONQUEVILLERS.
Rations for tomorrows breakfast will not be sent up to the trenches but will be issued to Coys tonight as usual. Coys will make arrangements for cooking men's breakfasts with Camp Kettles.
Camp Kettles will be stacked tomorrow morning at O. Room at 8. 30 am.
1 Cook per Coy will accompany the cookers and rations and remain with them.
The 5th Lincolns will use the cookers for their breakfasts tomorrow morning.

Operation Order No. 59 By Lt.Col. G.A. Yool, Commanding 1/4th
Bn. Lincolnshire Regt.   In the field.
                                      16.12.16.

1. The Bn. will be relieved tomorrow (17th inst) and will go into Divisional Reserve at SOUASTRE.

2. A" C & D Coys when relieved will proceed by FONQUEVILLERS-Track 3 to SOUASTRE by platoons, at 200 yards interval. The Platoon Commander will march in rear of his platoon and will be responsible for march discipline.
   B Coy, less Lewis Gun Teams, will proceed by CHISWICK AVENUE, HANNESCAMPS and BIENVILLERS.

3. Lewis Guns will be left at Bn. H.Q. FONQUEVILLERS under an escort of 1 N.C.O and 2 men to be provided by A Coy., and will be brought away by limber after dark.

4. All Officers kits will be stacked at H.Q. FONQUEVILLERS at 9.30 am.
   A" C & D Coy., stores to be at Bn. H.Q. by 9.30 am.
   B Coy., stores to be dumped at Cook House, HANNESCAMPS, under escort to be found by O.C. B.Coy.

5. Gum Boots Thigh on charge of A,C & D Coys., will be handed over by C.S.Ms. to the R.S.M., at Bn. H.Q. FONQUEVILLERS on leaving the trenches.
   B Coy., will dump their Gum Boots Thigh under suitable escort at Coy. Cook House, HANNESCAMPS, and hand them in to R.S.M. on arrival at SOUASTRE.

6. Any men sick and unable to march will be paraded at Regt. Aid Post at 9.30.am

7. 100 pairs Gum Boots Thigh will be handed over to 5th Lincs. by R.S.M.

8. Breakfasts at usual hour.
   Dinner will be served on arrival at SOUASTRE

9. "Relief Complete" Reports will be rendered to Bn. H.Q. FONQUEVILLERS.

10. Orderly Room will close at FONQUEVILLERS at 1.30.pm and will re-open on arrival at SOUASTRE.

                                           2/Lt & a/Adjt.
                             1/4th Lincs Regt.

Copy No. 1. Retained.
        2. A. Coy.
        3. B. "
        4. C. "
        5. D. "

Army Form C. 2118

WAR DIARY
or
INTELLIGENCE SUMMARY
(Erase heading not required.)

4th Lincolns. Vol 25

20.E.

Place	Date	Hour	Summary of Events and Information	Remarks and references to Appendices
HALLOY	Dec 1/16	2.30 pm	The 138th Brigade was inspected by Lieutenant General Sir T. D'O. SNOW Commanding VII Corps - accompanied by Major General W. THWAITES Commanding 46th North Midland Division. The G.O.C. presented Military Medals to the following N.C.O's & men of 1/4 LINCOLNS:- 1190 a/Cpl F. BILTON. 2644 C.S.M. HOWSON. A.B. 2284 Sgt H. CARTER. 2308 Sgt W. INMAN 1168 Pte T.A. CLAPHAM. 2849 Sgt W.F. LILLEY. 1078 Cpl G.H. PEET. 3690 Pte J.H. SLATER. 3939 Pte B.R. ROYS. 3767 Cpl P.S. WELLS. 1386 Sgt S.W. SMITH. The following notes has been received:- "The B.G.C. wishes all ranks to know that the Inspection Parade to-day was most satisfactory. Both the Corps & Divisional Commanders expressed themselves very pleased with the general turnout & steadiness of the ranks on parade, and during the March Past, which was most creditable to all, and stands to prove and maintain the position & credit of the Battalion and to the Brigade."	

Army Form C. 2118

WAR DIARY
or
INTELLIGENCE SUMMARY
(Erase heading not required.)

4th Kuendu

Instructions regarding War Diaries and Intelligence Summaries are contained in F.S. Regs., Part II. and the Staff Manual respectively. Title Pages will be prepared in manuscript.

Place	Date	Hour	Summary of Events and Information	Remarks and references to Appendices
HALLOY	Dec 2/16		Company training during the forenoon, went marched to DOULLENS for entertainment Y during afternoon evening.	
	" 3rd		Church parade.	
	" 4th		Company training in the morning. Marched to PAS to billets during afternoon. Lieut-Col. B.A. YOOL returned from C.O's. conference at AUXI-LE-CHATEAU & took over the command of the Battalion vice Major R.M. EARL evacuated. 2/Lieuts A.W. COULSON & C.C. RICE transferred to Machine Gun Corps. Heavy Branch.	
	" 5th		Platoon training, Squad fighting & various training.	
BIENVILLERS	Dec 6th		Battalion moved into billets at BIENVILLERS. Route via PAS and SOUASTRE.	
	" 7 "			
	" 8 "			
	" 9 "		LIEUT-COL. B.A. YOOL, Officers and Platoon Sergeants examined the trenches to go on HANNESCAMPS — FONQUEVILLERS front previous to taking over this portion of the line on 11th inst.	
	" 10th		MAJOR R.M. EARL evacuated to MERICOURT-SUR-SOMME on 9 inst. to take on the command of 12th Bn DUKE OF CORNWALL'S LIGHT INFANTRY LABOUR BATTALION. The enemy shelled BIENVILLERS from 9.30 p.m. — 10.30 p.m.	

WAR DIARY
or
INTELLIGENCE SUMMARY

Army Form C. 2118

Place	Date	Hour	Summary of Events and Information	Remarks and references to Appendices
BIENVILLERS	Dec 10th		3 men killed & 5 wounded.	
TRENCHES (FONQUEVILLERS)	11th	11 a.m.	The Battn relieves the 5th Lincolns on Y1 Sector – the trenches occupied were continuous with the 6th Sherwood Foresters at BERLES – OWL LANE running East from there, being H.Q's, Hdqrs Post Posn huts, CRAWL BOYS AVENUE – the main communicating trench being an extension. 7th & 8th Cos on Northern portion of FONQUEVILLERS	
	12th		During the morning the enemy fired about a dozen 9.2" shells into OTT'S Post & into CRAWL BOYS – between 4 – 10 p.m. the enemy fired 25-77 mm's into & around Tank Redoubt, our Right Company Support. 2/Lt R.C. Street returned from Base Conference.	
	13th		With the completion of this Battery the enemy has four emplacements Figured during the day. He continued about 100 - Whizzbangs and 4.2 shells along our front line - the majority of the others were fired from PIGEON WOOD and QUESNOY FARM. At 8 p.m. 2/Lt R.E. Hansen took out a patrol consisting of 1 Cpl & 4 O.R.s. His orders were to enter a ditch down the HANNESCAMP – ESSARTS Rd. They were challenged by a rifle fusilier of about 8 enemy, who fired three shots at close range, according (the Germans were very)	

Army Form C. 2118

WAR DIARY
or
INTELLIGENCE SUMMARY
(Erase heading not required.)

Instructions regarding War Diaries and Intelligence Summaries are contained in F.S. Regs., Part II. and the Staff Manual respectively. Title Pages will be prepared in manuscript.

Place	Date	Hour	Summary of Events and Information	Remarks and references to Appendices
	Mar 13"		No enemy attacks - Rain in the night. Maj. R.T. Thomson took out a whaler last but no trace of the enemy could be found. The R.O.C. sent 20P. R.T. Thomson & Pipeman complimenting him on the effort.	A. Smithers
	14"		An exceptionally quiet day.	
	15"		With the exception of a fire A.3.9 RHA fired on an enemy line the enemy was very quiet.	
	16"		Quiet day	
SOUASTRE	17"		The Battalion was relieved by the 5" Lincolns & moved into DIVISIONAL RESERVE at SOUASTRE. Capt. E.J.S. Naples promoted to F.R. Major Fielding-Johnson, 4" Leicester R.S., joined the Regiment & was appointed Second in Command. Capt. E.H. Marr3 transferred to Field Ambulance. Lieut. P.W.J. Cannon promoted to Hospital. Marched from Pipe Foley Reserve.	
	18"			
	19"			
	20"		Start went march. The Battalion relieved the 5" Lincolns in Y1 Sector.	
TRENCHES (FONQUEVILLERS)				

Army Form C. 2118

WAR DIARY
or
INTELLIGENCE SUMMARY
(Erase heading not required.)

4th Lincolns

Instructions regarding War Diaries and Intelligence Summaries are contained in F.S. Regs., Part II. and the Staff Manual respectively. Title Pages will be prepared in manuscript.

Place	Date	Hour	Summary of Events and Information	Remarks and references to Appendices
TRENCHES FONQUEVILLERS	Apr 22		Quiet day.	
	23		The enemy fired about 40 aerial darts on our front line and about 40 - 4.20 pm the Germans blew in FONQUEVILLERS.	
	24		Quiet day. Small parties of Germans were observed working about "THE Z" during the morning. Fires quickly dispersed by our Lewis Gunners.	
			The enemy distributes a Gas T.M.A. shell along our right company front line. About 10.40 pm. 20 mn round of flare are sent up by the enemy - sent light trench mortar shells of no lights - no apparent action took place. About 9 pm. the enemy was heard in the Pond line; at mid-night Retaliation of Rifle Communication trench fires in Head Quarters Area.	
	25		The Battalion was relieved by the 5th LINCOLNS Y MOOR and Rangers Groupe at	
BIENVILLERS			BIENVILLERS. 2/17 H.Q. SIMPSON joined the Regiment - Strangers from S. Lincolns	
	26		Interior economy, cleaning clothes &c - a large proportion of the Battalion being	
	27		required for various working parties.	
	28			

1875 Wt. W593/826 1,000,000 4/15 J.B.C. & A. A.D.S.S./Forms/C. 2118.

WAR DIARY or INTELLIGENCE SUMMARY

Army Form C. 2118

1/4 Lincolns

Place	Date	Hour	Summary of Events and Information	Remarks and references to Appendices
TRENCHES (FONQUEVILLERS)	Dec 27th	11 am	The Battalion relieved the 5th LINCOLNS in Y1 SECTOR. Several small parties of Germans were noticed working about "THE Z" - (They were carrying small sized cops) - our lewis gunners quickly dispersed them.	
	28th		The Scout Patrols are evidently carrying dogged lifts van our the enemy parts of the enemy lines running on their parapets in short distances & can observe & can specimens of humanity (?) can be seen unseen emptying buckets of earth.	
	29th		During the afternoon the enemies artillery fired a few rounds of 77mm shells from E33 A7B at our front company front line. The Germans were again heard sniping during the south part of the night. Owing to the heavy rain the trenches are in a very bad state - the front line trenches are knee deep with subside, the support line is nearly as bad - the dug-out are very wet & keep falling in. We have seen very little enemy aircraft recently.	

J.C. Fielding Johnson Major
for Col Comdg 1/4 Lincolnshire Regt

Army Form C. 2118

WAR DIARY
or
INTELLIGENCE SUMMARY
(Erase heading not required.)

1/4 Lincoln Regt
Nov 26
21.w

Place	Date 1917	Hour	Summary of Events and Information	Remarks and references to Appendices
TRENCHES. (FONCQUEVILLERS)	JAN 1st		Our artillery commenced the barrage of opening the Raid at 5.50am approx. From this 18 pdr, 60 pdr, & 4.5" Howitzer Batteries, the artillery concentrated it distributing to the Wisgzstange along our Battalion frontage for this & other of our firing line.	
SOUASTRE	2nd	11 a.m.	The Battalion was relieved by the 5th Lincolns & moved out previous to Souastre. During the morning (8 - 10.20 a.m.) the Battalion Reserve of Souastre. Spaciousness of humanity was overseen taking units out of the area before thrown in the HQ.	
	3, 4, 5		DIVISIONAL RESERVE AT SOUASTRE.	
TRENCHES. (FONQUEVILLERS)	6th		The Battalion relieved the 5th Lincolns in Y1 Sector; at 11am. the H.Q. Platoon was proceeding up CRAWL BOYS AVENUE, a 77 m.m. shell hit the side of the trench & killed 3 men also wounding 7 O Ranks. Strength Ration State:- 18 Officers. 3 Sergeant Officers. 25 Sergts. - 467 Other Ranks.	

Army Form C. 2118

WAR DIARY
or
INTELLIGENCE SUMMARY
(Erase heading not required.)

Instructions regarding War Diaries and Intelligence Summaries are contained in F.S. Regs., Part II. and the Staff Manual respectively. Title Pages will be prepared in manuscript.

Place	Date	Hour	Summary of Events and Information	Remarks and references to Appendices
	Jan. 6.		The following names appeared in the New Years Honours List:— Major A.A. Eastwood was awarded the Military Cross. 2104 Sergt. J.S. Blakey was awarded the D.C.M. 2229 Sergt. R. Burton, & 1918 Appn. G.F. Ray & were mentioned in despatches.	
	" 7—			
	" 8—	11 a.m.	Each morning from about 10·15 a.m. to 11·30 a.m. the enemy shelled at few 777mm & 105mm. Q.H.Rs along our front line & supports - no material damage was done to the trenches.	
	" 9—			
BIENVILLERS	" 10—	11 a.m.	The Battalion was relieved by the 1/5th Lincolns Ymoed and Rffs in BIENVILLERS.	
	" 11—			
	" 12—		The Reserve Brigade of BIENVILLERS — repairing the existing Battalion was employed in repairs existing Paris & sent line & communication trenches, the enemy shelled the BIENVILLERS Army night from 7.30 p.m. — 11.30 p.m.	
	" 13—		2/Lt. A.B. HARDY; T.W. EDGE; V.N.D. SELBY; L.W. DOBBY; H.C. CHASE; and W. CHEER joined the Battalion.	

Army Form C. 2118

WAR DIARY
or
INTELLIGENCE SUMMARY
(Erase heading not required.)

Instructions regarding War Diaries and Intelligence Summaries are contained in F. S. Regs., Part II. and the Staff Manual respectively. Title Pages will be prepared in manuscript.

Place	Date	Hour	Summary of Events and Information	Remarks and references to Appendices
TRENCHES S. (FONQUE-VILLERS)	JAN. 14th	11a.m.	The Battalion relieved the 1/5 LINCOLNS in Y.1. SECTOR.	
	" 15th " 16th		The night was exceptionally quiet; front line & support trenches improved, wire placed in overhead & at work. Abandoned trenches wired in.	
	" 17th		During the *[illegible]* the enemy fired about 50 — 77m.m. shells along our lines. Did no material damage. One shell "Over" did damage to Rang of our men.	
	" 18th	10.30pm	The Battalion moved into DIVISIONAL RESERVE in SOUASTRE. Being relieved by the 1/5 LINCOLNS.	
	" 19th " 20th " 21st		Close rest. Both nights carrying fatigue parties for ranges of St. AMAND wood only.	
TRENCHES S. (FONQUE-VILLERS)	" 22nd	11a.m.	The Battalion relieved the 1/5 LINCOLNS in Y.1. SECTOR; situating the WARLIETTES R.so were connected up to the Road at *[illegible]* — The other *[illegible]* were now being shown.	
	" 23rd " 24th		The enemy the day occasionally quiet — with the exception of the usual *[illegible]* our lines continued from our own lines — we had also about 11a.m. a hostile plane flew over the Y lines and our front line trenches.	

Army Form C. 2118.

WAR DIARY
or
INTELLIGENCE SUMMARY.
(Erase heading not required.)

Instructions regarding War Diaries and Intelligence Summaries are contained in F. S. Regs., Part II. and the Staff Manual respectively. Title pages will be prepared in manuscript.

Place	Date	Hour	Summary of Events and Information	Remarks and references to Appendices
TRENCHES (FONQUEVILLERS)	Jan. 25.		During the afternoon the enemy fired a few 77 mm. shells along the front line.	
BIENVILLERS	" 26	11 a.m.	The Battalion was relieved by the 1/5 Lincolns & moved into Brigade Reserve at Bienvillers. 2/Lt. S. Lee rejoined the Battalion	
	" 27			
	" 28		At Bienvillers. The majority of the men remaining	
	" 29		out of the billets baths in Y1 Sector.	
TRENCHES (FONQUEVILLERS)	" 30	11 a.m.	The Battalion relieved the 1/5 Lincolns in Y1 Sector	
	" 31		2/Lt. W.N. Scott rejoined the Battalion.	
			Enemy very quiet.	

J. C. Spilling Johnson Major
Comdg 4th Lincs Regt

WAR DIARY
or
INTELLIGENCE SUMMARY.

Army Form C. 2118.

Vol 27

22.E

Place	Date	Hour	Summary of Events and Information	Remarks and references to Appendices
FONQUEVILLERS	FEB 1ST		SECTOR. HANNESCAMPS - ESSARTS RD to LA BRAYELLE RD. We were much less troubled by enemy artillery fire though he continued to fire heavy trench mortars on the advanced trench in front of our right company. Owing to a favourable wind considerable movement was heard behind the enemy lines during the night. During dinner the 2/16TH LONDONS arrived for instruction. Two companies arrived at FONQUEVILLERS and proceeded to the front line, the second in command (MAJOR TUCKER) stayed at HDQRS.	
	2ND		A readjustment of the Bde front. We take over BRUSHWOOD DRIVE from the LEICESTERS on our left and hand over RIGHT COY sub-sector and BALLY HOOLY strong point to 139TH BRIGADE. BATTN HDQRS moves to HANNESCAMPS; COLONEL YOOL proceeds on leave & MAJ. T.P. FIELDING JOHNSON takes over command	
	3RD		Considerable movement of men in small groups, behind the enemy lines, especially in the direction of ADINFER WOOD. BATTN relieved by 5TH LINCOLNS and proceeds to billets in DIVISIONAL RESERVE at SOUASTRE.	
SOUASTRE	4TH 5TH 6TH		Bathing and Interior Economy. The companies commence training in the new method of TRENCH ATTACK as laid down in S.S. 135. B Coy was inspected by the B.G.C. who expressed himself well pleased with the operations.	

Army Form C. 2118.

WAR DIARY
or
INTELLIGENCE SUMMARY.
(Erase heading not required.)

4th Lincolns

Place	Date Feb	Hour	Summary of Events and Information	Remarks and references to Appendices
HANNESCAMPS	7TH		Batt'n relieves 1/5th LINCOLNS in the trenches starting from SOUASTRE at 5.30p.m. HANNESCAMPS had been heavily shelled during the day and consequently the afternoon relief was cancelled.	
	8TH		Enemy artillery have been exceptionally active. Shells of 77 m.m. 105 m.m & 150 m.m. fell on HANNESCAMPS. A Coy of 2/6th LONDONS relieved by C Coy 4TH LINCS in front line & proceeds to BIENVILLERS in Bde Reserve. At night one company of 2/8th LONDONS arrives for instruction. Two platoons proceed to C Coy and two to B Coy in front line.	
	9TH		Enemy artillery have quietened down but his aeroplanes remain over our lines throughout the day, though at a great height. In the afternoon one came down quite low and fired his M.G. into our trenches.	
	10TH		Batt'n relieved by 2/6th LONDONS who had been in Bde Reserve at BIENVILLERS. Relief commenced at 5 p.m. and was completed by 8 p.m. Enemy aeroplanes active throughout the day.	
BIENVILLERS	11TH 12" 13"		Brigade Reserve at BIENVILLERS. Inauguration of 10 mins daily exercises by Sir Ivor Maxse (XVIIIth Corps Commander) 10 mins " Rapid Loading, Bayonet Fighting, Bomb Throwing" confirmed in their work (12th).

R/Lts H.C. CHASE, W. CHEER and A.B. HARDY

Army Form C. 2118.

WAR DIARY
or
INTELLIGENCE SUMMARY.
(Erase heading not required.)

Instructions regarding War Diaries and Intelligence Summaries are contained in F.S. Regs., Part II. and the Staff Manual respectively. Title pages will be prepared in manuscript.

4th Leicester

Place	Date Feb	Hour	Summary of Events and Information	Remarks and references to Appendices
HANNESCAMPS	14TH	5.0 P.M.	BATTN moves into trenches to relieve 2/10TH LONDONS. The "doc" goes scavenging and in the rubbish heap finds 6 bags of fuel — for which we pass a vote of thanks to LONDONS.	
	15TH		Walls of CHISWICK AV. gradually meeting each other, necessitating working parties both by day & by night. Unfortunately a party of 4TH LIECESTERS observed and fired on by BOSCHE, resulting in four slight casualties. On night of 15TH a patrol of C Coy men under 2/LT J.R. NEAVE proceeded along the HANNESCAMPS – ESSARTS RD. At 600 hundred yards from our lines they were met and surrounded by strong enemy patrols. With the help of a trench Gun under SGT DOE we managed to fight our way through some old gun pits, where we established ourselves. On examining the ground one dead BOSCHE was found. The rest had dispersed. We returned to our trenches carrying the corpse. Telegrams of congratulation followed from the B.G.C. and the G.O.C. SGT DOE and CPL FLUKE awarded the MILITARY MEDAL. No casualties to our own patrol.	
	16TH		Witnesses of a spectacular but unvarying effort by the enemy to flatten the trenches of the BATTN on our right. Bunches of red, green & yellow lights were the signal for an intense trench mortar bombardment, as many as two bombs being seen in the air at one time. On our left number of gas trench mortars were included but few casualties resulted. Times of bombardment 6.15 P.M., 6.15 P.M., 1.15 A.M. & 3.30 A.M. 2/LT BAUMBER arrives from base & is posted to A Coy.	

Army Form C. 2118.

WAR DIARY
or
INTELLIGENCE SUMMARY.
(Erase heading not required.)

5th Lincolns

Instructions regarding War Diaries and Intelligence Summaries are contained in F. S. Regs., Part II. and the Staff Manual respectively. Title pages will be prepared in manuscript.

Place	Date	Hour	Summary of Events and Information	Remarks and references to Appendices
HANNESCAMPS	17TH 18TH		Quiet days, marked by thick fog throughout day with consequent lack of observation and artillery fire. The continued thaw is gradually bringing down the walls of the trenches and all hands are needed to cope with the fall.	
SOUASTRE	19TH		Fog continues so also does the thaw and the fall of earth. Battn is relieved at night by 5th Lincolns and proceeds to Divisional Reserve at Souastre.	
	20TH 21ST 22ND		Daily Training in Attack.	
HANNESCAMPS	23RD		Battn relieves 5th Lincolns in Hannescamps Sector. The sector now consists of the old La Brayelle Rd – Essarts Rd trenches together with Colingbourne Av & Brushwood Drive.	
	24TH		Enemy artillery quiet. Considerable amount of smoke seen to rise from 2nd line of Big Z. At night orders come through from Bde to send out a strong patrol of 2 full platoons to reconnoitre the Z and if practicable, make an entry. The patrol found the Z normally garrisoned and returned to report same. Patrol drawn from A Coy in support.	

Army Form C. 2118.

WAR DIARY
or
INTELLIGENCE SUMMARY.
(Erase heading not required.)

A. Lincoln

Place	Date	Hour	Summary of Events and Information	Remarks and references to Appendices
HANNESCAMPS	25TH		News comes of the evacuation by the enemy of ground from S. of GOMMECOURT to BAPAUME. In our sector the enemy artillery is particularly active but it is noticed that all his active batteries lie between QUESNOY FARM and ADINFER WOOD. There is considerable movement in small parties between QUESNOY FARM and enemy front line - presumably the enemy has grown bold in the continuous fog which has now somewhat lifted. Our Lewis Gunners give him an unpleasant surprise, and much fun is caused in our trenches by his efforts to evade the bullets. At night A Coy is detailed to determine if the enemy has evacuated the Z and if possible make an entry. 2/Lt DAY moves off his company down the POPLAR RD with 2 platoons in front and 2 in support. When within 100 yds of enemy lines numerous flares went up and thick rifle fire is opened by the enemy. 10 casualties are suffered and the Commander decides to withdraw his men. Evidently the Z is still strongly held by the enemy.	
	26TH		Enemy artillery is still more active and shells of various calibres fall on HANNESCAMPS throughout the day. 4 men are observed in GOMMECOURT and PIGEON WOOD. Strong patrolling along the line in front of the Z throughout the night. 1st Platoon of B Coy under Platoon Commander report that Z is still occupied & all come under & are come under enemy rifle fire. No casualties.	

Army Form C. 2118.

WAR DIARY
or
INTELLIGENCE SUMMARY.
(Erase heading not required.)

4 Lincolns

Place	Date Feb.	Hour	Summary of Events and Information	Remarks and references to Appendices
BIENVILLERS	24th		Battn relieved by 5th Lincolns. Battn Hdqrs, less Maj. T.P. Fielding Johnson, Battn Hdqrs, less Maj. T.P. Fielding Johnson, together with C & D Coys move to Bienvillers. A & B Coys under Maj. Johnson proceed to billets in Fonquevillers. Battn is congratulated on work of patrols by B.G.C. At 1.30 a.m. a telegram arrives at Hdqrs telling of successful entry by 4th Leicesters into Gommecourt. Battn (C & D Coys) immediately moves off to take over line from 4th Leicesters. During the night A Coy provides the carrying parties for the Leicesters and B Coy dig a trench across No Mans Land immediately S of Fonquevillers - Gommecourt Rd. The B.G.C. expresses himself pleased with the promptness which Maj. Johnson displayed in organising & despatching working parties and also with the way in which the men N.C.O's & platoon commanders carried out their duties. The 4th Leicesters establish themselves firmly in the evening lines & take possession of Gommecourt Park, Wood & Village.	
	28th			

Army Form C. 2118.

WAR DIARY or INTELLIGENCE SUMMARY.

4Th Lincolns Rgt.

(Erase heading not required.)

Place	Date March	Hour	Summary of Events and Information	Remarks and references to Appendices
FONQUEVILLERS	1st		D Coy and part of C withdrawn from line leaving only 3 posts as left flank guard to 4th Leicesters who had advanced to hedge of Pigeon Wood. C Coy in dug outs in Sniper's Square; A, B & D Coys in cellars at Fonquevillers.	
St Amand	2nd	10.30 A.M.	Battn relieved by 5th Sherwood Foresters and moves into billets in St. Amand. Relief complete by 10.30 A.M. We are very comfortable in our billets and are not molested by enemy artillery fire.	
	3rd		Coys under Coy Commanders. Rafting and Interior Economy.	
	4th		Morning taken up with Church Parades and Bathing. In the afternoon the Cinema is reserved for the Battn and the expenses are met out of the Canteen Profits. The men thoroughly enjoy the entertainment, and they badly needed it after their strenuous fatigues of the last week. Announcement of the award by Commander in Chief of Military Cross to 2/Lt J.R.Neave.	
	5th		2/Lts A.W. Wilson and H.P.L. Dawson join Battn from Base. 2/Lt Wilson posted to D Coy & 2/Lt Dawson to C Coy. Lecture by Brigadier on "What has been done + what might have been done", in reoccupation of Gommecourt. 2/Lt J.R. Neave, Sgt P.W. Doe and Cpl G.W. Fluke parade at Whizz Bang's Yard, Souastre and are decorated by G.O.C.	

Army Form C. 2118.

4/F Lincoln Rgt.

WAR DIARY
or
INTELLIGENCE SUMMARY.
(Erase heading not required.)

Instructions regarding War Diaries and Intelligence Summaries are contained in F.S. Regs., Part II. and the Staff Manual respectively. Title pages will be prepared in manuscript.

Place	Date March	Hour	Summary of Events and Information	Remarks and references to Appendices
St. Amand	6th		Training by Companies in TRENCH ATTACK.	
	7th		Combined attack by two Companies. B & C at 2.0 p.m. A & D at 3.15 p.m. Issue of new pattern goggles to be kept in satchel with P.H. Helmet. Lt. F.A. PHILLIPS proceeds as instructor to Divl. Depot and 2/Lt. P.W. HALLIDAY returns to Battn. Formation of Battalion Scouts under 2/Lt. J.R. NEAVE. Four picked men per company to form basis.	
	8th		A draft of 50 men arrives from Divl. Depot.	
	9th		Day spent in platoon & company training.	
	10th		Companies practice TRENCH ATTACK.	
	11th		Church Parade in CINEMA HALL, St AMAND. Outpost Scheme carried out between 10 a.m & 2 p.m. An enemy force is retiring in a W direction to a line running N & S through GAUDIEMPRE. Outposts are pushed out and PICQUET LINES established. The operations are favoured by a bright spring morning, the first of the year.	

Army Form C. 2118.

WAR DIARY
or
INTELLIGENCE SUMMARY.   1/4 Lincoln Rgt
(Erase heading not required.)

Instructions regarding War Diaries and Intelligence Summaries are contained in F.S. Regs., Part II. and the Staff Manual respectively. Title pages will be prepared in manuscript.

Place	Date	Hour	Summary of Events and Information	Remarks and references to Appendices
ST. AMAND	MARCH 12TH		All Coys at disposal of 134TH BDE. The 134TH BDE are detailed to provide the assaulting battalions for an attack on BUCQUOY. The 1/4TH LINCOLNS are lent to the BDE. to be used by them as moppers up or carriers. Coys. march to CHATEAU DE LA HAIE to rehearse the operations with the battalions of 134TH BDE.	
	13TH		The Bath again at the disposal of the 134TH BDE. Training to be completed by 15TH inst. There were of evacuation by enemy of GREVILLERS and trenches in front of ACHIET-LE-PETIT. All scouting orders are cancelled, we return for duty with 138TH BDE and receive orders to be ready to march off at short notice. On the night of 13TH 134TH BDE make their attack. They are partially successful but the BUCQUOY GRABEN is strongly held & before dawn they withdraw, having suffered heavy casualties.	

Army Form C. 2118.

WAR DIARY
or
INTELLIGENCE SUMMARY.   4th Lincoln Rgt.

(Erase heading not required.)

Instructions regarding War Diaries and Intelligence Summaries are contained in F. S. Regs., Part II. and the Staff Manual respectively. Title pages will be prepared in manuscript.

Place	Date	Hour	Summary of Events and Information	Remarks and references to Appendices
ST AMAND	MARCH 14TH		In the early morning come orders from BDE to the effect that we must be ready to move at one hours notice, later the situation becomes normal and we are able to continue our training as laid down by orders of previous day. Coys are under Coy Commanders. We receive notice that we may have to take over sector held by 139TH BDE., left battalion; and the C.O., Coy Commanders + H.Q. Staff proceed to PIGEON WOOD to reconnoitre the ground.	
	15TH		The morning is taken up by a route march, men carrying their haversacks & overcoats. In the afternoon the TRENCH ATTACK is practised by Coys.	
	16TH		The 138TH BDE is detailed to repeat the attack on BUCQUOY. The 4TH LINCS REGT are the left assaulting battalion & is detailed to take BUCQUOY GRABEN and press on to PREUSSEN GRABEN & HILL 155. The 4TH & 5TH LINCS in conjunction, practise the attack on the	

Army Form C. 2118.

WAR DIARY
or
INTELLIGENCE SUMMARY.
(Erase heading not required.)

4 Lincolns Rgt

Place	Date	Hour	Summary of Events and Information	Remarks and references to Appendices
ST AMAND	MARCH 16TH		Prepared ground at CHATEAU DE LA HAIE. From there the C.O. 9H.Q's staff proceed to BIEZ WOOD to select site for BATTN. HQs and reconnoitre ground & trenches to be occupied. The artillery are raining shells of various calibres on the wire & particular strong posts of the defence. It is almost impossible to make oneself heard.	
			Due to cancelling of orders on previous night the 138TH BDE is notified that it will relieve the 139TH BDE in the trenches. The 4TH LINCS will relieve the left battalion.	
		4pm	The first party leaves at 3.0 P.M. and relief is timed to be completed by midnight. When we arrive there however we find that the Boche has made a sudden retirement and the 139TH BDE have temporarily lost touch.	
			The advanced line runs roughly E & W through QUESNOY FM and we take over posts there & prepare to push forward at dawn.	

Army Form C. 2118.

WAR DIARY
or
INTELLIGENCE SUMMARY.
(Erase heading not required.)

Place	Date	Hour	Summary of Events and Information	Remarks and references to Appendices
Essarts	18th		Battn Hq's in dug-out immediately S. of Essarts. At dawn patrols push forward towards Adinfer Wood and Douchy. Three of the enemy are seen and fired on, one man running severely wounded in our hands. Patrols find that Adinfer Wood Adinfer (village) and Douchy are evacuated & nothing of the enemy rearguard has been seen. Battn H.Q's move to Quesnoy Fm. and we are detailed to hold an outpost line Douchy – Adinfer Hameau Fm.	
Quesnoy Fm.	19th		Battn H.Q's move to Douchy. The whole village is a mass of ruins. Houses have been demolished, fruit trees cut down and roads damaged by mines. Surrounding villages present a similar appearance and the whole country bears the smear of "Hun Kultur". Companies are concentrated in Douchy and B + D Coys perform excellent work in clearing & repairing the roads through the village. The pursuit of the enemy rearguards is taken up by the Corps Mounted Troops.	
Douchy				

Army Form C. 2118.

WAR DIARY
or
INTELLIGENCE SUMMARY.

4 Lincoln Regt.

(Erase heading not required.)

Instructions regarding War Diaries and Intelligence Summaries are contained in F.S. Regs., Part II. and the Staff Manual respectively. Title pages will be prepared in manuscript.

Place	Date March	Hour	Summary of Events and Information	Remarks and references to Appendices
St Amand	20th		The Battn moves into billets at St Amand via Essarts, Hannescamps and Bienvillers. We are met at Pommier by the Brigadier who expresses his pleasure at the clean appearance & fine marching of the battalion, also at the excellent way in which they adapted themselves to the new conditions, and the thoroughness with which they carried out all orders given to them. The latter half of the march is made in a blinding snowstorm, nevertheless the men are in extremely high spirits and very much appreciate the presence of the BDE band on the outskirts of St Amand. We are played through the village & prove quite a draw to the french population.	
	21st		This day is spent in bathing & reclothing the battalion. Coys are under Coy Commanders for training during the afternoon	

Army Form C. 2118.

WAR DIARY
or
INTELLIGENCE SUMMARY.
(Erase heading not required.)

4 Linc'ln Rgt

Place	Date	Hour	Summary of Events and Information	Remarks and references to Appendices
BERTRANCOURT	22ND		According to Bde orders of previous night the Battn moves in Bde march to BERTRANCOURT. The march is via COUIN, ST LEGER, BOIS DU WARNIMONT and BUS-LES-ARTOIS; a distance of about 9 miles.	
ARQUÈVES	23RD		We had thought it possible that we might spend one day in BERTRANCOURT but at breakfast orders arrive from Bde to the effect that we are destined for another short march. We accordingly set out — with no definite knowledge of our destination. We arrive at ARQUÈVES in the evening where good billets have been arranged for us.	
MIRVAUX	24TH		We again set out on the march with the same uncertainty as to our destination. After a very good march we arrive at MIRVAUX, a distance of about 9 miles. We march past the Brigadier who compliments the Colonel on our march, specially mentioning A Coy who marched home in grand style under CAPT E. ELLIOT. At night we receive a message from the Vth CORPS COMMANDER thanking the 46TH DIVISION for the excellent work which they did in the advance from PIGEON WOOD — ESSARTS — QUESNOY FM to DOUCHY and AYETTE.	

Army Form C. 2118.

WAR DIARY
or
INTELLIGENCE SUMMARY.
(Erase heading not required.)

Instructions regarding War Diaries and Intelligence Summaries are contained in F.S. Regs., Part II and the Staff Manual respectively. Title pages will be prepared in manuscript.

Place	Date MARCH	Hour	Summary of Events and Information	Remarks and references to Appendices
GLISY	25th		After a march of 4½ miles to VILLERS BOCAGE the 4TH & 5TH LINCS. embussed for GLISY and LONGUEVAL respectively. The ride was via AMIENS and proved both a welcome and an interesting diversion.	
GLISY	26th		Throughout the morning the battalion stood by awaiting definite orders from B.O.E. At 12.45 P.M., in accordance with orders, we set out for SALEUX but when about 2 miles on our way a motor cyclist orderly arrives with news that we are to remain in our present billets. We return to GLISY and in the evening a number of officers and men are given passes for AMIENS.	
	27th		We move off from GLISY at 3 P.M. Due to the fact, no doubt, that we are allowed to make our own arrangements, everything goes without a hitch. Tea is ready for the men on our arrival & all coaches are apportioned. We set out from SALEUX STATION at 9 P.M. to entrain at SALEUX at 9 P.M. During the night we pass through ABBEVILLE and AUXI-LE-CHATEAU	

Army Form C. 2118.

4 Tank Bn

WAR DIARY
or
INTELLIGENCE SUMMARY.
(Erase heading not required.)

Place	Date	Hour	Summary of Events and Information	Remarks and references to Appendices
Estrée Blanche	28th		Daylight finds us well on our way to St Pol where we duly arrive in the afternoon. Happily the day is warm and bright and the men thoroughly appreciate the rest. At 6p.m. we arrive at Lillers where we detrain. Officers have tea at the Hotel de Commerce, the men at the Y.M.C.A. and we then set out on our march for Estrée Blanche, a distance of 10 miles. We arrive at about 11p.m. and by midnight the men are settled down in the spacious "Sucrerie", the officers sleeping at the school, this due to the fact that the inhabitants, giving us up, had locked their doors and gone to bed.	
	29th		Coys at disposal of Coy Commanders. B & D Coys are moved from the "Sucrerie" into more suitable & congenial billets. All officers have very comfortable billets by night and the school is not required any longer.	
	30th		Owing to the fact that there is very little uncultivated land in the district we find some difficulty in obtaining a suitable training ground. Eventually we decide on the ground of the New Aerodrome immediately N.W. of the village.	

Army Form C. 2118.

WAR DIARY
or
INTELLIGENCE SUMMARY.
(Erase heading not required.)

4/Lincoln Rgt

Instructions regarding War Diaries and Intelligence Summaries are contained in F. S. Regs., Part II. and the Staff Manual respectively. Title pages will be prepared in manuscript.

Place	Date	Hour	Summary of Events and Information	Remarks and references to Appendices
ESTREE BLANCHE	30TH		The day is spent in close order drill — from 11.15 A.M. — 12.30 P.M. Battalion Drill under C.O.	
	31ST		All officers of the 138TH BDE are met by the 2ND CORPS COMMANDER. Every officer present was encouraged by the note of calm confidence which his address conveyed. The afternoon is observed as a half holiday	

Copy No.

Operation Order No 97 by Lieut.Col. G. A. Yool, Commanding
1/4th Battalion Lincolnshire Regiment.
———————————— In the Field 10.4.17.

1. **Information.**   Vide General & Special Ideas.

2. **Intention.**   The 4th Bn. Lincolnshire Regiment will attack on a front of 400 yards with A & B Coys in front line and C & D Coys in support.
   Right of Battalion will direct and will be on CUHEM - BOMY Road.

3. **Order of Battle.**   Right to Left.

        4th Lincolnshire Regiment.
        5th Lincolnshire Regiment.
        5th Leicestershire Regiment.
        4th Leicestershire Regiment (less 1 Coy) & Machine Gun Coy (less 1 section) in Reserve.

   1 Company 4th Leicestershire Regt. & 1 Section M.G. Coy is ready to move for Eastern edge of BOMY.

4. **Assembly.**   Position of assembly, a North & South Line through the last 'E' in LAQUETTE R. to the Eastern Entrance to BOMY.

5. **Route.**   To place of assembly ENQUIN LES MINES - Road Junction 'J' in JULIEN.

6. **March.**   Battalion will march in following order:-
   Hd.Qrs., A. B. C. D. Coys.
Head of the column to pass starting point at 9.0a.m.
Coys will parade as strong as possible.

7. **Starting Point.**   400 yards E. of Railway Crossing on ESTREE BLANCHE - ENQUIN LES MINES Road.

8. **Parade States.**   Usual parade states to be at Orderly Room by 8.30a.m.

9. **Lewis Guns.**   Lewis guns and ammunition will be carried on limbers which will march in rear of Companies. Lewis guns will be man handled from assembly place.

10. **Cookers.**   Will rendezvous at CUHEM at 12.30p.m. under Brigade Transport Officer who will issue the necessary orders direct to Sergeant Master Cook.

11. **Enemy.**   Is represented by T.M.Battery to be in position on trench line 800 yards N.W. of 'C' in CUHEM by 11.0a.m.

                                                          Capt & a/Adjt.,
            1/4th Bn. Lincolnshire Regiment.

Copy No 1 Office Copy
      2 Hd.Qr.Mess
      3 A Coy
      4 B Coy
      5 C Coy
      6 D Coy
      7 Transport Officer
      8 Quartermaster
      9 R.S.M.

No 99.

Operation Order by Lieut.Col.G. A. Yool, Commanding 1/4th
Battalion Lincolnshire Regiment.
In the Field 15.4.17.

Ref.Map HAZEBROUCK 5A.

1. Move.   Battalion will move into billets at VENDIN les BETHUNE.

2. March.   Battalion will march in column of route in the following
order: Hd.Qrs., C. D. A. B(less 1 platoon)Coys. Echelon
A & B Transport.
Head of the column will be at the starting point at 8.50a.m.
when the customary hourly halt will be observed.
ROUTE: LILLERS: CHOCQUES: VENDIN.
Sgt Pioneer & 3 men will report to Q.M.Stores at
6.30 a.m to act as loading party.
Remaining Pioneers, Hd.Qr.Signallers & Runners will parade
outside Bn.Hd.Qrs at 8.25a.m. under 2/Lt. T.W.HARRISON.
Coys will not include them on parade states. All other
details will be included. Parade states to be handed to
R.S.M. at Starting Point. Transport Officer will render
parade state to Coys by 7.30 a.m.

3. Starting Point.   Cross Roads near Orderly Room.

4. Lewis Guns.   Lewis Gun Handcarts are allotted as follows:-
A Coy   --   3 carts
B.C.& D Coys   1 cart each.
A Coy will carry all three guns on handcarts.
1 Lewis Gun Limber will be at B.C. & D. Coys billets
to load all Coys guns at following times:-
B Coy   ---   7.45 a.m.
C & D Coys   8. 0 a.m.

5. Billeting Party.   2/Lt W.CHEER & 2 NCOs per Coy and Cpl BILTON
for Hd.Qrs will parade at Orderly Room at 7.45 a.m. with
bicycles. 2/Lt CHEER will report to Town Major VENDIN les
BETHUNE at 9.0a.m.

6. Transport.   Echelon A & B Transport will march with Battalion.

7. Baggage Guard.   B Coy will detail 1 strong platoon to act as
baggage guard and march in rear of Echelon B.

8. Blankets.   1 G.S.Wagon each will collect B & C Coys blankets
and Officers valises. Blankets to be ready at Coy Hd.Qrs.
by 7.0a.m.
Coy Commanders will be responsible that the blankets
are carefully packed when the wagons will return to Q.M.
Stores.
A & D Coys blankets will be delivered to Q.M.Stores by
7.30 a.m.

9. Stores.   Will be at Q.M.Stores as under:-
Other Officers Valises   7.30 a.m.
Tailors   )
Shoemakers   ) Gear   8.0 a.m.
Armourers   )
O.Room   )

10. Mess Gear.   Mess Cart will call for B Coys mess gear at 7.0 a.m.
A. D.C.Coys & Hd.Qrs will have their mess gear ready
ready outside Messes at 7.45 a.m. when the mess cart
will call for them.

11. Canteen.   Canteen Cpl will report to Transport Officer for
instructions for loading up canteen stores.

12. Reports.   Usual march reports to be rendered to O.Room on
arrival at destination.

P.T.O.

2.

13. Orderly Room.   Will close at LE CORNET BOURDOIS at 8.50 a.m.
                    and open at destination on arrival.

                              A.H. Holmes, Capt & a/Adjt.,
                              1/4th Bn. Lincolnshire Regiment.

Copy No 1 Office Copy
        2 Hd.Qr Mess
        3 A Coy
        4 B Coy
        5 C Coy
        6 D Coy
        7 Transport Officer
        8 Quartermaster
        9 R.S.M.

No 100
Operation Order by Lieut.Col. G. A. Yool, Commanding 1/4th
Battalion Lincolnshire Regiment.
In the Field 19.4.17.

Ref.Map.HAZEBROUCK, 36 C,1/40,000, LENS 11.

1. Move.   The Battalion will relieve 5th Lincolnshire Regiment
             in reserve positions about FOSSE 16 & FOSSE 11.
             No movements East of MAROC to take place till dark.

2. March.   Battalion will march in column of route in the following
             order:- Hd.Qrs. D. A. B. C. Coys, Transport.
             Head of column will be at starting point at 12.50 p.m.
             when the customary hourly halt will be observed.
             Hd.Qr.Details will report to 2/Lt HARRISON outside
             Orderly Room at 12.40p.m.
             DRESS: Light Fighting Order with Greatcoat.
             ROUTE: BETHUNE: NOEUX les MINES: Cross Roads 1100
                      yards N.W. of 'B' in BULLAY GRENAY: MAROC:
                      500 yards N.W.-of FOSSE dite de LOOS
             Movements East of NEUX les MINES will be by parties not
             larger than Coys and forward of the AIX NOULETTE, BULLY
             GRENAY, MAROC Road will be by parties not larger than
             Platoons

3. Starting Point. Cross Roads 500 yards S.E. of VENDIN Church.

4. Lewis Guns.   Will be loaded up on Coy Limbers as demonstrated
                 yesterday, by 10.30 a.m. Limbers will march behind Coys.

5. Advance Party. 1 NCO & 10 men per Coy under 2/Lt J.R.NEAVE,M.C.
                 will proceed at 10.0 a.m. to reserve billets for the Bn.

6. Transport.   S.A.A., Tools, and Grenade Limbers will proceed to
                 Transport Lines in LES BREBIS in advance and unload.
                 These limbers will then load up with rations.

7. Blankets.   Will be delivered to Q.M.Stores by 10 a.m. 1
                 Blanket per man will be left at the store and 1 taken to
                 the new area.

8. Packs.   Clearly marked to be delivered to Q.M.Stores as under:-
                 A Coy   10.15 a.m.   B Coy   10.30 a.m.
                 C Coy   10.45 a.m.   D Coy   11. 0 a.m.

9. Stores.   Officers Valises to be at Q.M.Stores by   10.30 a.m.
                 Tailors   )
                 Shoemakers   ) Gear   10.30 a.m.
                 Armourers   )
                 Orderly Room Gear   12 noon.

10. Mess Cart.   Will call for mess gear at 11.15 a.m.

11. Canteen.   Will proceed to Transport Lines.

12. Bicycles.   All serviceable bicycles will be taken up by Hd.Qr.&
                 Coy Runners.

13. Teas.   1 Hours halt for teas at 5 p.m.

                                                  ,Capt & a/Adjt.,
                                         1/4th Bn. Lincolnshire Regiment.

Army Form C. 2118.

WAR DIARY
or
INTELLIGENCE SUMMARY.
(Erase heading not required.)

1/4 Lincoln Rgt

St 29

24.E

Instructions regarding War Diaries and Intelligence Summaries are contained in F. S. Regs., Part II. and the Staff Manual respectively. Title pages will be prepared in manuscript.

Place	Date	Hour	Summary of Events and Information	Remarks and references to Appendices
ESTRÉE BLANCHE	1ST APRIL		We held church service in the Suérne. The building makes a spacious improved cathedral and there is plenty of room even when the 4th Lincs Regt, R.E's, M.G's & T.M.B's have marched in. We were wearing the Box Respirator & Smoke Helmet, which before had always been carried on the person athlete on parade.	
	2ND		Platoon training under Platoon Commanders.	
	3RD		Platoon & Company Drill	
	4TH		Reorganisation of Sectors. Parades are as strong as possible & at 11.15 A.M. the Companies are ready for inspection by the C.O. The Second in Command & one officer per company carry out tactical exercises under the Brigadier. The Brigadier has kindly offered to present a Cup, to be called the Lebrun Cup, for an inter-company football cup-tie. Battalion & will play inter company matches trainine at Reg List train	

Army Form C. 2118.

WAR DIARY
or
INTELLIGENCE SUMMARY.
(Erase heading not required.)

Instructions regarding War Diaries and Intelligence Summaries are contained in F. S. Regs., Part II. and the Staff Manual respectively. Title pages will be prepared in manuscript.

Place	Date	Hour	Summary of Events and Information	Remarks and references to Appendices
ESTREE BLANCHE	5TH		We pass the starting point at 10 A.M. to take part in a Bde Route March. We join the Bde beyond CUHEM and thence we pass through LAIRES, BONCOURT, FLECHIN, & return to ESTREE BLANCHE, having covered a distance of roughly eleven miles.	
		6TH	The Battn marches to the Training Area allotted to 138TH BDE and carries out tactical exercises. The large wood proves too wet for some Platoon Commanders & readjustment is needed before exit is made on the farther side. D Coy prove the victors in a well contested match with A Coy & have to meet C Coy who have already vanquished B Coy.	
	7TH		The Battalion practises the TRENCH ATTACK on B training Area, then remaining in ESTREE BLANCHE march to the mine at FLECHINELLE where are excellent shower baths.	

Army Form C. 2118.

WAR DIARY
or
INTELLIGENCE SUMMARY.
(Erase heading not required.)

Instructions regarding War Diaries and Intelligence Summaries are contained in F. S. Regs., Part II. and the Staff Manual respectively. Title pages will be prepared in manuscript.

Place	Date	Hour	Summary of Events and Information	Remarks and references to Appendices
ESTRÉE BLANCHE	8TH		Church Parade in SUCRERIE. Easter Sunday is favoured with a warm bright sun. The first Spring Day of the year.	
	9TH		A Divisional Route March. The Battalion joins the 138th Bde at FLECHIN and the Division at the cross roads 1 mile S.E. of FEBVIN PALFART. The march is then by WESTREHEM, AUCHY, RELY & ESTRÉE BLANCHE. At RELY the whole Division marches past the Corps Commander, who expresses his pleasure at the marching and general appearance of the men.	
	10TH		The Battalion spends the day on the training ground. Open Warfare, under rules laid down in S.S. 144, is practised.	
	11TH		The 4th LINCOLNS take part in a Bde attack across open country. The breaking up into artillery formation by platoons & diamond formation by sections is very successful as is also the extension formation of waves. In the later stages of the attack however, the leadership by platoon section commanders is severely criticised. The G.O.C. attends & addresses the officers after the practice.	

A5834 Wt.W4973/M687 750,000 8/16 D.D.& L.Ltd. Forms/C.2118/13.

Army Form C. 2118.

WAR DIARY
or
INTELLIGENCE SUMMARY.
(Erase heading not required.)

Place	Date	Hour	Summary of Events and Information	Remarks and references to Appendices
ESTRÉE BLANCHE	12TH		Coys under Coy Commanders. Specialists at their subjects. 2/Lt H.R.GREENWOOD arrives from the Base and is posted to A Coy.	
	13TH		The Battalion marches to LE CORNET BOURDOIS, 2 miles N. of LILLERS. ESTRÉE BLANCHE is left at 8 A.M. and we arrive at our new billets at 12.30 P.M. LE CORNET BOURDOIS is remarkable for the quantity & quality of its waters. There are springs at every house & the duration is enthusiastic in its praise.	
	14TH		Parades under Coy Commanders. Coys will be ready to move at short notice.	
	15TH		Church Parade is ordered but owing to the unsettled weather the parade is cancelled. Very little rain is needed to convert the fields into marshes. The Battn. has the Thresh Disinfector for 2 days & makes full use of it.	
VENDIN lez BÉTHUNE	16TH		The Battn. marches to VENDIN (ez BETHUNE) a distance of less than 9 miles. The route is by LILLERS and CHOCQUES. We leave LE CORNET BOURDOIS at 9 A.M. & arrive at VENDIN shortly after midday.	

Army Form C. 2118.

WAR DIARY
or
INTELLIGENCE SUMMARY.
(Erase heading not required.)

Place	Date	Hour	Summary of Events and Information	Remarks and references to Appendices
VENDIN lez BETHUNE	17TH		Platoons under platoon commanders. Special attention paid to small tactical exercises & solutions as laid down in S.S. 143	
	18TH		Regs under Coy commanders. Bad weather prevents carrying out of tactical schemes on training ground S.W. of CHOCQUES.	
	19TH		Starting at 1 P.M. the battalion marched from VENDIN to CITÉ ST PIERRE via the IRON GATES ROUTE. Rivers passed at 4.30 P.M. and the battalion reached its destination soon after 8 o'clock. The total distance was about 14 miles.	
CITÉ ST PIERRE	20TH		A fairly quiet day. Ignorant of the country and of the exact enemy positions we explored ourselves needlessly.	
	21ST		The enemy bombarded the place intensely from 2 P.M. until 8 P.M. 6 or 200 - 8.5" shells fell on the railway just to S. of billets. It was evident that the enemy were searching for a 4.5 inch battery immediately W. of our billeting area. We had no success.	

Army Form C. 2118.

WAR DIARY
or
INTELLIGENCE SUMMARY.
(Erase heading not required.)

Instructions regarding War Diaries and Intelligence Summaries are contained in F. S. Regs., Part II. and the Staff Manual respectively. Title pages will be prepared in manuscript.

Place	Date April	Hour	Summary of Events and Information	Remarks and references to Appendices
CITÉ ST. PIERRE	22ND		On the 22nd we supply carrying parties to the 4TH LEICESTERS who are the left battalion on the BRIGADE FRONT. They are successful in capturing COOPER TR. with 10 prisoners.	
		23:00	We believe the 5TH LINCS REGT in right battalion sector. The method of holding the line is entirely new to us & most interesting. Trenches serve only as a means of approach and advanced posts are concealed in houses which occupy commanding positions. There is little protection in the way of wire & obstacles, this necessitates a super alertness. The men are helped much by knowing that they are top dog & are ready to track encounters.	
	24TH		It is evident that the enemy It is very nervous. We see the entrances in this sight of a magnificent display of red, green & white enemy lights followed by an intense defensive barrage which must have stretched two or three miles to the south. 2nd D. 1st 2nd D. 23rd rdms.C.2/15/1311 an N.C.O's patrol of A Coy attacked enemy sentries in a strong post were successful in killing one man	

WAR DIARY
or
INTELLIGENCE SUMMARY.
(Erase heading not required.)

Army Form C. 2118.

Place	Date	Hour	Summary of Events and Information	Remarks and references to Appendices
CITÉ ST PIERRE	25TH		The enemy continues his plan of intermittent shelling with some success. A carrying party under 2/Lt BAKER, in CORKSCREW TR were unlucky with a shell; one man was killed, one wounded & 2/Lt BAKER was badly bruised.	
	26TH		We side step to the right and take over the front hitherto held by one battalion of the STAFFORDS and for the last two days by the 5TH LINCS REGT. C & D Coys take their place in the line, A & B Coys are in support. A telegram of congratulation from the B.O.C. on the good work of A Coy's patrol of the night of 24/25th. We do not have our advanced posts in any definite system of trenches and too many visitors during the daytime only invite disaster. We see hardly any movement in the enemy line and it is our intention that he shall see little of us. With a view to further operations from battalion scouts reconnoitre	
	27TH		by night a number of houses beyond our advanced posts.	

Army Form C. 2118.

WAR DIARY
of
INTELLIGENCE SUMMARY.
(Erase heading not required.)

Instructions regarding War Diaries and Intelligence Summaries are contained in F. S. Regs., Part II. and the Staff Manual respectively. Title pages will be prepared in manuscript.

Place	Date April	Hour	Summary of Events and Information	Remarks and references to Appendices
CITÉ ST PIERRE	27TH (Cont)		They return with the information that 3 or 4 of the enemy are patrolling Mine Houses; this confirms information already gained by 2/Lt. P.S. HALLIDAY.	
	28TH		The early morning of the 28th is marked by an intense enemy bombardment which develops into nothing more serious. At night 2/Lt P.S. HALLIDAY takes out a fighting patrol, the object being to capture the enemy patrollers seen the previous night, but with no success. The patrol then proceeds to examine a supposed strong point but finds no one there, within signs of occupation. In returning they are fired on by enemy M.G. but have no casualties.	
LIÉVIN	29TH		We are relieved by the 5TH LINES REGT and move into billets at LIÉVIN. There is ample cellar accommodation and facilities for bathing of which we make full use.	

WAR DIARY
or
INTELLIGENCE SUMMARY.

Army Form C. 2118.

Place	Date	Hour	Summary of Events and Information	Remarks and references to Appendices
LIÉVIN	April 30th		The day is spent in cleaning up & interior economy. The men have been 10 days without packs and are much in need of a rest. Since leaving VENDIN-LEZ-BETHUNE we have had particularly fine warm weather - a sudden change from the unpleasantly cold & wet weather up to April 20th. 2/Lt R.J. HALLIDAY received a telegram of congratulation from the G.O.C. on his patrol of the night of the 28th inst.	

Lt Col
Commanding
1/4

No 96.   Copy No. 1

Operation Order by Lieut.Col. G. A. Yool, Commanding 1/4th Bn.
              Lincolnshire Regiment.
              ------------------   In the Field 8.4.17.

Ref.Map HAZEBROUCK 5A.

1. March.   The 46th Division will carry out a march exercise
                   tomorrow.
                   Bn. will pass starting point at 8 a.m. in the following
                   order:-
                        Headquarters, C.D.A.B.Coys. D Coy will join
                   the column as it passes their parade ground.

2. Starting Point.   Opposite D Coy Hd.Qr Mess.

3. Strength.   Coys will parade as strong as possible.
                   The following will be on parade:-
                        C.Q.M.Sgts, Pioneers, All Signallers & Hd.Qr Runners
                   (less Pte A Munns, A Coy, & Pte A.Noble, B Coy), all
                   servants less 1 mess cook per Coy and 1 for Hd.Qrs;
                   Hd.Qr Guard to be supplied by D Coy; Sanitary men less
                   2 per Coy.

4. Parade States. Accurate states to be handed in to Orderly Room
                   by 7.30a.m., on forms attached.

5. Lewis Guns.   3 Guns and their ammunition per Coy to be carried
                   by Transport, and will be delivered to Transport by
                   6.45a.m.
                        1 Gun and ammunition of B. C. & D.Coys will be
                   carried on Handcarts which will march in rear of the
                   Battalion.
                        Coys will each detail 6 Lewis Gunners to man these
                   carts.
                        Sgt. DOE will be in charge.

6. Transport.   Echelon 'A' will march behind Battalion and Echelon 'B'
                   will be Brigaded under arrangements made by Brigade
                   Transport Officer.

7. Pack Animals: will march behind Battalion.

8. Haversack Rations.   A bread and cheese ration will be carried.

9. Leather Jerkins.   Will not be carried.

10. Baggage Guard.   Will be detailed by Transport Officer.

                                    [signature]
                                    ....Holmes, Capt & a/Adjt.,
                                    1/4th Bn. Lincolnshire Regiment.

Copy No 1 Office Copy
       2 Hd.Qr Mess
       3 A Coy
       4 B Coy
       5 C Coy
       6 D Coy
       7 Transport Officer
       8 Quartermaster
       9 R.S.M.

Army Form C. 2118.

1/4 Lincoln Rgt
9 of 30

25.E

WAR DIARY or INTELLIGENCE SUMMARY.

(Erase heading not required.)

Place	Date May	Hour	Summary of Events and Information	Remarks and references to Appendices
LOOS (HARTS CRATER)	1st		We receive orders to relieve 91st Bde in the line. Our left is the OLD GERMAN FRONT LINE and our right is near FOSSE 11 de LENS. The relief is completed by night without incident.	
	2nd		In the early morning of the 2nd a bombing post of A Coy in NETLEY TRENCH raided by enemy STURMTRUPPE. We suffer somewhat heavily and casualty list being 1 killed, 4 missing, 11 wounded. The wounded men were bombed whilst resting in the dug-out, the post having been captured, the four men on duty in the line were all hit by the first salvo; one 2nd Lieut J Rushby was killed by a sniper while leaving his advanced post in Neri trench.	
	3rd.		At about the same time as on the previous morning D Coy bombing post in NERO TRENCH is raided by the enemy. They numbered about 20 strong and after fierce fighting the post was forced to fall back against odds. Three men were taken prisoners by the enemy, one was killed & four wounded. Casualties were inflicted on the enemy but the exact number is not known.	

Army Form C. 2118.

WAR DIARY
or
INTELLIGENCE SUMMARY.
(Erase heading not required.)

Place	Date	Hour	Summary of Events and Information	Remarks and references to Appendices
LOOS. (HARRISON'S CRATER)	3RD		On the night of the 3RD we are relieved by the 5TH LINCOLNS. and proceed to support dug-outs with HARRISON'S CRATER as headquarters. The burial takes place in LOOS CEMETERY of 2/Lt J ROONEY who had been shot by a German sniper soon after our relief of the 41ST BDE. He was a fine type of the South African sportsman and one of our most enthusiastic officers. The padre, CAPT LOWNDES, officiated ~~at the funeral of my friend~~	
	4TH		The battalion remains in support to 5TH LINCS.	
	5TH		BATTN H.Q. moves to "EWASTON CASTLE", a palatial dug-out off UNION ST. The "contractors" were the SHERWOOD FORESTERS & every officer notes that it is the best British dug-out we have yet been in. Company H.Q's remain as before	
	6TH		The Bde. is relieved by the 139TH BDE & proceeds to billets in BULLY GRENAY. We reach these billets at 3 A.M on the 7TH inst.	

Army Form C. 2118.

WAR DIARY
or
INTELLIGENCE SUMMARY.
(Erase heading not required.)

Instructions regarding War Diaries and Intelligence Summaries are contained in F. S. Regs., Part II. and the Staff Manual respectively. Title pages will be prepared in manuscript.

Place	Date	Hour	Summary of Events and Information	Remarks and references to Appendices
BULLY GRENAY	7TH 8TH		These days are observed as rest days, by order of G.O.C.	
	9TH		Tactical Operations by Coys. At night the Battn. is engaged in wiring of Divl. Line.	
	10TH		We lose the services of our Medical Officer M.O. Capt M.H. PATERSON M.C. who returns today to the Canadians. Capt E.E. HERGA takes his place. 2nd Lieut J.R. NEAVE M.C. leaves us to take up the more responsible duties of Brigade Intelligence Officer	
	11TH		A composite Coy from the Battn. proceeds to SAINS-EN-GOHELLE where an exhibition of trench stores takes place	
LIEVIN	12TH		We relieve the 5th Bn. NORTH STAFFORDSHIRE REGT. in an outpost line in W. of LENS extending from the Railway N. of CITE ST THEODORE down to the Main LIEVIN LENS Road: our front line running from the junction of COWDEN trench with the railway on N. Westerly direction then along CRIMSON TRENCH including CROOK Redoubt and CRAZY trench on our extreme right flank; our reserve and support Coys are located in LIEVIN	

Army Form C. 2118.

WAR DIARY
or
INTELLIGENCE SUMMARY.
(Erase heading not required.)

Instructions regarding War Diaries and Intelligence Summaries are contained in F. S. Regs., Part II. and the Staff Manual respectively. Title pages will be prepared in manuscript.

Place	Date	Hour	Summary of Events and Information	Remarks and references to Appendices
LIEVIN	13TH		Daylight makes very apparent the havoc wrought by shelling in this town since our departure on May 1st; but previous Bn Headquarters and the adjacent cross roads have suffered severely. Enemy trench Mortars are very active today.	
	14TH		The Brigade Commander Lt. Col. EVILL visits CROCUS trench and CRAZY Redoubt in the early hours of the morning. In the afternoon Bn. H.Q's and immediate neighbourhood were heavily shelled – about 125 shells falling within an hour. We are visited by the Senior Chaplain of the Division Major HALES	
	15TH		The Bn. are relieved without incident by 5TH LINCOLNS and move to support area in centre of town of LIEVIN. Bn H.Qs are on the ANGRES – LIEVIN – LENS Road; 2 Platoons being at Bn. HQs and accommodated in dug-out on S. side of road. B Coy occupying cellars some three hundred yards from H.Qs. C & D Coys South in the neighbourhood of the demolished church [illegible] Souchez River – C and D Coys being in cellars between CABIN and CALDRON Trenches.	
	16TH		Breakfast throughout the Battn is somewhat late: men rest	

A5834 Wt.W4973/M687 750,000 8/16 D. D. & L. Ltd. Forms/C.2118/13.

Army Form C. 2118.

WAR DIARY
or
INTELLIGENCE SUMMARY.
(Erase heading not required.)

Instructions regarding War Diaries and Intelligence Summaries are contained in F. S. Regs., Part II. and the Staff Manual respectively. Title pages will be prepared in manuscript.

Place	Date	Hour	Summary of Events and Information	Remarks and references to Appendices
LIEVIN	MAY (16TH)		for the greater part of the day	
	17TH		Several operations are in progress - but down gunners take advantage of the natural butts formed by the high railway embankment for "live ammunition" practice	
	18TH		Our down gunners practice again - Revolver shooting is indulged in by several of the Officers. We return to our former positions on the line relieving the 5th LINCOLNS.	
	19TH		There was very heavy shelling by the enemy on our immediate left - it appears to have been without any attacking object. CRAZY disappointment receiving much attention from enemy trench mortars - happily we have no casualties. 2ND LIEUT. C.F.E. DEAN joins the Batt. and is posted to B Coy.	
	20TH		The weather today is very bright and aerial activity on both sides is great. 2 LIEUT. W.N SCOTT is wounded in the left hand by an shell fragment - he leaves us for F.A.	

Army Form C. 2118.

WAR DIARY
or
INTELLIGENCE SUMMARY.
(Erase heading not required.)

Instructions regarding War Diaries and Intelligence Summaries are contained in F.S. Regs., Part II. and the Staff Manual respectively. Title pages will be prepared in manuscript.

Place	Date	Hour	Summary of Events and Information	Remarks and references to Appendices
LIEVIN	MAY 21ST		After an uneventful day we were relieved by 5TH LINCOLNS and return once more to the support Battn area in LIEVIN - we occupy seven posts in the BRIGADE DEFENCE LINE which run from COWDEN Trench - along the E side of CITÉ ST AMÉ - through the E outskirts of LIEVIN - through CITÉ DES BUREAUX to a post on the SOUCHEZ River N.E. of CITÉ DE ABATTOIR	
	22ND		We supply various fatigues for Trench Mortar company - wire carrying and watering parties. The enemy this evening did a great deal of counter battery work	
	23RD		A party of 2 Officers and 10 O.Rs proceeded to SAINS EN GOHELLE to hear a lecture on "Aerial and Ground Patrolling" by Capt. COZENS-HARDY of the NORFOLK Regt.	
	24TH		The Enemy shell our front area today - various buildings in vicinity of Bn H.Qs. are damaged - so also are houses near B Coy H.Qs. We find a large working party for purpose of making a trench in CITÉ DE RIANMONT. This trench may have particular interest for the Battn in forward attack	

A5834 Wt.W4973/M687 750,000 8/16 D.D. & L. Ltd Forms/C.2118/13.

Army Form C. 2118.

WAR DIARY
or
INTELLIGENCE SUMMARY.
(Erase heading not required.)

Instructions regarding War Diaries and Intelligence Summaries are contained in F. S. Regs., Part II. and the Staff Manual respectively. Title pages will be prepared in manuscript.

Place	Date MAY	Hour.	Summary of Events and Information	Remarks and references to Appendices
LIEVIN	25TH		The enemy today shell the vicinity of the Railway Bridge over the CITÉ DE LA PLAINE — LIEVIN — LIEVIN-LENS road. We are relieved by 7th SHERWOOD FORESTERS — 139TH BRIGADE taking over this area. We moved to BULLY GRENAY in our former billets there	
BULLY GRENAY	26TH		This - the first day of "48 Hours Rest" is devoted in technical inspection and paying of the men; in the evening we are placed at the disposal of the 137TH BDE.	
	27TH		Divine service in the afternoon interrupted this morning by the advent of enemy aircraft — after an interval of fifteen minutes. Afterwards we resumed Medical Officers duty with us as LIEUT. S. DOWLING reported to Brigade today CAPT. E.E. HERGA who leaves french to trench attack training in undergone under Coy Commandants — after tea the Baum move to BOUVIGNY-BOYEFFLES — a pleasant	
BOUVIGNY	28TH		village in woody country. The CHATEAU finds accommodation for Bn H.Q. Staff and for three of Two Companies in addition. We experience excellent WHIT-MONDAY weather.	

Army Form C. 2118.

WAR DIARY
or
INTELLIGENCE SUMMARY.
(Erase heading not required.)

Place	Date MAY	Hour	Summary of Events and Information	Remarks and references to Appendices
BOUVIGNY	29TH		This morning Coy indulge in intense "Trench to Trench attack" training over a marked course at MARQUEFFLES FARM. The afternoon is devoted to Bathing. 2 LIEUT W.F. MASKELL joins us and is posted to "D" Coy.	
	30		Battalion training at MARQUEFFLES FARM.	
	31		Training at MARQUEFFLES FARM continues — an al fresco concert is enjoyed in the training ground; the Brigade Band enhancing the pleasure we experience in lunching amidst lovely surroundings.	

Operation Order No 107 by Lieut.Col. G. A. Yool. Commanding
1/4th Bn. Lincolnshire Regiment.
In the Field 1. 5. 17.
Ref Map LENS 36C S.W.1/10,000.

1. The 138th Inf. Brigade will take over a portion of the 6th Division front tonight from the present left to M.6.b.9.8.

2. The Battalion will relive the 9th NORFOLK & 2nd NOTTS & DERBY Regt tonight on Line Railway N.1.c.50.40(inclusive) to M.6.b.9.8.

3. 4th Leicestershire Regt is taking over the line on our right tonight and touch must be obtained with them by the Right Coy.

4. Order of March. Hd.Qrs., D. A. B. C. Coys in order of platoons 14, 16, 13, 15: 1, 2, 3, 4: 5, 7, 6, 8: 9, 10, 11, 12. Route: LIEVIN Road through M 16.a. M. 10.c & a., M.4.c. to Road Junction M.3.b.5.6. North East along PICCADILY to its junction with LENS-BETHUNE Road thence CROSS ROADS M.5.a.5.9., to rendezvous for guides at point where LENS-BETHUNE Road crosses old German front line.
200 yards intervals will be maintained between platoons Hd.Qr.party to move at 9 p.m.

5. The Line will be held D Coy from Railway Line inclusive along NOVEL ALLEY as far as its junction with NETLEY exclusive.
A Coy NOVEL ALLEY from NETLEY inclusive to NATAL exclusive.
B Coy from NATAL inclusive to point M.6.b.9.8.
C Coy in Support in M.6.d.

6. Packs will be carried.

7. Grenades will be taken over in the line.

8. Cooked Rations will be brought up by Transport to Ration Dump at M.6.a.65.30.

9. Coys will send a guide for ration parties, which will be provided by C Coy, to Bn.Hd.Qrs.

10. Relief Complete will be notified by the word PUNCH and time.

11. Coys will report when their last platoons are leaving LIEVIN.

12. Hd.Qrs. will close at LIEVIN at 9 p.m. and open at M.6.a.7.1. on arrival.

Sd. ...., Capt & a/Adjt.,
1/4th Bn. Lincolnshire Regiment.

Operation Order No 118 by Lieut.Col. G. A. Yool, Commanding
1/4th Battalion Lincolnshire Regiment.
                                    In the Field 23.5.17.

1. **Move.**   Battalion will move to new billets in BOUVIGNY today.

2. **Order of March.** Bn. will pass the Road Junction at R.10.b.80.10
                        as under:-
                        Hd.Qr.Details   4.10 p.m.
                        B Coy   4.20 p.m.
                        C Coy   4.30 p.m.
                        D Coy   4.40 p.m.
                        A Coy   4.50 p.m.
                        All movement by platoons at 200 yards distance.
                        Route: Road Junction R.10.b.88.10 & thence track
                        through R.10.d. & c., R.9.d & c, R.8.d, R.14.b & a,
                        thence Road to BOUVIGNY.

3. **Lewis Guns.**   Coy Lewis Gun limbers will be at Coy Billets at 3.30p.m
                        1 Lewis Gunner per Lewis gun team will accompany each
                        limber.

4. **Blankets.**   All blankets to be at Shoemakers Shop by 3 p.m. The
                        blankets will be taken to the Thresh Disinfector at
                        PETIT SAINS.
                        A Coy will supply a guard of 1 NCO & 3 men to remain
                        with the blankets till the disinfection is completed.
                        Guard to be at Shoemakers Shop by 3 p.m.

5. **Stores.**   Orderly Room, Signallers, Shoemakers & Tailors and
                        Armourers Gear to be at Shoemakers Shop by 3 p.m.

6. **Canteen.**   To be ready to move at 3 p.m.

7. **Medical Stores.** To be ready to move at 4 p.m.

8. **Officers Valises.** To be at Shoemakers Shop at 3.30 p.m.

9. **Mess Gear.**   The Mess Cart will call at Coy Messes in the following
                        order:- C. B. D. A. Hd.qrs. C Coy to be ready at
                        4.0p.m.

10. **Teas.**   The Cookers will move at 2.30 p.m. and will have tea
                        ready for the Battalion on arrival.

11. **Orderly Room**   Will close at 5 p.m. and re-open on arrival at
                        destination.

                                            Capt & a/Adjt.,
                                    1/4th Bn. Lincolnshire Regiment.

Copy No 1 Office Copy
       2 Hd.Qr.Mess
       3 A Coy
       4 B Coy
       5 C Coy
       6 D Coy
       7 T.O.
       8 Q.M.
       9 R.S.M.

Army Form C. 2118.

26.E

1/4 Lincoln Regt
Vol 31

WAR DIARY
or
INTELLIGENCE SUMMARY.
(Erase heading not required.)

Instructions regarding War Diaries and Intelligence Summaries are contained in F. S. Regs., Part II. and the Staff Manual respectively. Title pages will be prepared in manuscript.

Place	Date MAY	Hour	Summary of Events and Information	Remarks and references to Appendices
	28th		On May 28th the 138th Brigade (Lincolns and Leicesters) was withdrawn from the line the 4th Bn. LINCOLNS taking up billets at BOUVIGNY-BOYEFFLES. Here it was that striking news reached them. The Battalion was honoured by the command to take part in an extensive enterprise on a 2000 yds front N.W, W. and S.W. of LENS, the 138th Infy Brigade being further represented by the 5th LEICESTERS. Our Battn was thrilled with the news and one heard repeatedly the remark "Our first real chance since HOHENZOLLERN."	
BOUVIGNY- BOYEFFLES	29th to JUNE 3rd		Training began in earnest. A replica to scale of the ground over which the attack would be launched was planned and laid out at MARQUEFFLES FARM a mile or so S.E. of BOUVIGNY. From "ASSEMBLY TRENCHES" one my ranged forward to penetrate notice boards announcing in bold letters "RAILWAY CUTTING" and "BRIDGE DESTROYED" on past enemy wire entanglements to objective trenches first and second line strongholds of the enemy strangely quiescent and labelled according to their map designation, AHEAD, AGNES, ALEOPE, ARCHIE, ALICE, AMY, ADMIRAL & ANNIE. Such were the communications and trenches guarding HILL 65. These it was the Battn was to storm. Daily to the practice ground went the Battn. joined by D.Coy (Capt WANSLEY) of the 4th LEICESTERS - our "MOPPERS-UP" elect. The Artillery and Machine Gun Barrage to cover our advance and keep the impetuous in check was indicated by flagmen and thus the progress of the attacking waves was directed.	
	4th		One was successful always the ground was covered, forward at zero to the "CUTTING," half right form to face the objective trenches, A Coy then edging away to the left, half D Coy inclining to the right and joining up with C Coy on that flank. "Moppers-up" in position behind the third wave - gradually the movement attained a flock work precision and every man was capable of pursuing his part blessed with arms, spades, picks, bombs, lights and flares the "attack" began. The repeated "look out" of a "Klaxon" from a Contalt plane aloft completed the programme. Flares were lighted to announce	

On progress of our advance.

WAR DIARY
or
INTELLIGENCE SUMMARY.
(Erase heading not required.)

Army Form C. 2118.

Instructions regarding War Diaries and Intelligence Summaries are contained in F. S. Regs., Part II. and the Staff Manual respectively. Title pages will be prepared in manuscript.

Place	Date JUNE	Hour	Summary of Events and Information	Remarks and references to Appendices
	4th		The Higher Commands were satisfied & only remained to form up and receive the confident good wishes of the staff, and with a full day's rest on the morrow all were ready and impatient for the Real Thing.	
	5th		A day of well earned rest.	
	6th		On the morning of June 6th the C.O. announced to the Battn. at a special parade that plans had been altered, and instead of the premeditated operation the attack was to be a series of destructive raids. The same evening the Battn. marched away from BOUVIGNY, and billed in the ruins of CITÉ DES BUREAUX, LIÉVIN.	
CITÉ DES BUREAUX LIÉVIN	7th			
CITÉ DES RAUMONT	8th		The 8th of June arrived – a perfect summer day. The afternoon was spent in moving up to cellars in CITÉ DE RAUMONT adjoining the Assembly Trenches. All Coys reached there without mishap except D Coy, which lost the services of 2/LT E.A. DENNIS (13 Platoon) wounded by one of the enemy's shells that were already finding our starting zone. Time crept on towards ZERO. "Savages" returned the waiting period as they slashed on and around the ruins which sheltered us. Well before 3 p.m. 'C', 'D' and 'B' Coys. were in position in their respective assembly trenches. In some way the enemy seems to have known our timed movements and intentions. The intensity of the barrage to which the assembled troops was subjected was an experience no one on the spot is likely to forget. D Coy paid worst as, while the bombardment of their sector was accounts to a degree, on the flank sector its was sufficiently close to make the assembled platoon.	
			At ZERO – 3 Capt R.D. ELLIS commanding D Coy and Capt WAKELEY, 2nd in Succession mopping-up Coy, were caught by the same shell as they came into position in their trench. Both were killed outright.	
			At 8.30 p.m. the synchronised signal to advance was given. C Coy on the right got away without mishap, two platoons S. of CUTTING and one under 2/LT A.B. HARDY, who was wounded almost immediately bringing covering fire from CUTTING. D Coy in the centre as soon as they jumped off try scored ranks and withdrew intervals to lessen gaps, showed the effects of their baptisme in the Assembly Trenches. B Coy on the left were a joy to behold as they went over on time. The CUTTING was reached.	

WAR DIARY
or
INTELLIGENCE SUMMARY.
(Erase heading not required.)

Army Form C. 2118.

Place	Date	Hour	Summary of Events and Information	Remarks and references to Appendices
			B Coy, by this time reduced by half its number, and C Coy, already caught by the enemy's guns, scaled the further slope of the CUTTING together and advanced to their objective. Capt E.T.S. MAPLES commanding B Coy was at this juncture struck in the forearm by an ugly piece of shell case but continued the advance with his men. Owing to a portion of their line being obliged to the Wst Barrage and the others having withdrawn this sector being put out of action the enemy had time to man his trenches from his dug-outs. C Coy with the platoon of the 5th LEICESTERS on their right was completely held up. When the first wave of "B" & "C" Coys reached the Wst German Trench the barrage was already on it and a temporary check occurred until the reinforcing waves came up. Owing to this check we were unable to keep up with our barrage and the enemy had lined his second trench before our arrival there. Hand to hand fighting ensued and after a further advance of D Coy to the SOUTH and B Coy to the EAST the odds became overwhelming & we fell back first to AHEAD and then to the CUTTING. Meantime Sgt QUINTON, with his platoon got further afield than the rest. It was during this stage of the fight that B Coy lost 9427 R.T. THOMSON and 3/4 H.C. CHASE, both of whom died gloriously, the former as a result of a second wound and the latter from a shell burst. Sgt E. QUINTON B Coy, and his platoon after several attempts to rejoin their comrades, in which they repeatedly bumped up against strong parties of the enemy, finally succeeded in making an opposition post and fighting their way back to our line after having been in the German lines for four hours; a triumph of leadership on the part of Sgt. E. QUINTON. The demolished bridge on the Right Flank was at once manned, and under 2/Lt W.F. MASKELL (D Coy 14 Platoon) kept the enemy at respectful distance, killing work being done by the Lewis Gun. The Front of the CUTTING was lined by the remnant of B & D Coys under Capt. E.T.S. MAPLES, and was held until orders for withdrawal to ASSEMBLY TRENCHES was received. A Coy, having manned our original line of posts. It was not till then that Capt. E.T.S. MAPLES. withdrew from the fight and that his arm was properly dressed, some 3 hours after he was wounded. The greatest assistance had been rendered throughout by the 138th Machine Gun Company under Major A.A. ELLWOOD, a 4th LINCOLN Officer, and particularly by a detachment of two of his guns under Lieut. STENTIFORD manned by 4th LINCOLNS. The attack on the right had gone well. A Coy. 4th LEICESTERS having reached their objective early and sent back 24 prisoners.	

WAR DIARY or INTELLIGENCE SUMMARY.

Army Form C. 2118.

Place	Date	Hour	Summary of Events and Information	Remarks and references to Appendices
CHATEAU (LIÉVIN)	9TH		The day was spent in reorganising coys. To evacuation of wounded continued and by night search parties went out, discovering two more wounded men and a number of dead, who before had been reckoned as missing. On the night of the 9th we were relieved by the 5th Lincolns and moved to billets in AIX NOULETTE. There we rested that night and also the following day.	
AIX NOULETTE	10TH		In the afternoon we were honoured by the visit of the G.O.C. the Battalion paraded in clean fatigue and were addressed by the General. He expressed himself well pleased with the excellent fighting qualities our men showed, and with the number of Boches they killed. On the night of the 10th we moved into support in LIÉVIN	
LIÉVIN Bn. HQ M.22.d.65.15	11TH 12TH 13TH 14TH		These four days were spent in support to left battalion. The battalion was rested and reorganised prior to its occupation of the line. On the night of the 14th we relieved the 4th Leics R in the left subsector	

Army Form C. 2118.

WAR DIARY
or
INTELLIGENCE SUMMARY.
(Erase heading not required.)

Place	Date	Hour	Summary of Events and Information	Remarks and references to Appendices
LIÉVIN. Bn H.Q. M 26 c 20.10	15TH		The Battn holds the sub-sector stretching from the MAIN LINE, N of CITÉ DE RIAUMONT to the MAIN LENS-LIÉVIN RD. A new trench is taped out, running roughly along our outpost line.	
		16h.	There is less enemy shelling than usual and much more attention is paid to counter battery work than to the shelling of our forward positions. The digging of the trench is commenced at night and 1,000 men are engaged. They include South Irish Horse, Cyclists and men of the HK Leics Regt.	
		17h.	Again the day is marked by the quietness of the enemy's artillery on our front. He continues his trench mortar activity however, and at night, work on the new trench is much interrupted. Casualties are caused to the S.I.H. and to the Cyclists.	
		18h.	Bn. H.Q. was made a target for the enemy's artillery. Shooting commenced at 10 A.M. and with only one short rest continued until night. It is calculated that in that time 400 shells	

Army Form C. 2118.

WAR DIARY
or
INTELLIGENCE SUMMARY.
(Erase heading not required.)

Instructions regarding War Diaries and Intelligence Summaries are contained in F. S. Regs., Part II. and the Staff Manual respectively. Title pages will be prepared in manuscript.

Place	Date	Hour	Summary of Events and Information	Remarks and references to Appendices
M22b 20.10 LIÉVIN	18th		feel on the vicinity. We are relieved by the 4th Leics Regt and move to cellars in LIÉVIN with Bn H.Q. at M 22d G5.	
M22d 6515.	19th		(while the 5th Lincs Regt unsuccessfully attack and hold BRICK and BOOT trenches. A total of 28 prisoners is sent back to Div: Cages. The Battn supplies each night a full company to act as covering party to special digging parties on the left subsector.	
	20th		The new trench there is drawn the attention of the enemy and	
	21st		he shells it every night. An evening parties move well forward	
	22nd		and we have only few casualties but the diggers are less fortunate. In consequence the work is much interrupted and little progress made	
			We are relieved on the night of the 22nd/23rd and march to billets at Fosse 10. The 5th S. Staffs R. take our place in support to left battalion.	
FOSSE 10	23rd 24th		These two days are observed as rest days. Church Parade is held in the Church Army Hut at Fosse 10.	

Army Form C. 2118.

WAR DIARY
or
INTELLIGENCE SUMMARY.
(Erase heading not required.)

Instructions regarding War Diaries and Intelligence Summaries are contained in F. S. Regs., Part II. and the Staff Manual respectively. Title pages will be prepared in manuscript.

Place	Date	Hour	Summary of Events and Information	Remarks and references to Appendices
FOSSE 10	25TH		The Brigade has been ordered to carry out an attack on ADJACENT. The 4th and 5th Leic. R. are the assaulting battalions, that the lines R. will be used for carrying, and wiring of strong posts and that 3th lines R. will be in reserve. When the changing and wiring is completed the 4th line R will be in support. Accordingly training is carried out on the ground at MARQUEFFLES FARM. Coys are practised in rapid wiring, and in addition musketry firing of rifle grenades form part of the programme. The G.O. presents nine men (Sgt QUINTON, L/Cpl THORPE, Ptes OAKLAND GOTT, BRACKENBURY and BROOM) with cards from the G.O.C. at the same time informing them that the CORPS COMMANDER has awarded them the Military Medal.	
	26TH		Special training at MARQUEFFLES FARM. The G.O.C. holds a ceremonial parade and presents MILITARY MEDALS to the above mentioned men.	

Army Form C. 2118.

WAR DIARY
or
INTELLIGENCE SUMMARY.
(Erase heading not required.)

Place	Date	Hour	Summary of Events and Information	Remarks and references to Appendices
Fosse 10	27th		The Brigade held a final rehearsal at MARQUEFFLES FARM. The 4th and 5th LEICESTER REGT are the assaulting battalions and we supply one whole company for carrying, the other Coy's, B, C & D, are in position for moving. On the night of 27th/28th we take up battle positions in the line. The Battn is in support in CITÉ DES GARENNES.	
CITÉ DES GARENNES	28th		At 4.10 p.m. the 4th and 5th Battns Leicestershire Regt attack the enemy trenches ADJUNCT and ADJACENT. An hour previous to this our men had got into position. A Coy under the SLAG HEAP, D Coy to their rear and C and D Coy's in the CUTTING. [For full details of operations see attached sheet].	
	29th		We remain in support in CITÉ DES GARENNES, B Coy being in immediate support under the SLAG HEAP.	

Army Form C. 2118.

WAR DIARY
or
INTELLIGENCE SUMMARY.
(Erase heading not required.)

Instructions regarding War Diaries and Intelligence Summaries are contained in F. S. Regs., Part II. and the Staff Manual respectively. Title pages will be prepared in manuscript.

Place	Date	Hour	Summary of Events and Information	Remarks and references to Appendices
CITÉ DES GARENNES.	30TH		The Battalion spends the day in resting previous to relieving the 4th Lines R on the forward position. On the night of the 30th June/1st July we move into battle positions taking the line over from the 4th Lines. We have been ordered to consolidate a line of outposts some 500 yds in advance of our present positions and at 2.47 A.m. the advance is commenced. [For detailed account see attached sheet on Diary for July.]	

E. G. Fielding Johnson Major
Comdg 1/4 th Lincolnshire Regt

REPORT ON OPERATIONS OF 28th JUNE - 2nd JULY.

4th. LINCS. REGT.

For the operations of the night of 28th June the Battalion was placed in Support to the two assaulting Battalions, and in addition, found carrying and wiring parties.

Battalion Hd.Qrs. remained at CITE des GARENNES throughout the operations.

'A' Company, under Capt. E. ELLIOTT, was detailed to carry for the 5th LEICS. REGT. on the Right, and B, C and D Companies jointly supplied five wiring parties of One Officer and Thirty Men each. These were given the wiring of definite strong posts in ADJUNCT, selected to cover the Brigade Front, where at least 50 yards of "quick fence" was needed for each post.

At the last moment, however, D Company as a whole were required to wire under R.E. arrangements and 'B' Company had to find the men for the post vacated by them. Thus the whole of the Battalion was at one time employed in carrying or wiring.

Dispositions before ZERO were as follows:-

A Company in position immediately under the SLAG HEAP and under the orders of O.C. 5th LEICS. REGT.
B Company in a trench running S. from ASSIGN and immediately behind 5th LEICS. HD.QRS.
C and D Companies in CUTTING in M.30.b.

Once operations had commenced A Company moved forward on order of O.C. 5th LEICS. REGT., B and C Companies awaited orders from Brigade Hd.Qrs. and D Company were found guides by the R.E. who took them to their allotted task.

On completion of their work, if considered necessary,
A and B Companies were to return to the SLAG HEAP where they would be in immediate support to the Right Battalion;
C and D Companies were to return to the CUTTING where they would be in a position to support the Left Battalion.

Owing to the complete success of the operations this was not necessary

Consequently A, C, and D Companies returned to CITE des GARENNES leaving B Company in immediate support under the SLAG HEAP.

The O.C. 5th LEICS. REGT. expressed himself particularly well pleased with the despatch of the carrying parties supplied by 'A' Company. Bombs and S.A.A. reached the front line in advance of requirements and the organisation under Capt. E. ELLIOTT won the success and praise which it justly deserved.

The wiring parties acquitted themselves well, devoting themselves strenuously to their task under a heavy shrapnel fire. Their efforts require particular commendation when it is remembered that they had spent four hours in the CUTTING, a target which the enemy shelled consistently as opposed to his otherwise erratic bombardment.

OPERATIONS OF JULY 1st - 2nd.

In the advance by the 46th DIVISION on LENS, on a three Brigade front, the Battalion was placed on the extreme right with its right flank resting on the SOUCHEZ RIVER. On our left was the 5th BN. LINCS. REGT.

The enemy trenches ADJUNCT, ADJACENT and ACORN had been won by the 4th and 5th LEICS. REGT. on the 28th June, and a suitable line immediately in front of ACORN was chosen for assembly. A and C Companies were detailed for the assault with B and D Companies in support.

ZERO hour was 2.47 a.m. and an hour before this all Companies were in position.

The artillery barrage commenced, and on our front, was stationary for seven minutes. In this time the assaulting Companies moved forward and crept close under the barrage, preparatory to following it as it crept onward.

The enemy reply was tardy and erratic, and our men reached their objectives with few casualties and little opposition.

The outposts quickly commenced to dig themselves in and a picquet line was established to their rear. When daylight came our men had firmly established themselves on the captured ground, with intentions to hold it at all costs.

Our scouts did good work in gaining touch with the Canadians on the Southern bank of the SOUCHEZ RIVER, and later, touch was also gained with the 5th LINCS. REGT. on our left. The latter, however, had more difficult country to negotiate and found the houses in CITE de MOULIN strongly garrisoned and fortified with wire and machine guns. Accordingly they did not reach their objectives and our left flank was exposed to enfilade fire from snipers in houses and from machine guns.

In consequence our left had to fall back in line, as by this time it was broad daylight and the position was untenable. The attack would probably have gone better had ZERO been a little later, for on more than one occasion in the house to house fighting, both the 5th LINCS. REGT. and our own men were handicapped in the half light. Parties of the enemy beyond bombing distance were indistinguishable from our own men. Had there been more light there is no doubt that the enemy would have been much more severely punished.

When daylight came our posts were overlooked by the excellent enemy observation posts. He was not long in getting his artillery into action and the whole of the forward slope, containing both outpost and picquet lines, was subjected to an intense bombardment. The fire was accurate and our men found their prepared defences being gradually destroyed. They were reluctantly compelled to withdraw, taking shelter in the numerous shell holes to their rear. At 10 a.m. Capt ELLIOTT crawled forward and established his advanced posts in their original positions.

There they stayed through an enemy bombardment, which lasted, with few and short intervals, for 48 hours. In the course of this time hundreds of tons of explosives ranging from 77 m.m. to 210 m.m. and including light trench mortars, were hurled at our men.

Another operation was ordered for the night of July 1st/2nd to enable the line on our left to be further rectified but this was eventually cancelled at the eleventh hour.

The 5th LEICS. REGT. was ordered to relieve our Battalion on the same night but owing to the delay of a message that operation was cancelled.

There was insufficient time to get back guides for the forward groups which were, in consequence, not relieved that night. The Bde was relieved on the night of 2nd/3rd July by the 25th CANADIAN BATTALION without further fighting.

(Sd) G.A.Yool, Lt.Col.

Copy No.

1/4th BATTALION LINCOLNSHIRE REGIMENT ORDER No 128.

In the Field 27.6.17.

1. **Information.** The 138th Infantry Brigade will attack ADJACENT on June 28th. Canadian Corps and Corps on their Right are attacking further South, and 137th & 139th Brigades of this Division are attacking to the North. The Battalion(less 1 Company) will be in Support.
A Company will be attached to the 5th LEICESTERSHIRE REGT. for carrying.
B Company will be in direct support to the 5th LEICESTERSHIRE REGT. and under the orders of the O.C. this Battalion from ZERO until further orders.

2. **Assembly.** A Company reports to O.C.5th LEICESTERSHIRE REGT. at RED MILL at 10 p.m. 'Y' day and will return to the Battalion at CITE des GARENNES when ordered to do so by O.C. 5th LEICESTERSHIRE REGT. on completion of his carrying duties. Hd.Qrs for this Company will be at M 30 a 52.07.
B Company will move up to trench running South from A Coy Hd.Qrs and come under the orders of O.C. 5th LEICESTERSHIRE REGT. as his Reserve Coy. This Coy will be in position by ZERO minus 1 hour.
C Company will move from billets at CITE des GARENNES at 3 p.m. on 'Z' day and proceed by platoons via ASSIGN: ASIATIC: ASIA: to cellars in row of houses about M 24 c 63.33, and will be available to reinforce assaulting Battalions on demand by their Commanding Officer's, and will move forward to wire when ordered to do so by Bn.Hd.Qrs. Platoons will move at 10 minutes intervals and will take over cellars from,or vacated by, 5th S.STAFFORDSHIRE REGT. On completion of wiring tasks, or when ordered to do so by Hd.Qrs.,this Coy will return to its billets in CITE des GARENNES.
D Company will move from billets at CITE des GARENNES at 3.40 p.m. 'Z' day, and proceed by platoons via ASSIGN: ASIATIC: ASIA: to cellars in row of houses about M 27 c 70.10, and will be available to reinforce assaulting Battalions on demand by their Commanding Officers, and to move forward to wire when ordered to do so by Bn.Hd.Qrs. Platoons will move at 10 minutes intervals and will take over cellars from, or vacated,by,5th S.STAFFORDSHIRE REGT. On completion of wiring tasks, or when ordered to do so by Bn.Hd.Qrs., this Coy will return to its billets in CITE des GARENNES.
Bn. Hd.Qrs. will remain at M 29 d 20.35.

3. **Rations.** A Company will draw rations and water for the 28th from Bn. Dump at M 29. d.10.53 on the way up on the evening of the 27th and for the 29th after returning to the Battalion.
B Company will draw rations and water for the 28th and 29th from Bn.Dump on the evening of the 27th and will carry those of the 29th up the assembly trenches with them on 'Z' day.
C & D Coys will draw rations and water for the 28th at Bn.Dump on the evening of the 27th and for the 29th after returning to their billets at CITE des GARENNES. Coy Commanders will arrange for every man to be in possession of a sandwich(cheese or bacon) at ZERO hour. A Reserve of water will be held at Bn.Hd.Qrs.

(2)

4. <u>Grenades.</u> Grenades No 5 & 23 will be drawn by all 4 Coys in bulk from QUARRY DUMP on the night 27th/28th. These will be issued on production of an indent signed by an Officer.
No 5 Grenades. 2 per man will be carried and 10 per Bomber.
No 23 Grenades. 10 per Rifle Grenadier will be carried.

5. <u>Lewis Guns & Magazines</u> will not be carried by carrying and wiring parties, but will be taken up to assembly position and left in charge of Nos.1 & 2.
32 Magazines per Gun will be carried in packs by 4 men per team.

6. <u>Equipment.</u> Carrying Companies. Light Fighting Order, 50 Rounds S.A.A., 2 No 5 Bombs per man.
For other Companies as laid down in S.S.135 except 120 rounds S.A.A. only will be carried.

7. <u>Dress.</u> All Officers will be dressed the same as their men except that badges of rank will be worn on their shoulder straps.

8. <u>B.A.B.Code Books</u> will not be taken into action.

9. <u>Company Stores</u> not actually required in action will be dumped at Company Hd.Qrs. before moving forward to assembly position.

10. <u>Wiring Parties.</u>

No 1 Party.   N.25 central   supplied by B Coy.
No 2 Party.   N.25 a 70.20   "   " D "
No 3 Party.   N.25 a 55.40   "   " C "
No 4 Party.   N.25 a 50.60   "   " C "
No 5 Party.   N.19 c 45.10   "   " C "

Each party will be composed of 1 Officer & 30 men. In every party 10 men will each carry 1 coil of wire and 15 men will each carry 3 long and 2 short pickets.
50 yards of "quick fence" will be wired in front of each post, and, time permitting, a stay will be added on the near side and entanglements strengthened by cross and loose wires.
Each party will carry a proportion of wire cutters.

11. <u>R.E.Stores.</u> Stores required for wiring parties will be drawn on the night of 27th/28th June from the LIEVIN SQUARE Dump, and will be carried up the assembly trenches on 'Z' day.

12. <u>Aid Post.</u> Will be at CITE des GARENNES at a place to be notified later.

13. <u>Stragglers Posts.</u> Will be found at:

M. 29.c.05.65 (Quarry Dump)
M. 29.c.50.15 (Assign Trench)

Strength:- 1 NCO & 3 men each to be found from Bn.Hd.Qrs.

14. <u>Dumps.</u> S.A.A., Grenades & Fireworks.
Advanced Brigade Dumps. - M.30.a.35.62
M.30.a.09.49

(3)

<u>Dumps contd.</u>(S.A.A.,Grenades & Fireworks).

    Right Bn.   M.30.b.05.10
    Centre Bn.   M.30.a.65.38
    Left Bn.   M.24.c.40.45

  <u>R.E.Stores</u>. Advanced dumps will be placed as follows:-

    Right Bn.   M.30.b.05.05
    Centre Bn.   M.30.a.40.55
    Left Bn.   M.24.c.18.45

15. <u>Communications</u>. Signal Offices will be established at all Battalion Hd.Qrs., and be in communication with Brigade Hd.Qrs. at M.29.a.65.20.
Telephone & Fullerphone communication will be established to all Battalions in a six foot bury.
<u>Runners</u>. Each Battalion will send 4 extra runners to report to Advanced Brigade Hd.Qrs. at 9 a.m. on 'Z' day. Runners will work in pairs and are not to be sent alone.

 The following position calls will be used:-
  Brigade Hd.Qrs   'Z'
  Brigade Visual   'V'
  Left Bn.   'A.C.49'
  Centre Bn.   'A.C.75'
  Right Bn.   'R'
  Support Bn.   'A.C.48'
  Reserve Bn.   'A.C.47'
  M.G.Company.   'M.G'

16. <u>Distinguishing Marks</u>: will be worn as laid down in S.S.135.

17. <u>Prisoners</u>. Prisoners will be taken by escort to RED MILL, LIEVIN, where they will be taken over by the A.P.M. and conducted to the Divisional Cage at FOSSE 10.

18. <u>Synchronisation of Watches</u>. 2/Lt T.W.HARRISON will attend at Advanced Brigade Hd.Qrs at 12 noon and 4 p.m. on 'Z' day with at least two watches. Coys will be notified of the time later.

              J.R.Keave 2/Lt & a/Adjt.,
     1/4th Bn. Lincolnshire Regiment.

Copy No. 1 Office Copy
2 Retained
3 A Coy
4 B "
5 C "
6 D "
7 T.O.
8 Q.M.
9 R.S.Maj.
10 War Diary

Operation Order No 119 by Lieut.Col. G. A. Yool, Commanding 1/4th Battalion Lincolnshire Regiment.

In the Field 6.6.17.

1. **Move.** The Battalion will take over the Battle front from M.30.a.88.62 exclusive to ABSALOM inclusive from 5th Sherwood Foresters on the night 6/7th June.
    'A' Company will take over front line Posts in this Sector as at present held.
    'C' Company will be in close support about CHATEAU and New Dugouts.
    B & D Companies in houses and cellars in Squares M.23.c & M.29.a. South of the LENS-ANGRES Road.
    Guides will meet A Company at Red Mill at 9.30 p.m.
    Guides for remaining 3 Companies will be at Red Mill by 9.45 p.m.
    Order of March will be Hd.Qrs., A, C, B, D Coys in following order of Platoons:-
    1,3,4,2,9,10,11,12,6,8,7,5,13,14,15,16.
    All movement will be by platoons at 200 yards interval.
    Headquarters will pass Church at 7.30 p.m. and first platoon of Coys as under:-
    A Coy 7.35 p.m. C Coy 7.40 p.m. B Coy 7.50 p.m.
    D Coy 8.0 p.m.
    Route: AIX NOULETTE, main SOUCHEZ Road to COLONELS HOUSE, ANGRES, RED MILL.
    Dress: Light Fighting Order except for Lewis Gunners who will wear their haversack at their side and empty packs on their backs.
    Officers will be dressed as the men.

2. **Lewis Guns etc.** Ammunition will be taken out of boxes and will be loaded up on to limbers by 6.30 p.m. 1 Lewis gunner per team will accompany limbers.
    Limbers will dump the ammunition in sixteen dumps together with 2 days rations, artillery discs etc. at RED MILL.
    Reserve Lewis Gun ammunition will be taken together with all Hd.Qr.Gear and rations and reserve of water and will be dumped as far as possible up LIEVIN-LENS Road.

3. **Advance Party.** 1 Officer per Coy has proceeded to billeting area.

4. **Packs.** The packs of men who are going up the line will be stacked at the CHATEAU in 4 Coy Dumps by 2 p.m.

5. **Other Stores.** Officers Valises, Shoemakers & Tailors Gear etc. will be ready at the CHATEAU at 7.45 p.m.

6. **Cookers.** Will return to Transport Lines at 6 p.m.

7. **Medical Room** to be ready to move at 7 p.m.

8. **Mess Gear** for Transport Lines & Trenches to be ready by 8 p.m.

9. **Bn. Hd.Qrs** will close at BOUVIGNY at 8.15 p.m. and proceed to 5th Bn. Sherwood Foresters Hd.Qrs about M.28.b.25.10 to which place relieve complete reports will be sent. Relief complete will be notified by the words SAME AGAIN. On receipt of this message far from all Coys Bn.Hd.Qrs. will move to the CHATEAU about M.23.d.60.55. where it will remain during Operations.

,Capt & a/Adjt.,
1/4th Bn. Lincolnshire Regiment.

Operation Order No.120 by Lieut.Col. G.A.YOOL, Commanding 1/4th
Battalion LINCOLNSHIRE Regiment.
                                                In the Field 10.6.17.

1. Bn. will move into billets in LIEVIN tonight, and will take
   over billets now occupied by 4th LEICESTERSHIRE Regiment

2. Leading Platoons of Companies will pass the Church as under :
                A Coy - 11.15 p.m.
                B "   - 11.25 p.m.
                C "   - 11.35 p.m.
                D "   - 11.45 p.m.
   All movement to be by platoons at 200 yards interval.
      Route : COLONELS ROAD, ANGRES.
      Dress : Light Fighting Order.

3. <u>Advance Party.</u> 2/Lt. SUMMERBELL and 4 O.Ranks per Coy. will
   proceed to take over billets at 6.30 p.m.
      Coys. will occupy the same billets as they did when in
   the area before. Guides will not meet them unless the
   billets are changed.

4. <u>Lewis Guns.</u> Lewis Guns and all ammunition in tin boxes to
   be dumped at church by 9 p.m. One Lewis Gunner per team
   will accompany limber.

5. <u>Rations.</u> will be delivered at Coy. Dumps with Lewis Guns.

6. <u>Water.</u> Water Tins may be drawn from the dump East of
   SHRAPNEL PLATZ used by Bn. yesterday.

8. <u>Stores.</u> All stores, officers valises etc. for trenches and
   transport lines will be dumped in two dumps at the Church
   by 9 p.m. R.S.M. will arrange for a guard on these dumps.
   The Guard will accompany the limbers to LIEVIN.
      Mess Cart will call for Officers Mess Gear at 9 p.m.
      Packs will be collected at Coy. Billets at 7 p.m.

9. Headquarters will close in AIX NOULETTE at 11.30 p.m. and re-
   open at M 22 d 65.20 on arrival.

                                          [signature] Capt & a/Adjt
                                                1/4th Bn. Lincs. Regt.-

Copy No. 1 Office Copy.
         2 Retained.
         3 A Coy.
         4 B "
         5 C "
         6 D "
         7 Transport Officer.
         8 Quartermaster.
         9 R.S.Major.

Operation Order No 12 by Lieut.Col. G. A. Yool, Commanding
1/4th Bn. Lincolnshire Regiment.

In the Field 26.6.17.

1. <u>Move</u>. The Battalion will move into the Line on night of 27th/28th June.
   'A' Company will be under the orders of the O.C. 5th LEICESTER REGT.
   B. C. & D. Coys will move into cellars in CITE-des-GARENNES.

2. <u>Order of March</u>. Order of march will be as follows:-

Hd. Qrs.	9.35 p.m.
A Coy	9.40 p.m.
B Coy	9.50 p.m.
C Coy	10. 0 p.m.
D Coy	10.10 p.m.

   March will be by platoons at 200 yards interval, and will not reach QUARRY DUMP before 11.30 p.m.

3. <u>Billeting Party</u>. 1 NCO & 1 Servant for Hd.Qrs and 2 Other Ranks per Company (less A Coy), will report to 2/Lt W. CHEER outside Orderly Room immediately after dinner.
   They will proceed to CITE-des-GARENNES to find accomodation for the Battalion, less A Company.
   They will then meet the Battalion at RED MILL and act as guides to billets.

4. <u>Assembly</u>. Assembly in CITE-des-GARENNES will be complete by 4 a.m.
   Coys will report completion of assembly by runner.

5. <u>Stores</u>. Stores will be collected and dumped as per orders already issued.

6. Orderly Room will close at FOSSE 10 at 10 p.m. and re-open at CITE des GARENNES on arrival.

                    2/Lt & a/Adjt.,
1/4th Bn. Lincolnshire Regiment.

Copy No 1 Office Copy
       2 Hd.Qr.Mess
       3 A Coy
       4 B Coy
       5 C Coy
       6 D Coy
       7 Transport Officer
       8 Quartermaster
       9 R.S.M.

Army Form C. 2118.

WAR DIARY
or
INTELLIGENCE SUMMARY.
(Erase heading not required.)

Place	Date	Hour	Summary of Events and Information	Remarks and references to Appendices
CITÉ DES GARENNES	JULY 1ST		On the morning of JULY 1ST at 2.47 A.M. the batt. advanced on a two company front and established a line of outposts immediately W of the LENS-ARRAS RD and between CITÉ DE MOULIN and SOUCHEZ R. [Detailed account will be found at the end of Diary for June]	
	2ND		On the morning of the 2nd we were relieved by the 5th LEICS RGT in the line, and again took up our position in reserve. In these operations two officers, 2/Lt SUMMERBELL and 2/Lt BAKER were both slightly wounded. On the night of the 2nd the battalion was relieved by a company of the 25th CANADIAN BATTN. We marched out to AIX-NOULETTE where 'buses were waiting to take us to HOUVELIN. A few men were left behind due to lack of accommodation and these slept for the night in prepared billets in BULLY GRENAY, proceeding to HOUVELIN on the following day.	27.E

Army Form C. 2118.

WAR DIARY
or
INTELLIGENCE SUMMARY.
(Erase heading not required.)

Place	Date	Hour	Summary of Events and Information	Remarks and references to Appendices
HOUVELIN	3rd		We arrived at HOUVELIN (about 5 miles S. of BRUAY) in the early morning of the 3rd. The peace and quiet was much appreciated after the strenuous fighting at LENS. The day was appropriated for rest a luxury which the men had not been able to fully enjoy for many days.	
	4th		Bathing and Kit Inspection. Rest continued.	
	5th		Training is commenced on a splendid ground 2 Kilos S.W. of HOUVELIN. Special attention is paid to training in skilled subjects.	
	6th		Continuation of training on above lines.	
	7th			
	8th		At a Bde. PARADE SERVICE held on the training ground the G.O.C. attended and complimented all ranks on the excellent fighting qualities they had shown in the recent operations before LENS. The 4th Battn. LINCS. REGT. received special mention for the tenacity they displayed in holding ground won on JULY 1ST.	

Army Form C. 2118.

WAR DIARY
or
INTELLIGENCE SUMMARY.
(Erase heading not required.)

Instructions regarding War Diaries and Intelligence Summaries are contained in F.S. Regs., Part II. and the Staff Manual respectively. Title pages will be prepared in manuscript.

Place	Date	Hour	Summary of Events and Information	Remarks and references to Appendices
HOUVELIN	9th		Continuation of training under Major T.P. Fielding-Johnson.	
	10th		Rocourt Rifle Range is allotted to the Battn. for the firing of the Div. Musketry Course. The range has 20 targets and is in excellent condition.	
	11th			
	12th		Bathing. Arrival of reinforcements to number of 67. O. Rks.	
	13th		The Battn. is paraded for the C.O.'s inspection. Generally, the turn-out is good, the laurels going to A Coy.	
	14th	2.45pm	Inspection by the Brigadier-General, who expresses himself well pleased with the bearing and appearance of the men. Coys are normally organised and not sized or equalised.	
	15th		A Parade Service is held, Rev. Lowndes officiating.	
	16th		The 138th Inf Bde is inspected by the G.O.C. The Bde is drawn up in lines of Battns in close column of companies in line. Companies are normally organised. We are later honoured by the presence of the Army Commander	
	17th		who expresses his pleasure at the success of our recent operations	

A5834 Wt.W4973/M687 750,000 8/16 D.D.&L. Ltd. Forms/C.2118/13.

Army Form C. 2118.

WAR DIARY
or
INTELLIGENCE SUMMARY.
(Erase heading not required.)

Place	Date	Hour	Summary of Events and Information	Remarks and references to Appendices
	17th		and his confidence in us for the future. Arrival of Lt. P.W.J. CANNON from BASE. - posted to B Coy	
	18th		Three hours are allowed us to complete the Div¹ MUSKETRY TEST. We have now only the last practice before and consequently are easily able to finish.	
	19th		These two days are set aside for the Div¹ RIFLE MEETING. Excellent competitions are arranged and the meeting is much appreciated. The Battn wins its share of prizes in individual competitions but our team is not successful in lifting the G.O.C's Cup. Lt. Col. G.A. YOOL returns from leave+resumes command of the battn.	
	20th			
VERQUIN	21st		We march to VERQUIN, a distance of about 11 miles, starting from HOUVELIN at 9 A.M. Very good billets are found for us and we wish our stay could be longer.	
MAZINGARBE	22nd		The march is resumed to MAZINGARBE (5½ miles). It is a relief to know that the march is short for the heat is overpowering. We act as BRIGADE SUPPORT, the 5th LINCS and 5th LEICESTERS relieving the 16th INF BDE in the line.	

Army Form C. 2118.

WAR DIARY
or
INTELLIGENCE SUMMARY.
(Erase heading not required.)

Place	Date	Hour	Summary of Events and Information	Remarks and references to Appendices
MAZINGARBE	23RD		The Battn remain in Bde Support and working parties for the line.	
	24TH			
	25TH		2/Lt C.V. LONGLAND arrived from Base on 25th and reposted to C Coy. C Coy proceeds to the line on the night of the 26th coming under the orders of O.C. Left Battalion as a tactical reserve and also for work. A platoon of D Coy moves up to the right sub-sector for a similar purpose.	
	26TH			
	27TH		2/Lt R.D. UTTING reports from the Base y is posted to "B" Coy.	
TRENCHES	28		MAJOR T.P. FIELDING-JOHNSON RWK Regiment to bring over the command of the 4th LEICESTERSHIRE REGIMENT. The Battalion relieved the 5th LINCOLNSHIRE REGT. on the line during the night - taking over the Right Sub-sector - the Battalion frontage being about 1200 yards - extending from POSEN ALLEY to ESSEX LANE.	

WAR DIARY or INTELLIGENCE SUMMARY

Army Form C. 2118.

1/4 Lincoln Regt.

Place	Date	Hour	Summary of Events and Information	Remarks and references to Appendices
TRENCHES LOOS - HULLUCH SECTOR	August 1st		The enemy fired about 10-15mm trench mortars shots into our front & support trenches 5-7pm. We also retaliated with Priester Bombs along the front lines, supports & trenches. After another fine, quiet, the enemy bombarded with Priester Bombs the minenwerfer enemy depot lifting their firing into the trenches.	
	"2"		About 4pm a very strong bombing post was seen in trenches. 2nd Lt F.J. Peacock & M Corporal Slater were sent there immediately. Unable to see what was happening, until Boyen & 10 Mly found a white patch on the ground, which appeared to be the mouth of a white man. 2nd Lt F.J. Peacock and two of his patrol. Cpl Pte J.A. Slater were tried in (?) enemy party of 44 persons. Cpl Pte J.A. Slater returning one of the enemy out of a big big gun & firing his revolver at him. He could not account for more of the enemy. The machine made by the enemy was Mr No Mans Land, this initial blow.	
	"3"		During the night the Battalion was relieved by the 1/5th S. Stafford Prince Regt. and marched into Divisional Reserve (HQr in Fosse Nouville) lez Bethune via Mazingarbe - y Hoedy - les - Mines. Arrival in billets at 4.30 am. Battalion was probably (?) (?) (?) (?) As the Battalion was being billeted during the day 1.11.16.	28e

WAR DIARY or INTELLIGENCE SUMMARY

Army Form C. 2118.

Place	Date	Hour	Summary of Events and Information	Remarks and references to Appendices
TRENCHES.	July 28-		POSEN ALLEY - The Southern Boundary to about 1500 yds. N. of LOOS; ESSEX LANE - the Northern Boundary to about opposite the Southern edge of HULLUCH village; the enemy trenches are about 200 yds. from our front line, which is held by a team of posts. Kept up the usual minor bombardment throughout. POSEN ALLEY & VENDIN ALLEY - both are sufficient to employ fire from the back area, comprising the time of the year the trenches are in a bad state and wet indeed. the enemy annoying about 15"mls throughout the trench system. The relief was delayed for a short time owing to both P.H.Green & Lachowski Gens. being detached from Covve Maris. it was necessary to bring Captain E. Elliott & 2/Lt. W. Cheer to Field Ambulance for a time as they were affected by the fumes. The CANADIANS are holding the lines on our Right the L. Leicesters on the Left. The Regiment endeavoured to capture the trenches during the night, the enemy carried out numerous attempts with PRIESTER BOMBS	
	29-		Lieut. P.W.J. Cannon attached to Field Ambulance. 2/Lieuts A. Melville & R.G. Harris reported from the Base, notes to D & R. Coys. respectively.	
	30-		9 W.W.O. detailed to & 1/ m. n. O. Felt very ill on two shells hitting the bay.	
	31-		Y PRIESTER BOMBS during the night.	

Army Form C. 2118.

WAR DIARY
or
INTELLIGENCE SUMMARY.
(Erase heading not required.)

Place	Date	Hour	Summary of Events and Information	Remarks and references to Appendices
TRENCHES	Aug 3"		In early rounds up to 4 a.m. 6am, ambulance was on roadway & enemy at MAZINGARBE to enemy arrive into our trench to march; the Battn. marched peacefully till the whole 10 mile something they had been again went without casualties for a halt off 9mm Army arrived to ambulance which	
			Platoons up Hastings; the following Officers reported from the base:—	
			2Lt W. PHYPERS - posted to "A" Bn; 2Lt D.A. JACOB - posted to "B" Bn.	
			2Lt A.P.H. BAIN - posted to "C" Bn; 2Lt J.R. FISH - posted to "D" Bn.	
			Stuart Pullam.	
	5"		MAJOR T.P. FIELDING-JOHNSON rejoined the Regiment.	
	6"		Capt A.M.E. Physical Training Recuit-training = attacks and Machetes	
	6"		on running order and arranged North of POSNAY.	
FOUQUIERES	7"			
	8"			
	9"		2Lt W.B. KEY rejoined from the Base from posted to "D" Bn.	
	10"		Training continued	
	11"			

WAR DIARY or INTELLIGENCE SUMMARY

Army Form C. 2118.

Place	Date	Hour	Summary of Events and Information	Remarks and references to Appendices
FOSQUIERES	July 12. 1917		Brigade Group Church Parade at DROUVIN, after the service Major-General W. THWAITES C.B. presented Military Medals to 200840 Sergt. H. CARTER, 202244 Sergt. E.E. HARRISON & 201493 L/Sergt. J. WARD for gallantry and good service in action on July 1st 1917 during an attack on the 46th Division on western edge of LENS.	
	13		Training continued as per M.R.G. POSNAY. During the evening the Battalion again supplied a company advance (2nd Lt. J.G. QUIRK — travelling guide) to the working party & quartermaster to Officers, N.C.O.s & Men.	
			Coys C, D & H.Q., F. Coy. office and two companies. Training — Bombing during afternoon.	
	14		Training on the Huluch — Bombing during afternoon.	
	15		Training continued on BOIS DES DAMES — West of POSNAY.	
			2/Lt. J.P. MURRAY reported from Reserve of Officers 6/R. Coy. The Battalion adopts the 6. Notts / Derbys in Brigade Reserve in PHILOSOPHE.	
PHILOSOPHE	16		C, B, and D Coys proceeding to the trenches in support Coys to Right and Left Front line Battns respectively.	
	17 R 18 R 19 R 20 R		Battn H.Q. and A & B Coys remain in PHILOSOPHE. Work hurriedly consists of carrying parties for Trench Mortars & Gas Cylinders	

Army Form C. 2118.

WAR DIARY
or
INTELLIGENCE SUMMARY.
(Erase heading not required.)

Instructions regarding War Diaries and Intelligence Summaries are contained in F. S. Regs., Part II. and the Staff Manual respectively. Title pages will be prepared in manuscript.

Place	Date	Hour	Summary of Events and Information	Remarks and references to Appendices
PHILOSOPHE	AUG 21ST			
	22ND		The Battn remains in PHILOSOPHE, all available men being employed in working or carrying parties. Every man in the battalion is bathed and given a clean change of clothes before proceeding to the line.	
	23RD		On the night of the 22/23rd the Battn relieves the 5th Lincs Regt in the line — holding the right sub-sector, St ELIE SECTOR. 2/Lt STEPHENSON A.E. & 2/Lt ELLIS F.R. arrive from Base and are posted to B and D Coys respectively.	
	24TH		Our sub. sector is a novelty to everyone. Such an extensive tunnel system has not been seen before. It is possible to go round most of the battalion sub-sector without using the trenches. C, D & A Coys from the right, centre & left Coys. respectively & B Coy in support.	
	25TH		One of the peculiarities of this sector is the small amount of artillery fire on both sides. In consequence there are proportionately more trench mortars. Our "footballs" and "Stokes" are always busy pounding the enemy trenches. No MAN'S LAND was thoroughly searched but no enemy were seen moving about their wire. A few light enemy patrols were seen moving about their wire, but on approaching they disappeared into their trench.	

A.S.34 W.W4973/M637 750,000 8/16 D. D. & L. Ltd. Forms/C.2118/13.

WAR DIARY
or
INTELLIGENCE SUMMARY.

(Erase heading not required.)

Army Form C. 2118.

Place	Date	Hour	Summary of Events and Information	Remarks and references to Appendices
TRENCHES	26TH		Contrary to his usual custom the enemy discloses his movements in this sector. It is quite a common thing to see his troops in column fours on the roads, & accounts of his movements take a large part in the Intelligence Summary. We send out three patrols during the night but no enemy patrols are encountered.	
	27TH		Owing to the continued activity of enemy trench mortars our artillery carry out a destructive shoot. In consequence their activity falls below normal and for the next two days there is comparative quiet.	
	28TH		On the night of the 28th we are relieved by the 5TH LINCS R. Owing to operations on our right relief is complete by 7 P.M. Headquarters Staff marches out last, passing the batteries as the barrage commences. The dull glow of the setting sun, the flashes of the guns, the silhouettes of the ruins of VERMELLES make a real war picture. The march to FOUQUIERES is without incident except that a halt is made at LABOURSE for tea.	
FOUQUIERES	29TH		A rest day spent in cleaning up & bathing. 2/Lt A.J.C. HARVEY and R.G. EEDES arrive from Base. Posted to C & D Coys respectively	

Army Form C. 2118.

WAR DIARY
or
INTELLIGENCE SUMMARY.
(Erase heading not required.)

Instructions regarding War Diaries and Intelligence Summaries are contained in F. S. Regs., Part II. and the Staff Manual respectively. Title pages will be prepared in manuscript.

Place	Date	Hour	Summary of Events and Information	Remarks and references to Appendices
FOUQUIERES	Aug 30th		Training commenced with Close Order & Setting up Drill.	
	31st		The Battn marches through HESDIGNEUL and practises the Platoon in the "Attack" as per S.S. 143.	

Colonel McClary
of Inverness
9.a. York

Army Form C. 2118.

WAR DIARY
or
INTELLIGENCE SUMMARY.
(Erase heading not required.)

1st Lincoln Regt   Vol 34

29.E

Instructions regarding War Diaries and Intelligence Summaries are contained in F.S. Regs., Part II. and the Staff Manual respectively. Title pages will be prepared in manuscript.

Place	Date	Hour	Summary of Events and Information	Remarks and references to Appendices
FOUQUIERES	Sept 2		The Battalion marched through HESDIGNEUL and passed through 4th Trench's Brigade	
"	2	11am	Church Parade. Chicard visit to Col. BLACKBURNE M.C.	
			The C.O. C.E. 18W inspected the Battalion.	
			The Battalion relieves 8th Lincoln Regiment in the line holding the heights overlooking	
TRENCHES	3		St ELIE SECTOR.	
			2nd Lt. S.L. PEACOCK been over and made contact on faction & missions to reconnoitering	
"	4		ditto from the G.O.C.	
	5		He made the enemy wire were in condition. Reported to Brigade HQ & reported on support line. See 2nd Lt. PHYPHERS's own good work in putting ?? in condition in the B.G.C.	
			CAPT. S. LEE & two company & relief marching party. 2nd Lt. PHYPHERS in command ?? his trench party. Enemy in sight. No enemy sniper seen today. 6 to ??? ??? received in all his trench work over sent to ??? safely. (2nd Lt. LEATHERSTONE having a ??? advised for conspicuous gallantry to this field.)	
	5		Pte Snipers & 2/9 & Pte 2A Lincoln Prizes ??? to ??? no ordering form Trench 78. Pte ??? Green ???	

A5834 Wt W4973/M687 750,000 8/16 D. D. & L. Ltd. Forms/C.2118/13.

Army Form C. 2118.

WAR DIARY
or
INTELLIGENCE SUMMARY.
(Erase heading not required.)

Instructions regarding War Diaries and Intelligence Summaries are contained in F.S. Regs., Part II. and the Staff Manual respectively. Title pages will be prepared in manuscript.

Place	Date	Hour	Summary of Events and Information	Remarks and references to Appendices
TRENCHES	Sep 8/9		Entailed much work & preparation. With reference to this raid O.C. 5th Gwalk Regt sent a message to O.C. "H" Co Lt Col G.A. Yoon expressing appreciation of help given & arrangement made to accompany the Gurkas to Coy Commander.	
"	9		The Battalion is relieved in the Line by 1/5 Gwalk Regt. A Coy is relieved by Jamandar Coy, B Coy left forward support Coy. C & D Coy g. o. to PHILOSOPHE	
PHILOSOPHE	Sept 10/11/12		The time in BDE SUPPORT is spent in improving dublin & providing everything possible to special importance happening. There is very little shelling. Fairlie artillery to appears then lines.	
TRENCHES Squre 18 (ST ELIE RIGHT SUBSECTOR)			On the night of Sept 13th the Battalion relieved 5th Batt Lines Regt in the line. There are no incoming men punches with this section relief unless quite a simple problem. On completed much entire than previously.	
"	17		Returning to stabilisation for 5th Lines Regt, enemy artillery to much more active. Apparent attention is paid to DEVON LANE the main communication trench forward.	

A.5834 Wt. W.4973/M657 750,000 8/16 D. D. & L. Ltd. Forms/C.2118/13.

Army Form C. 2118.

WAR DIARY
or
INTELLIGENCE SUMMARY.
(Erase heading not required.)

Instructions regarding War Diaries and Intelligence Summaries are contained in F.S. Regs., Part II. and the Staff Manual respectively. Title pages will be prepared in manuscript.

Place	Date	Hour	Summary of Events and Information	Remarks and references to Appendices
TRÉNCHÉS (Bus)	Sept 19		Continued shelling by the enemy of DEVON LANE in the morning, fairly of this trench are blown in for a length of 50 yds.	
		18/noon	Nothing of importance to report.	
		21	On last day of the Tour companies proceeded with the other tasks reported, been improved & work in dug-out changes. During this tour a many of our dead close to enemy wire were reported & references to Hostile Offensive patrols have been kept out during the nights. No patrols have been thoroughly searched and no enemy patrols encountered. One the nights 20/21 & 21/22 were the relieved by the 5th Devon Regt. & marched to FOUQUIÈRES.	
FOUQUIÈRES	22nd		Sec 2nd Lt A. G. VIVIAN joins the Battalion. This officer is proceeding to duty.	
	23rd		Sec Lt L. J. PEACOCK leaves the Battalion to join the R.F.C. This officer is very highly sympathic, he is all times very conscious to arrange concerts, games & army amusements for the men, & music in the Bivouacs to keep up all ranks spirits to support & hearten every where	

Army Form C. 2118.

WAR DIARY
or
INTELLIGENCE SUMMARY.
(Erase heading not required.)

Instructions regarding War Diaries and Intelligence Summaries are contained in F. S. Regs., Part II. and the Staff Manual respectively. Title pages will be prepared in manuscript.

Place	Date	Hour	Summary of Events and Information	Remarks and references to Appendices
FOUQUIERES	Sept 23		Wm his energy & evident interest shown also a good & keen soldier. Has deficiencies in fibre heavily dwelt on.	
"	24		2nd Lt H.E. HUBBLE joins the Battalion & is posted to A Coy. 2nd Lt J.W. BRETT joins the Battalion & is posted to A Coy. 2nd Lt R. HANSEY " " " " B Coy.	
"	26		1 Officer & 320 O.R. supplied to carrying party for Gen & hudson. Moving carry carrying them to PHILOSOPHE & doing them back when work is completed.	
"	27		On the night of the 27th we march from FOUQUIÈRES for the line. Relief is greatly facilitated owing to moonlight moon.	
"	29		This tour the work has been carried very quietly. The weather being fairly misty for ow time than there has been recently but no spent chiefly Artillery. On the night 28/29th 2nd Lt R.J. FISH takes no 6 patrol to reconnoitre enemy wire & when actually in the enemy wire this Officer was shot by an enemy sentry. He was a most promising young Officer, & his death is greatly regretted.	

A5834 Wt.W4973/M687 730,000 8/16 B.D.&L. Ltd. Forms/C.2118/13

Army Form C. 2118.

WAR DIARY
or
INTELLIGENCE SUMMARY.
(Erase heading not required.)

Instructions regarding War Diaries and Intelligence Summaries are contained in F. S. Regs., Part II. and the Staff Manual respectively. Title pages will be prepared in manuscript.

Place	Date	Hour	Summary of Events and Information	Remarks and references to Appendices
TRENCHES	Apr. 30.		There is nothing special to report. Both snipers & they are murdered by guardsmen. human beings presents great observation of trench absence. Hence probably inactivity of artillery.	

C.S. Hopkinson
Lt Col. Comdg 1/4.

WAR DIARY
or
INTELLIGENCE SUMMARY.

(Erase heading not required.)

Army Form C. 2118.

Vol 35

30.E

Place	Date	Hour	Summary of Events and Information	Remarks and references to Appendices
TRENCHES	Oct. 1		There is enemy shelling at the usual targets by day with increased fire by machine guns and light trench mortars at night.	
	2			
	3		On the night of the 3rd we are relieved by the 5th Lines Regt and move into Brigade Support with Battn H.Q. at PHILOSOPHE. C & D Coys remain in immediate support.	
PHILOSOPHE	4		Capt L.A. Phillips leaves for Base subsequent transfer to England. He has been selected to act as an instructor to U.S.A. forces. the loss in him one of its veteran officers who was successively platoon commander, adjutant and company commander.	
	5		2/Lt Andrews returns from Base and is posted to D Coy. The Boche engages in counter-battery work on front-line round PHILOSOPHE but happily we suffer no casualties.	
	6		Marked by quietness.	
	7		Lieutenants R.J.C. Crowden and S. Lee are appointed acting captain (additional) vide Scrut that no 154 dated 22.9.17.	
	8		There is nothing of special interest to report.	

Army Form C. 2118.

WAR DIARY
or
INTELLIGENCE SUMMARY.
(Erase heading not required.)

Instructions regarding War Diaries and Intelligence Summaries are contained in F. S. Regs., Part II. and the Staff Manual respectively. Title pages will be prepared in manuscript.

Place	Date	Hour	Summary of Events and Information	Remarks and references to Appendices
PHILOSOPHE	Oct 9th		On the 9th we relieved the 5th Lines Regt in the line. The weather has completely changed since the last tour and we have a fortnight of winter.	
	10th		On the morning of the 10th Lt. T.W. HARRISON proceeded to England for six months. He was badly in need of a rest though every officer in the battalion was sorry to lose him. He was typical of the honest, straightforward & somewhat blunt English countryman and wherever he moved was held in high esteem. He had held the post of signal officer to the battalion for over 12 months.	
	11th		The period is marked by exceptional quiet and dry cold damp weather. There is little enemy artillery fire by day or night. On the nights of the 12th/13th we suspect a relief of the enemy division opposing us and consequently bursts of artillery & machine gun fire are directed on their roads, tracks, and communication trenches.	
	12th			
	13th			
	14th			

A5834 Wt.W4973/M687 750,000 8/16 D.D. & L. Ltd. Forms/C.2118/13.

Army Form C. 2118.

WAR DIARY
or
INTELLIGENCE SUMMARY.
(Erase heading not required.)

Place	Date	Hour	Summary of Events and Information	Remarks and references to Appendices
FOUQUIÈRES	15th		We are relieved by the 5th Leics Regt and move to FOUQUIÈRES arriving there in the small hours of the 16th.	
	16th		A day of rest. In the afternoon A Coy & B Coy play a well contested football match. B Coy win by 2 goals to nil.	
	17th		Lt C.W. JOHNSON arrives from Base and is posted to B Coy. 4th Battn plays its first Divisional League match our opponents being the 2nd North Midland Field Ambulance. We win a one sided match by 2 goals to 1.	
	18th		We commence battalion training and march off at 9am for training ground beyond FOUQUEREUIL. A small class is exercised in the use of the lewis line, which turns in a novel form of carrying loads. After a little practice men are able to carry two boxes of S.A.A. with comparative ease.	
	19th		2/Lt CHEER takes over the duties of acting adjutant from 9.10.17. Lt STEPHENSON takes over command of B Coy from same date.	
	20th		Divisional League match with 5th Leic Regt. Defeated by 3 goals to nil. Major T.P. FIELDING JOHNSON takes over command of 5th Leics Regt during temporary absence on leave of Col. WARING.	

A5834 Wt. W4973/M687 750,000 8/16 D.D.&L. Ltd. Forms/C.2118/13

Army Form C. 2118.

WAR DIARY
or
INTELLIGENCE SUMMARY.
(Erase heading not required.)

Place	Date	Hour	Summary of Events and Information	Remarks and references to Appendices
TRENCHES	21st		We moved to the trenches halting for tea at NOYELLES.	
	22nd		The following officers arrived from Base and were posted to companies stated. 2/Lt F.G. BAKER "D" 2/Lt A.G. FISHER "A" 2/Lt A.G. BLACK "B" 2/Lt R.S. CREASEY. C" 2/Lt ELSTON "C" " E. TOMLINSON "B" " P. SHARPE "A" " G. TAYLOR "D" " A.R. LUNN "A" " F. DAWSON "B"	
	23rd		The three days under review were marked by exceptional quietness, there is little artillery or trench mortar fire by day and practically no machine gun fire at night. Curiously enough there are very few very lights at night. Our patrols go out and return with the report that not one flare has been sent up during their patrol. 2/Lt F.J. LEVI arrived from base on 23rd and is posted to C Coy.	
	24th			
	25th			
	26th		There is an increase in enemy activity and his machine guns fire on the old sap, leading us to believe that a relief has taken place.	
	27th		In the morning a H.V. gun not previously reported fired twenty shots rifled fuse about Battn H.Q. One shell hit in not more than 3yds from the M.O's dug out which has little more than 1 sheet of corrugated iron on top.	

Army Form C. 2118.

WAR DIARY
or
INTELLIGENCE SUMMARY.
(Erase heading not required.)

Instructions regarding War Diaries and Intelligence Summaries are contained in F. S. Regs., Part II. and the Staff Manual respectively. Title pages will be prepared in manuscript.

Place	Date	Hour	Summary of Events and Information	Remarks and references to Appendices
PHILOSOPHE.	28TH		Relief takes place on the night of 27/28 & and we move to PHILOSOPHE. A & C Coy's are in immediate support and B Coy undergoes special training at NOYELLES	
	29TH		We play the Divl Signal Coy at football there 1-2. A most keenly contested game.	
	30TH		B Coy continue their special training in view of a raid which it is intended they shall carry out on the following tour.	
	31st		October has seen the first signs of bad weather, but in spite of this the trenches are in excellent condition. We hope that the enemy permitting, they will continue so through the coming winter.	

C. W. Fishers Lt.
C. O. 7th Lincoln Regt.

1/4th Battalion LINCOLNSHIRE Regiment.

Order No.149.

Copy No.

In the Field 20.10.17.

1. **Relief.** The Bn. will relieve 1/5th Bn. LINCS. REGT in the line on the night 21/22nd October 1917.
   On relief distribution of Coys. will be :-
   A Coy. Right   D Coy Left.
   B Coy. Centre   C Coy. Support.
   Relief to be complete by 3 a.m.

2. **Move.** The Bn. will pass starting point (Bn. Hd. Qrs.) at 1.30 p.m. in the order D B A C H.Q.
   600 yards distance to be maintained between Coys. as far as SAILLY, thence 200 yds. between platoons.
   A halt will be made at NOYELLES for tea.

   Dress : Full marching order (less packs) - Steel Helmets.
   Caps will be worn as far as SAILLY by all ranks.

3. **Lewis Guns.** Lewis Guns and Ammunition will be stacked by all Coys. at Bn.Hd.Qrs. by 10.30 a.m. and inspected by 2/Lt. J.P.MURRAY.
   Lewis Guns will be carried from NOYELLES by Coys.
   Lewis Gun Ammunition will be taken over from 5th Lincs in the Line. 256 magazines will be handed over to 5th Lincs. Regt at PHILOSOPHE, and 256 magazines at Bn.Hd.Qrs in the Line.

4. **Stores.** Blankets will be neatly rolled up in bundles of 10, tied securely, and stacked in Bn.Hd.Qr.Yard by 10 a.m. Pioneer Sgt. will be in charge of Blanket Dump.
   Officers Valises, Coy.Mess Gear and all stores for Q.M. Stores to be dumped in Bn.Hd.Qr.Yard by 1.0 p.m.
   All Trench Gear, including officers' trench mess gear, to be dumped in Bn.Hd.Qr.Yard by 1.0 p.m. Police will take charge.

5. **Packs.** will be stacked by Coys. (Hd.Qrs. separately) just outside Bn.Hd.Qr.Yard by 11 a.m. They will be carried to NOYELLES in limbers.
   One N.C.O. and 2 men per Coy., and 2 scouts for H.Q., will accompany limbers.
   Provost Sgt. will be in charge and will move off at 12.30 p.m.

6. **Rations.** will go up by rail.

7. **Cookers** will move to NOYELLES in advance of Bn.

8. **Relief complete** to be signalled by "NO TOBACCO WANTED".

                                        2/Lt. & a/Adjt.,
                                        1/4th Bn.Lincolnshire Regt.

Copy No. 1 Retained.
         2 Office Copy.
         3 A Coy.
         4 B Coy.
         5 C Coy.
         6 D Coy.
         7 Transport Officer & Quartermaster
         8 5th Lincs.Regt.
         9 War Diary.

1/4th Bn. Lincolnshire Regiment.   Copy No. 1.
                Order No. 150.
                                    In the Field 26.10.17.

1. **Relief.** Battalion will be relieved by 5th Battn. LINCOLNSHIRE REGIMENT on night of 27/28th inst. Relief to be complete by 3 a.m.

2. **Move.** The Battalion (less A and C Companies) will move as follows:-
   H.Q. and D Coy.   PHILOSOPHE.
   B Coy.   NOYELLES.

   Route: via CHAPEL ALLEY to junction with STANSFIELD ROAD, thence by track to corner of SCREEN, CEMETERY and PHILOSOPHE, and NOYELLES respectively.

   C and A Companies will move into RIGHT and LEFT RESERVE respectively.

3. **Advance Parties.** One Officer per Company, and one N.C.O. per platoon of B and D Companies will report at Battn. H.Q. at 2 p.m., and proceed to billet their respective Companies. Corpl. BILTON will billet H.Q.

   One Officer per Company and one N.C.O. per platoon of A and C Companies will be at respective new Company H.Q. at 3 p.m. to take over.

4. **Brigade Guard.** One corporal and 3 men from D Company will proceed with advance party, and will mount at Bde. H.Q. at 5 p.m.

5. **Lewis Guns.** All Lewis Gun ammunition in the line will be handed over to 5th Bn LINCOLNSHIRE REGIMENT.

   A and C Company's advance parties will take over ammunition in RESERVE positions. B and D Coys. at PHILOSOPHE.

   2/Lieut. F DAY with Sergt. P.W. DOE will inspect all Lewis Gun ammunition in the Line tomorrow morning; in the afternoon, in RIGHT and LEFT RESERVE positions, and at PHILOSOPHE.

6. **Cookers.** 12 cookers will be handed over in the Line.
   A and C Coys. will take over 3 each in RESERVE positions.
   6 cookers will be taken over from 5th LINCOLNSHIRE REGT. at PHILOSOPHE by advance parties.

7. **Stores.** All H.Q. Stores. } will be handed over to Provost-Sergeant
   Coy. mess Gear, } at Battalion DUMP by 5.30 p.m.
   (B and D Coys)

   C and A Companies will carry their own to RESERVE positions.

(1).

(2).

8. Traffic.

Company Commanders are responsible for Tunnel Entrances being kept clear of traffic during relief. Companies will not commence to move out until the last platoon of relieving Battalion is clear of their respective sector.

Down traffic in DEVON LANE and CHAPEL ALLEY will be suspended from 5. ▮ p.m., until clear of relieving troops.

9. Handing-over Lists.

will reach Orderly Room by 9 a.m.

10. Relief complete.

will be notified by signalling "153 WANTED".

W Ellen 2/Lt & /Adjt.
1/4th Bn. Lincolnshire Regiment.

Copy No. 1   Retained
    2   A Coy.
    3   B Coy.
    4   C Coy.
    5   D Coy.
    6   T.O. & Q.M.
    7   R.S.M.
    8   War Diary

Copy No. 13

1/4th BATTALION LINCOLNSHIRE REGIMENT
ORDER No. 151.

In the Field 30.10.17.

Ref. Map QUARRIES 2.

1. **Information.** On night of 4/5th NOVEMBER a Raid will be carried out by 3 Officers & 80 Other Ranks of 'B' Coy. Commander - 2/Lt. R. D. UTTING.

2. **Objective.** Enemy First & Second Lines between HAWK and HOMER ALLEY'S, both inclusive.

3. **Object.** To kill and capture Germans, and to capture Machine Gun and Trench Mortar located.
   To obtain identification.

4. **Wire Cutting.** Gaps are being cut at

   H.7.c.10.14.   H.7.c.05.27.
   H.7.c.42.22.   H.7.c.35.38.

   and dummy gaps outside Raid Area.

5. **Poison - Training of enemy.** To train the enemy to put on his gas mask at the sound of firing projectors, and their noise in the air, poison will be projected into part of HULLUCH, and area immediately South of raid area on the night of NOVEMBER 1/2nd., wind permitting.

6. **Final Reconnaisance - Tapes.** After dark on 'Z' day patrols will inspect gaps, lay tapes to them, and report on their condition.

7. **Assembly.** The whole raiding party will be assembled in "NO MANS LAND" in front of BOYEAU 78 by ZERO - 15.

8. **Compositions of Parties, and Tasks.**

   Party 'A 1'. Strength - 1 Officer & 18 Other Ranks.
   Will enter by S. Gap, work up HAWK ALLEY, moving above ground, searching ground on either side of it to second line wire, through which it will pass by gap and (or) C.T., and enter and search enemy second line.

   Party 'A 2'. Strength - 1 Officer & 18 Other Ranks.
   Will similarly proceed, entering by N. Gap and working up HOMER ALLEY, and will have as special objective, T.M. located at H.7.c.40.45, and dugouts in second line trench.

   Party 'B'. Strength - Raid Commander & 17 Other Ranks.
   Will enter by N. Gap and select position about H.7.c.15.40 in which to lie up for any returning enemy in the event of Party 'A' failing to get an identification.
   It will also form blocks facing N. in front and traffic trenches, to cover Party 'A'.
   Raid Hd.Qrs. will be at H.7.c.16.28 until Party 'A' is clear.
   If Party 'A' fails to obtain an identification this party will lie up till they take a prisoner, or till half an hour before dawn.

2.

Composition of Parties contd.

    Party 'C'.   Strength - 1 Corporal and 6 Men.
    Task. To work up trench at point H.13.a.15.98, which is a believed M.G. Emplacement, and capture gun and crew. If this emplacement proves unoccupied, they will return and form block at H.7.c.10.10 to cover withdrawal of Party 'A', and then follow it back.

    Party 'D'.   Strength - 1 Corporal and 6 Men.
To block trench at point H.7.c.25.10.
To Cover Party 'A' and withdraw after it.

    Party 'E'.   Strength - 1 Lewis Gun & Team of 4 men, with 12 Magazines.
    Task. Facing South to cover S. Gap in "NO MANS LAND" and follow back after withdrawal of Parties A, C, & D.

    Party 'F'.   Strength - 1 Lewis Gun & Team of 4 Men, with 12 Magazines.
    Task. Facing North to cover N. Gap until Party 'B' has withdrawn.

Special men in each party will be told off to search for identification.

9. **Dress.** All ranks will wear Service Dress with badges of rank. Box Respirators in the "ALERT" position, dummy gas masks, steel helmets.
    All papers and Regimental badges will be left behind, and a Field Service Post Card will be carried in right breast pocket with a serial number marked on it.

10. **Arms & Equipment.** All Other Ranks will carry darkened Bayonet fixed on rifle (except No 1 Lewis Gunners). 5 rounds in the magazine - 1 in chamber, safety catch back, and 1 bandolier.
    Grenades will be carried as per table 'A' attached.
    Parties A 1 and A 2 will each carry 4 hand and 4 rifle wire cutters.

11. **Stretcher Bearers.** Will carry waterproof sheets in lieu of Stretchers, and will be attached to Raid Hd.Qrs.

12. **Dummy Gas.** At ZERO projectors filled with water will be fired on to line just behind enemy second line of raid area.
    A small amount of smoke will be included in the projection.
    The Raiding Party will go in under this dummy gas, while the enemy are putting on their respirators.

13. **Liaison.** The Brigade Intelligence Officer and a Liaison Officer R.A. have been warned to report at Advanced Bn. Hd.Qrs.

14. **Direction for Withdrawal.** Red Lights from Electric Torches will be shown from STONE O.P. to guide parties back.

15. **Artillery.** In the event of the Raiding Party needing assistance, the Artillery is "standing by" ready to put down a box barrage round the raid area, when called for.
    This will be done by 18 Pounders, with 4.5 Howitzers and Heavy Artillery neutralizing certain hostile guns, trench mortars and machine guns outside the box barrage.

3.

16. The 138th M.G.Company is putting a gun into BOYEAU 78 to cover the HULLUCH Road after Party 'A' has withdrawn, and is arranging to thicken the Artillery Barrage and engage enemy emplacements if called on to do so.

17. Stokes Mortars will co-operate if called on, by putting down a dummy barrage about points

    H.13.a.20.70.
    G.12.d.44.86.
    G.5.d.05.16.
    G.11.b.90.55.

with the object of confusing the enemy and drawing his fire away from raiding troops.

18. Smoke. Will similarly be put down in G.12.b.

19. Signal for Assistance. Coloured Very Lights will be fired nearly horizontally into our wire by the raiding party.
 On this signal a THERMITE Bomb will be fired from BOYEAU 78, and an agreed code sent back by wire to O.C. ST. ELIE GROUP, R.A.
 Artillery will open on seeing the THERMITE Bomb or on receipt of Code Word.
 T.M's and M.G's will open on their respective lines on seeing the THERMITE Bomb, or hearing the Artillery open.
 Very Pistols to be carried by the 3 Officers and C.S.M.

20. Prisoners. Any prisoners captured will be sent back under escort to Brigade Headquarters.

21. Synchronisation. A watch is being sent to Bn. Hd.Qrs. on 'Z' day at 6 p.m.

22. On Return of Party 'A'. If this party is unsuccessful the Coy Commander will take charge and stand by with it in BOYEAU 78, ready to return to the help of 'B' Party if required.

23. Reports. Will be sent to Advanced Battalion Hd.Qrs. which will be at present Centre Coy Hd.Qrs in DUDLEY TUNNEL.

         W. Cheer 2/Lt. & a/Adjt.,
        1/4th BN. LINCOLNSHIRE REGIMENT.

Copy No. 1 138th Inf. Bde
   2 C.O.
   3 A Coy
   4 B Coy
   5 C Coy
   6 D Coy
   7 Right Battalion
   8 5th Leicesters
   9 O.C.St.Elie Group, R.A.
   10 138th M.G.Coy
   11 138th T.M.Battery.
   12 War Diary
   13 Retained.

Army Form W.3091.

Cover for Documents.

20 Raid

Nature of Enclosures.

4th Lincolns

5/6 · 11 · 17

Notes, or Letters written.

Army Form C. 2118.

WAR DIARY
or
INTELLIGENCE SUMMARY.
(Erase heading not required.)

1/4 Tiverels YY
1 / 1 36

31.E

Instructions regarding War Diaries and Intelligence Summaries are contained in F. S. Regs., Part II. and the Staff Manual respectively. Title pages will be prepared in manuscript.

Place	Date	Hour	Summary of Events and Information	Remarks and references to Appendices
PHILOSOPHE	1ST		Last day in support. B Coy make a final rehearsal for raid to be carried out on the night of the 4th/5th of Nov.	
	2ND		The Battn relieves the 5th Lines Regt in the line.	
	3RD		The enemy now make a practice of sending over salvoes of 77 m.m. on Battn H.Q. at intervals during the night. DEVON LANE also is the centre of artillery activity.	
	4TH		On the night of the 4th conditions are adverse and the raid is postponed. Strong patrols are pushed out, however, and find the Boche "standing to" in the front line. An entry into their trenches cannot be made and our patrols return with two casualties - two men wounded.	
	5TH		Conditions favour us on the night of the 5th and the raid is carried out. The raiding party is assembled in No Man's Land by ZERO - 15 minutes. At Zero projectors filled with water are fired on to ground immediately behind raid area, accompanied by gas projectors on areas well to rear. The operation is a complete success. An enemy post is found in the front line all men wearing their respirators. Two prisoners are secured and brought back to our lines. Prisoners belong to the 13th Bavarian Regt, 6th Bavarian Division	

Army Form C. 2118.

WAR DIARY
or
INTELLIGENCE SUMMARY.
(Erase heading not required.)

Instructions regarding War Diaries and Intelligence Summaries are contained in F. S. Regs., Part II. and the Staff Manual respectively. Title pages will be prepared in manuscript.

Place	Date	Hour	Summary of Events and Information	Remarks and references to Appendices
TRENCHES	6TH		On the following day we receive retaliation fire from the enemy guns. This is chiefly directed on DEVON LANE and other communication trenches.	
	7TH		Whilst on patrol 2/Lt D.A JACOB of B Coy is shot by an enemy sentry. The wound proves fatal and he died in hospital. One other rank also is wounded but not seriously.	
	8TH		The Battn is relieved by the 5th Battn Lines Regt and proceeds to FOUQUIERES. At PHILOSOPHE we entrain on the light railway and are carried as far as SAILLY - LABOURSE where we detrain, obtain hot tea sprinkles and continue our march to FOUQUIERES.	
FOUQUIERES	9TH		At FOUQUIERES we are under 2 hours notice to move and consequently no passes can be granted to BETHUNE. Training must be done on ground near billets.	
	10TH		Adverse weather conditions prevent outdoor training and the time is utilised in bathing and inspections. B Coy working party is paraded and inspected by the G.O.C. who commends them on their success on the night of the 4th/5th inst.	
	11TH		Church Service in Church Army Hut followed in the afternoon by football match (league) with Divl. H.Q. We win the match by 3 goals to 2. Lt-Col. Foot goes on leave. Major Golding-Palmer takes over command.	

A 5924 Wt. W4973/M657 750,000 8/16 D. D. & L. Ltd Forms/C.2118/13.

WAR DIARY
or
INTELLIGENCE SUMMARY.
(Erase heading not required.)

Army Form C. 2118.

Place	Date	Hour	Summary of Events and Information	Remarks and references to Appendices
FOUQUIÈRES	12		Battalion Route March - including transport - to LABUISIÈRE and return. The morning is bright and dry and the route march is thoroughly enjoyed by all ranks. In the afternoon we play a League match against the 1st MONMOUTH REGT. and are beaten by 3 goals to 1. The Monmouths have the reputation of being the best team in the League and up to within 15 minutes from time they had not scored. Major Howis jerns & takes over 2nd in Command. Coy Commanders and a percentage of Coy officers reconnoitre tracks and main CT's on the Divisional Front.	
	13th		On the 13th the Battalion receives a surprise order to move to NOYELLES. The C.O. Intelligence Officer and Coy Commandants proceed to reconnoitre the night subsector of the HILL 70 SECTOR. On their return the move is completed and the battalion is billeted for the night in the huts at NOYELLES. A further move is made on the following day. The Battn moves	
	14th		by platoons into support positions of HILL 70 SECTOR. Battn H.Q. is in TOSH ALLEY on the LOOS - HULLUCH RD. Here we relieve the 5th Battn Sherwood Foresters.	
	15th		Once more we move forward, this time relieving the 6th S.F.'s in the front line. We are on the extreme right of the Divisional front and have on our right the 11th Division	

Army Form C. 2118.

WAR DIARY
or
INTELLIGENCE SUMMARY.

(Erase heading not required.)

Instructions regarding War Diaries and Intelligence Summaries are contained in F. S. Regs., Part II. and the Staff Manual respectively. Title pages will be prepared in manuscript.

Place	Date	Hour	Summary of Events and Information	Remarks and references to Appendices
TRENCHES	16th		Our first day in the line is spent in making a more complete reconnaissance than was possible before. HYTHE ALLEY is the only C.T. possessing duckboards and the enemy appear to know it. Our left is the stereotyped trench system but our right front line is the far lip of a QUARRY or wide railway cutting running approximately S.S.E. and open to the south. Movement in and out is under enemy observation and consequently is restricted to a minimum. The dug-out system is extensive and one alone is capable of holding 200 men. In close support on the right is one whole company which will counter attack in case of an attack on the QUARRY.	
	17th		On the night of the 17th harassing fire is directed on enemy C.T's, tracks and roads. The guns open with a strong burst at 5.30 A.M. and almost immediately red rockets are sent up from CITÉ ST AUGUSTE followed by two green lights. In reply an enemy barrage is put down on NO MANS LAND, RESERVE LINE and C.T's. It is evident that the enemy are extremely nervous and are evidently expecting an attack. Previous to this enemy bombardment 2/Lt A.J.C. HARVEY and 2 O.R's of C. Coy had been wounded in the QUARRY by enemy WING BOMBS. Capt H.G. LUDOLF R.A.M.C. proceeds on leave and is relieved by Captain ULLMAN an American M.O.	

WAR DIARY
or
INTELLIGENCE SUMMARY.
(Erase heading not required.)

Place	Date	Hour	Summary of Events and Information	Remarks and references to Appendices
	19th		One of our patrols under 2/Lt Levi was seen by an enemy sentry post when only 30 yds away. M.G. fire was directed on them and as a result 2 men were wounded. Great difficulty was experienced in bringing in the wounded men – both being stretcher cases – and 2/Lt Levi did especially good work.	
	20th		Fairly quiet – 4.2's occasionally on Hythe Alley. – 3.O.Rks wounded.	
	21st		The Batln is relieved by the 5th Batln Lines Regt and moves into support. The Coys are accommodated in OB1 & O.G.1., two companies acting as support to left batln and two to right batln.	
	22nd	6.8 A.M.	According to orders the support Coys Stand To in the Reserve Line on the morning after relief. On the morning of the 22nd B & D Coy's were moving to Stand To positions when an extremely heavy barrage opened on our Reserve Line. Men were got under cover as quickly as possible but not before it had been killed 4 & 6 wounded – all of B Coy. Included in the killed were 2/Lt W.F. Maskell and & 6t Peet, whilst 2/Lt F.R. Ellis was wounded in the head. A & C. Coys were not in position, fortunately, and escaped without casualties.	

Army Form C. 2118.

WAR DIARY
or
INTELLIGENCE SUMMARY.
(Erase heading not required.)

Place	Date	Hour	Summary of Events and Information	Remarks and references to Appendices
TRENCHES	23rd		Quiet days spent in support to front line battalions. As we find working and carrying parties for them.	
	24th		On the 24th we are visited by a reconnoitring party from the 11th Division. They have been holding the line with two Brigades that are now relieving us with their resting Brigade.	
	25th		On the night of the 25th relief takes place. The 6th York and Lancs Regt takes our place in support and we march out to PHILOSOPHE where we entbus for VAUDRICOURT.	
VAUDRICOURT	26th		An usual our first day out is made a complete rest. Bathing & reclothing is in progress.	
	27th		The baths at VERQUIN are condemned by our M.O. and our men go to ~~Verquin~~ DROUVIN. The baths here are quite small and bathing progresses slowly.	
	28th		The whole battalion marches out for training on the ground overlooking CHARTREUSE CHATEAU. Platoon training occupies the whole of the morning.	
	29th		A brigade inspection is held by the B.G.C. at 2.30 p.m. - is rehearsed ~~held~~ for an inspection which the G.O.C. intends holding on the 1st Dec	

Army Form C. 2118.

WAR DIARY
or
INTELLIGENCE SUMMARY.
(Erase heading not required.)

Instructions regarding War Diaries and Intelligence Summaries are contained in F. S. Regs., Part II. and the Staff Manual respectively. Title pages will be prepared in manuscript.

Place	Date	Hour	Summary of Events and Information	Remarks and references to Appendices
VADECOURT	30TH		The Battalion by Companies parade for bathing — medical inspection. Training is also continued.	

Major W. Holmes
O/C Lincoln Rgt

1/4th Bn. Lincolnshire Regiment
Order No. 161

Copy No. 1

In the Field, 20.11.17.

1. **Relief.** The Battalion will be relieved by 5th Battalion LINCOLNSHIRE Regiment on the night of 21st/22nd November, and will move into BRIGADE SUPPORT of the HILL 70 SECTOR.

2. **Dispositions.** On completion of relief, dispositions in Support will be as follows:-

RIGHT Company	C Coy.	relieved in the line by	B Coy. 5th LINCOLNS	
RIGHT CENTRE	A Coy.	— do. —	C — do. —	
LEFT CENTRE	D Coy.	— do. —	D — do. —	
LEFT Company	B Coy.	— do. —	A — do. —	

   Dispositions of 5th LINCS. REGT. in Support are:-
   RIGHT   B Coy.
   RIGHT CENTRE   C Coy.
   LEFT CENTRE   D Coy.
   LEFT   A Coy.

   Guides will reconnoitre respective SUPPORT Coy. H.Q.s in the morning.

3. **Guides.** 3 guides per Coy. and 1 for Headquarters will report to 5th LINCOLNS. Coy. and Battn. H.Q. in Brigade Support respectively at 4.30 p.m. to guide incoming Battalion.

4. **Advance Party.** One Officer & 1 cook per Company, one N.C.O. per platoon, and Lieut. F. DAY, Corpl. BILTON and two servants for Headquarters will report to Battn. H.Q. at 1.30 p.m. and proceed to take over for respective Coys. and Battn. H.Q. in SUPPORT.

5. **Lewis Guns.** All Lewis Gun ammunition will be handed over in the Line, and advance parties will take over a similar quantity in Support.

6. **Cookers.** 16 will be handed over, and the same number taken over in Support.

7. **Mess Gear.** H.Q. Mess Gear and stores to be on dumps by 5 p.m.
   They will be put on returning ration trolley.
   R.S.M. will detail a party to push all ration trolleys to TOSH DUMP, and then return them to CRUCIFIX DUMP.
   Company Mess Gear will be taken down under Company arrangements.

8. **Traffic.** All unnecessary DOWN traffic must be stopped in HYTHE ALLEY after 5 p.m. until relief is complete.

9. **Handing over lists.** To reach Orderly Room by 10.0 a.m.

10. **Relief complete.** will be signalled by "NOT HERE."

Capt. & /Adjt.

Issued by Orderly at 5.40 p.m. to:-
  Copy No. 1   Retained
         2   O.C. A Coy
         3   B
         4   C
         5   D
         6   R.S.M.

1/4th Lincolnshire Regt
Operation Orders

1/4th Bn. Lincolnshire Regt.
Order No. 153.

Reference Order No. 151.

2 Platoons of "D" Company will relieve "B" Company in Centre Sector on NOVEMBER 4th.
D Company in Support will be reinforced by 1 Platoon 4th BN. LEICESTERSHIRE REGT.
Relief to be complete by 4.30 p.m. and will be signalled by following message "NO WHITEWASH HERE".

Normal dispositions will be taken over after "Stand Down" on morning of 5th inst.

4/11/17.

2/Lt. & Adjt.
1/4th Bn. Lincs. Regt.

1/4th BATTALION LINCOLNSHIRE REGIMENT

ORDER No. 152.

In the Field 1. 11. 1917.

1. **Relief.** Bn. will relieve 5th BN.LINCS.REGT. in the line on night of 2/3rd inst. Relief to be complete by 3 a.m.

2. **Move.** By Platoons from PHILOSOPHE & NOYELLES at intervals of 400 yards.
   1st Platoon of 'B' Coy will pass Bde Hd.Qrs at 4.45 p.m
   1st   do.   do. 'D' do.   do.   do.   5.15 p.m.

   Order of March: B & D Coys, Headquarters.

   Route: via track to Railway thence by track to Junction of STANSFIELD ROAD & CHAPEL ALLEY.
   A & C Coys will arrange to be clear of tunnel entrance by 5.30 p.m. and 5.45 p.m. respectively.

3. **Dispositions** on relief will be as follows:-

   | Right | A Coy. | Centre | B Coy. |
   | Left | C Coy. | Support | D Coy. |

4. **Advance Party.** Coy Commanders will proceed at least one hour in advance of Companies.
   Signallers on duty will proceed with Coy Commanders.
   Snipers will proceed to the line at 11 a.m. and take over positions from 5th LINCS.REGT.

5. **Lewis Guns.** A & C Coys will carry their ammunition and hand over to 5th LINCS. at Bn.Hd.Qrs in the line.
   B & D Coys ammunition will be handed over by Q.M. to 5th LINCS.REGT. This will be ready to put on limber at Bn.Hd.Qrs at 4 p.m.
   Coys will take over as under:-
   Front Line Coys.   128 Magazines per Company.
   Support Coy.   96 Magazines.
   Lieut. F. DAY will inspect Lewis Gun Ammunition to be handed over by B & D Coys, and report on same.

6. **Cookers.** Six will be taken over in the line. A & C Coys will carry 3 each from Support to Bn. Hd. Qrs.

7. **Stores.** Blankets will be rolled neatly in bundles of ten and stacked outside respective Hd.Qrs as follows:-
   Bn.Hd.Qrs 10 a.m.   D Coy 10 a.m.   B Coy 10.30 a.m.
   Officers valises, mess gear and other stores for Q.M. Stores will be dumped at respective Hd.Qrs by 4 p.m.
   Stores for trenches will be handed in to R.S.M. by 3.30 p.m. and will be sent by train to trenches.
   The Provost Sergeant will be in charge.

8. **Relief Complete** will be wired by following message "NIL".

W. Cheer, 2/Lt. & a/Adjt.,
1/4th Bn. Lincolnshire Regiment.

1/4th Bn. Lincolnshire Regt.
Order No. 155.

1. **RELIEF.** The Bn. will be relieved by 5th LINCS. REGT. on the night of 8/9th inst., and proceed to billets at FOUQUIERES.

2. **MOVE.** On completion of relief platoons will move at intervals of 200 yards to PHILOSOPHE, thence by train to SAILLY-LABOURSE where a halt of 30 minutes will be made for tea and hot meal in field adjoining Q.M. STORES.

   Arrangements have been made for 2 trains to be at junction of Railway near Bde Hd. Qrs. at 8.30 p.m., and 2 trains at 10. p.m.

   Capacity of each train 140 Officers and men. Major T.P. Fielding-Johnson will supervise the entraining.

3. **TRAFFIC.** All down traffic in DEVON LANE and CHAPEL ALLEY will be suspended from 5 p.m.

   Tunnels and Entrances will be kept clear during relief and Coy Commanders are responsible that their Coys do not commence to move out until the last platoon of relieving Battalion is clear of their respective sectors.

4. **DRESS.** Soft Caps will be worn when LABOURSE is reached and Steel Helmets carried on shoulder.

5. **LEWIS GUNS.** All Lewis Gun Ammunition will be handed over in the line and a similar quantity taken over at FOUQUIERES. Receipts will be exchanged.

   Lewis Guns will be put on limber at junction of track with main road, PHILOSOPHE. Sgt DOE will be in charge of Dump.

6. **PACKS:** will be carried on limbers from LABOURSE.

7. **COOKERS.** 12 will be handed over in the line and a similar number taken over at FOUQUIERES.

8. **STORES.** All Hd. Qr. Stores and Coy Mess Gear will be handed in to R.S.M. at Bn. Hd. Qrs by 5 p.m.

9. **HANDING OVER LISTS** will reach Orderly Room by 10 a.m.

10. **RELIEF COMPLETE** will be notified by wire "FRESH FISH CERTAINLY"

7.11.1917.

1/4th Bn. Lincolnshire Regt.

REPORT ON RAID BY 1/4th LINCOLNSHIRE REGIMENT
immediately NORTH OF VERMELLES-HULLUCH ROAD
on night 5th/6th NOVEMBER, 1917.

1. Raiding Party.

        2/Lieut. R.D. UTTING. (Commander).
        2/Lieut. A.G. VIVIAN.
        2/Lieut. R. HAYSEY.
        and 82 Other Ranks.

2. General idea was to go in under a projection of "dummy gas", bombs filled with water, on raid front, while real gas drums were fired on to HULLUCH and ST ELIE.

3. Zero 10.5 pm.

Conduct of Operation.

(a). At 9 am 2/Lieuts. VIVIAN and HAYSEY went out to lay tapes to the gaps, which they successfully accomplished, one man being wounded on return journey.

(b). The projectors were fired punctually at Zero, also some gunpowder was let off in tins to increase the noise.

(c). The raiding party, who had completed their assembly in No Man's Land by Zero - 5 minutes, were delayed for about 20 seconds by a smoke bomb which fell short in front of them, preventing any movement until it had burnt out. Up to the moment of Zero there had been considerable and promiscuous and rifle and machine gun fire, mostly directed against back areas, but one burst of M.G. came low and wounded three men. When the projectors were fired there was complete quiet for a time on the part of the enemy: then flares were sent up from second line and promiscuous M.G. fire recommenced.

(d). The raiding party advanced and were observed by posts near top of HAWK and at top of HOMER ALLEYS, who opened on them with rifle fire and grenades. The right party under 2/Lt: HAYSEY replied with rifle fire on which the enemy ran away down HAWK ALLEY a little way, and then turned and fired again, thence conducting a deliberate rearguard action back towards his second line. 2/Lt: HAYSEY followed him up and did much rifle firing, two enemy are believed to have been hit. It is not certain whether this enemy post had on their respirators, it is probable that they did.

(e). A special party under Cpl. Boulton had for objective a M.G. Post south of the HULLUCH ROAD. They reached their objective and found it unoccupied, so rejoined.

(f). The left party, 2/Lt: VIVIAN, was greeted with rifle fire and bombs from a post at the top of HOMER. They returned the rifle fire, and the enemy fire lessening, they threw a few bombs into the post and rushed it, finding only two men of the 13th Bavarian Regt: both unwounded with their respirators on and ready to surrender. It appears these two men were a little distance away from the rest of their post, who ran back just before the rush, carrying with them, according to a statement by one of the prisoners, their company commander and two other wounded men.
    2/Lt: VIVIAN continued the advance and found himself confronted by a heavy rifle and grenade fire from HOMER, as well as M.G. and rifle fire from the 2nd Line.

4. Conclusion.

   The object of this raid was to alarm the enemy by firing dummy gas cylinders from projectors and thus make him put on his respirators. This was entirely successful, the enemy being found in respirators when our men entered his trench. There was no artillery or machine gun barrage.

   Prisoners captured: two - 13th Bav: Regt
   Our casualties: 5 other ranks wounded.

--- *** ---

46th Division No. G.
742/236.

Headquarters,
   I Corps.
****

I forward herewith report on Raid carried out by 1/4th Batt: Lincolnshire Regiment on the night 5th/6th November, 1917.

G. R. Sandeman Capt.
for
Major-General,
Commanding 46th Division...

8th November, 1917.

Headquarters G
46th Division.

46TH DIVISION, GENERAL STAFF.
No. G742/235
Date 6/11/17

SECRET

      With reference to my previous report of 40 Dummies being hit in the raid of 31st.October.
      I now find after a careful examination in the R.E.Yard that 92 Figures were hit, and that the number of hits, totals to 269, most of the hits were on a level with the elbow in the standing figures, though a fair proportion are at the level of the knee.
      The hits are difficult to see as the 3/8ths cardboard material they are made of closes up when hit, especially when wet.

C. Kingfiew Stutford.
Brig-General
C.R.E. 46th Division.

5/11/17.

CRE

How many figures were exposed? he said 120.

6.11

G. 46th Div

120

C. Kingfiew Stutford

7/11

138 J. B. Reid

QUARRIES

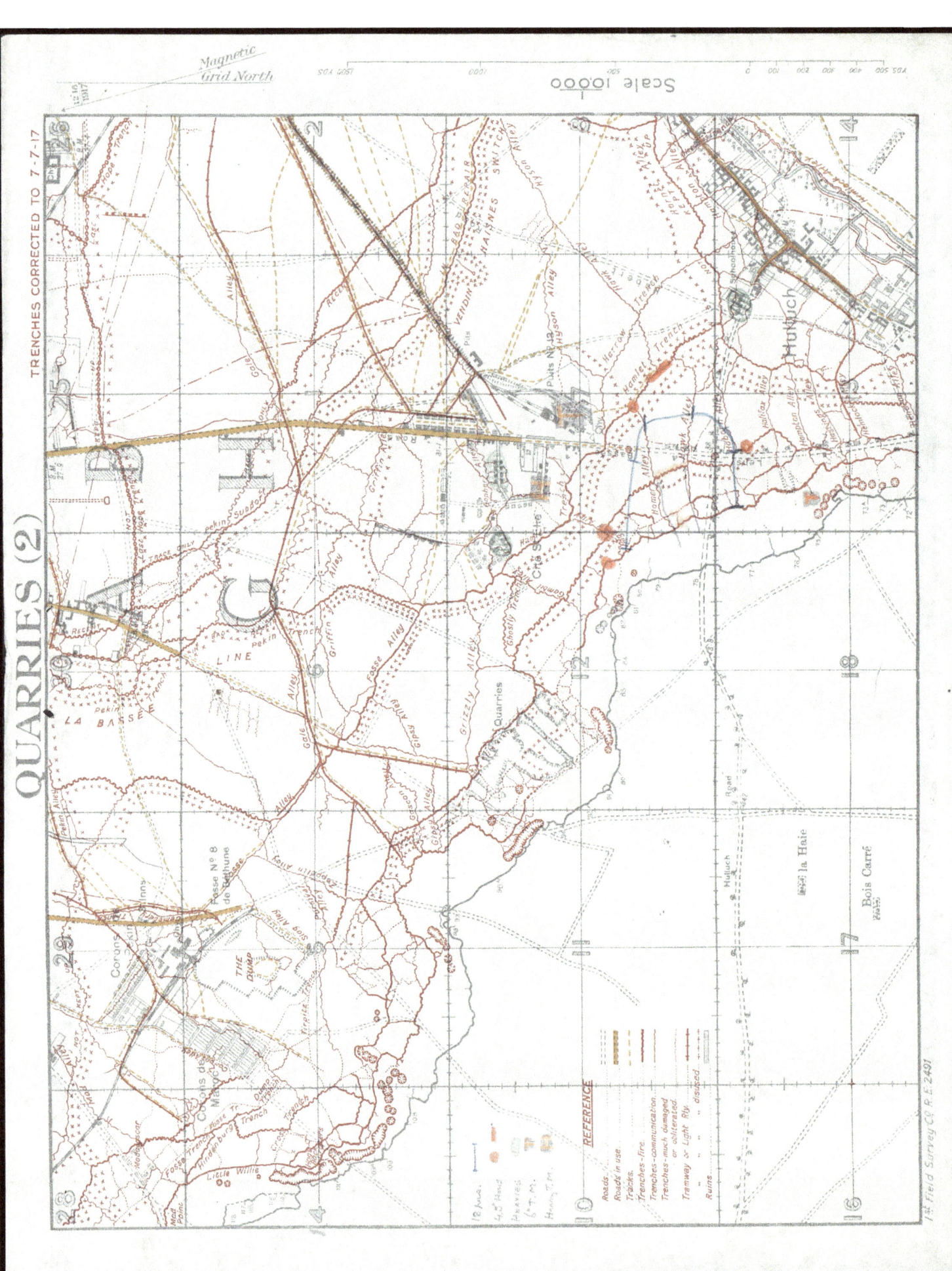

138 J. B. Reid

Quarries

S E C R E T.

G. 742/234.

1. With reference to 46th Division Order No. 251, of 17th October, 1917.—
The 4th Bn, Lincolnshire Regiment, 138th Infantry Brigade, Raid will take place to-night, 5th November, if the wind is favourable.

2. Zero hour will be 10.5 pm.

3. The Codes laid down in my G. 742/233 of 4th instant will be used.

4. ACKNOWLEDGE.

W.H.F. Adams Capt.
for Lieut-Colonel,
General Staff, 46th Division.

Issued at 12 noon, 5th November, 1917, to all recipients of 46th Division Order No. 251.

SECRET.

ARTILLERY ARRANGEMENTS FOR RAID OF 138th: INFANTRY BRIGADE ON NIGHT OF 5th:/6th: NOVEMBER.

--:--

(1) It was proposed that the Infantry should go in under a dummy Gas attack with the Artillery and Trench Mortars standing by ready to assist if necessary.

(2) (a) The 18 Pdr: Batteries were laid on a wide standing "Box" Barrage protecting both flanks of Raid, and forming a protective barrage well beyond the final objective.

(b) 4.5" Howitzers and one 6" Trench Mortar were laid on Machine Gun Emplacements on both flanks of the Raid, and also on selected points in HAMLET Trench which lies East of the 18 Pdr: Barrage Line.

(c) The other 6" Trench Mortar was to engage FOSSE 13 in H.7.a. whilst the Heavy Trench Mortar was laid on the nearest group of houses in CITE ST ELIE.

(d) Heavy Artillery was prepared to take on 2 groups of houses in CITE ST ELIE, and the Schoolhouse N.W. of HULLUCH.
All arrangements were also made for Counter Battery work.

(3) In order to prevent any suspicion on the enemy's part, registration was reduced to a minimum, lines being checked by occasional rounds at considerable intervals.

(4) Wirecutting was carried out by Trench Mortars and 4.5" Hows: (chiefly by the former) over a wide front for many days beforehand.

(5) The signal for Artillery Barrage to come down was to be a Thermite Bomb fired straight up from BOYAU 78.

(6) The Raid was carried out with Artillery standing by, but no assistance was required.

SECRET

ARTILLERY ARRANGEMENTS FOR RAID OF
138th: INFANTRY BRIGADE ON NIGHT
OF 5th:/6th: NOVEMBER.

--:--

(1) It was proposed that the Infantry should go in under a dummy Gas attack with the Artillery and Trench Mortars standing by ready to assist if necessary.

(2) (a) The 18 Pdr: Batteries were laid on a wide standing "Box" Barrage protecting both flanks of Raid, and forming a protective barrage well beyond the final objective.

(b) 4.5" Howitzers and one 6" Trench Mortar were laid on Machine Gun Emplacements on both flanks of the Raid, and also on selected points in HAMLET Trench which lies East of the 18 Pdr: Barrage Line.

(c) The other 6" Trench Mortar was to engage FOSSE 13 in H.7.a. whilst the Heavy Trench Mortar was laid on the nearest group of houses in CITE ST ELIE.

(d) Heavy Artillery was prepared to take on 2 groups of houses in CITE ST ELIE, and the Schoolhouse N.W. of HULLUCH.
All arrangements were also made for Counter Battery work.

(3) In order to prevent any suspicion on the enemy's part, registration was reduced to a minimum, lines being checked by occasional rounds at considerable intervals.

(4) Wirecutting was carried out by Trench Mortars and 4.5" Hows: (chiefly by the former) over a wide front for many days beforehand.

(5) The signal for Artillery Barrage to come down was to be a Thermite Bomb fired straight up from BOYAU 78.

(6) The Raid was carried out with Artillery standing by, but no assistance was required.

SECRET.

46TH DIVISION,
GENERAL STAFF.
No. G.742/239
Date. 10.11.17

46th Division.

No. 154. (G.O.). 10th November, 1917.

The Corps Commander makes the following remarks with regard to the raid carried out by the 1/4th Bn: Lincolnshire Regiment on the night 5th/6th November, 1917:-

"The raid was well carried out by the young Officers in command, and appears to have achieved its object."

Brig: General,
General Staff, I Corps.

46.Division. G.

> 46TH DIVISION.
> GENERAL STAFF.
> No. 4742/237
> Date 7.11.17

I enclose report of LT.C.D.STORRS,R.E. who was in charge of the combined dummy and gas projector attack carried out by the Company on the night 5th/6th.Nov.1917.

A tracing showing the projector positions and targets is attached.

> "K" SPECIAL COMPANY, R.E.
> No. 7/11/17.
> Date.

H.R. Wright. Capt.
O.C."K" Special Company, R.E.

O.C. "K" Special Company, R.E.

Reference Sheet LOOS 1/10,000.

Sir,

I have the honour to submit the following report on the projection on the night of Nov.5th/6th.1917., in conjunction with the raid on the area H.7.c. by the 1/4th.Lincolns.

1. PERSONNEL.   Lt.C.D.STORRS,R.E. and 2/Lt.S.GASKELL,R.E.,with Sections 47,48 and 49.

2. INTENTION.   The intention of the projection was to cause the garrison of the enemy trenches to put on their respirators, in the meantime the raiding party was to enter the enemy's trenches and secure prisoners.

For this purpose 50 drums (C.G.) each were fired into HULLUCH,H.13.d.5.8. and CITE ST.ELIE,G.12.b.8.7. and 45 drums filled water and 5 drums filled smoke onto the undermentioned points round the area to be raided:-

15 drums on to H.7.c.2.7.
15 ..   ..   .. 4.0.
20 ..   ..   .. 9.4.

3. LOCATION OF BATTERIES.

1. 50 guns on HULLUCH at G.18.b.3.3., 2'9" guns.
2. 50 guns on ST.ELIE at G.18.a.central, 2'9" guns
3. 50 guns for dummy drums at G.18.a.9.6., 2'6" guns.

Small base plates were used for all three positions with the exception of ten crimped base plates which were dug in with the light guns. There was no appreciable difference in the recoil taken by the crimped and light base plates.

All the guns were dug in, set and loaded by 2/Lt.S. GASKELL,R.E. and a party of 30 O.R. living in dug-outs in the HULLUCH TUNNEL.

4. CHARGES.

Improvised charges were used, made up by Workshops, Special Companies, R.E., First Army.

    For HULLUCH group.   45 ozs. B.P.
    For St. ELIE group   52 ozs. B.P.
    For Dummy group.   35 ozs. B.P.

To increase the flash, 40 biscuit tins filled B.P. were exploded.

5. ZERO&

Zero was fixed for 9.5.p.m. on the night of Nov. 4th/5th. 1917, but owing to adverse wind conditions the operation was postponed till 10.5.p.m. on the night of Nov. 5th/6th. at which time all the guns were fired, the wind being S.S.W., 6 m.p.h.

6. EFFECT.

Immediately upon the discharge all machine gun fire etc ceased and there was a complete absence of activity on the enemy's part till zero plus 3 minutes, when a considerable amount of machine gun fire was opened and lights were put up.

At zero plus 25 minutes a light bursting into two green stars was seen followed by several lights bursting into two pink stars. There was practically no artillery fire at all.

The object of the discharge was achieved in that the two prisoners taken by the raiding party were both captured wearing their respirators.

7. CASUALTIES.

I regret to report one casualty, No. 147142. A/Sgt. T. Ashley, who was shot behind the left knee by a machine gun bullet which passed right through his leg.

        I have the honour to be,
           Sir,
              Your obedient Servant,

SECRET.

[Stamp: HEADQUARTERS, 138TH INFANTRY BRIGADE. No. G.146/8 Date 6-11-17]

[Stamp: 46TH DIVISION, GENERAL STAFF. No. GHQ/236 Date 6.11.17]

G.O.C. to see
WHH

Headquarters,
46th. Division.

Herewith copy of Report by O.C. 4th. LINCOLNSHIRE REGIMENT on Raid carried out on the night 5th/6th November.

Brig. Genl.,
Commanding 138th. Infantry Brigade......

6/11/17.

REPORT ON RAID BY 1/4th LINCOLNSHIRE REGIMENT
immediately NORTH of VERMELLES-HULLUCH Road
on night 5th/6th November 1917.

1. Raiding Party:
  2/Lieut. R. D. UTTING. (Commander).
  2/Lieut. A. G. VIVIAN.
  2/Lieut. R. HAYSEY.
  and 82 Other Ranks.

2. General idea was to go in under a projection of "dummy gas", actually water on the raid front, with real gas projected in neighbourhood. bombs filled with water on raid front while real gas drums were fired onto Hulluch & Gr. Glen

3. Zero 10-5 p.m.

3a. Conduct of Operation
  At 9-0 p.m. 2/Lieuts VIVIAN and HAYSEY went out to lay tapes to the gaps, which they successfully accomplished, one man being wounded on return journey.

b. The projectors were fired punctually at Zero, also some gunpowder was let off in tins to increase the noise.

c. The Raiding party who had completed their assembly in 'NO MAN'S LAND' by -5, were delayed for about 20 seconds by a smoke bomb which fell short in front of them, preventing any movement until it had burnt out. Up to the moment of Zero there had been considerable and promiscuous rifle and M.G. fire, mostly directed against back areas, but one burst of M.G. came low and wounded three men. When the projectors were fired there was complete quiet for a time on the part of the enemy then flares were sent up from 2nd line and promiscuous M.G. fire recommenced.

d. The Raiding Party advanced and were observed by posts near top of HAWK and at top of HOMER ALLEYS, who opened on them with rifle fire and grenades. The Right Party, under 2/Lt. HAYSEY replied with rifle fire on which the enemy ran away down HAWK ALLEY a little way, and then turned and fired again, thence conducted a deliberate rear guard action back towards his Second line. 2/Lt. HAYSEY followed him up and did much rifle firing, 2 enemy are believed to have been hit. It is not certain whether this enemy post had on their respirators, probable that they did.

e. A special party under Corporal BOULTON had for objective a M.G. Post, S of the HULLUCH Road. They reached their objective and found it unoccupied, so rejoined.

f. The Left Party, 2/Lieut. VIVIAN, was greeted with rifle fire and bombs from a Post at the top of HOMER. They returned the rifle fire, and the enemy fire lessening, they threw a few bombs into the post and rushed it, finding only two men of the 13th. BAVARIAN Regt., both unwounded, with their respirators on, and ready to surrender. It appears these two men were a little distance away from the rest of their post, who ran back just before the rush, carrying with them, according to a statement by one of the prisoners, their Company Commander, and two other wounded men.

2/Lieut. VIVIAN continued the advance and found himself confronted by a heavy rifle and grenade fire from HOMER, as well as M.G. and rifle fire from the 2nd. Line.

The Raid Commander decided that the element of surprise being gone, the 2nd. Line was too strongly held to be rushed without excessive casualties, so, having obtained his identification he withdrew his party.

4. 6/11/17.

(Sd) G.S. YOOL. Lieut.-Colonel.,
1/4th. Battn. Lincolnshire Regiment.

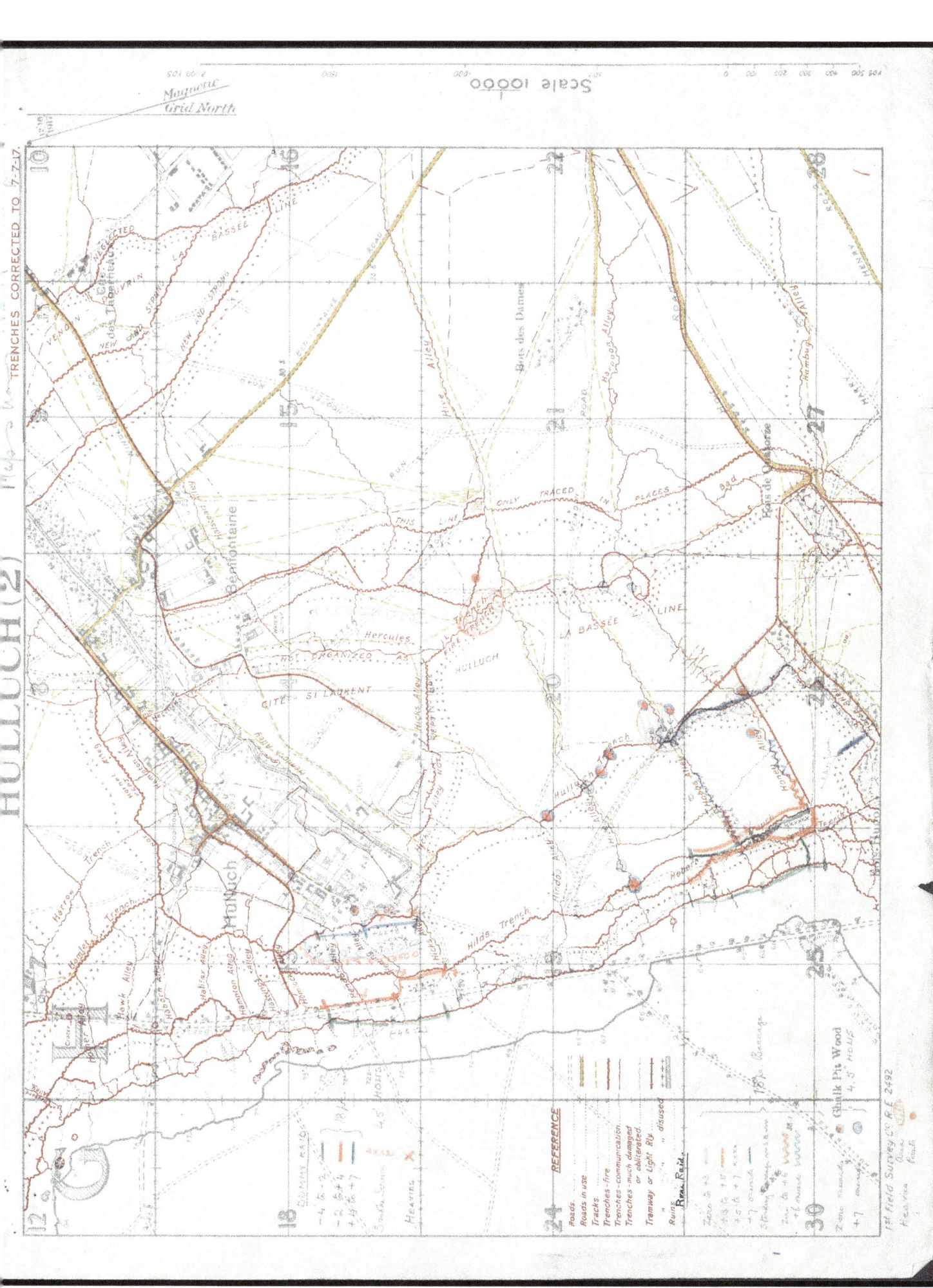

137th Bde Raid

Hulluch (2)

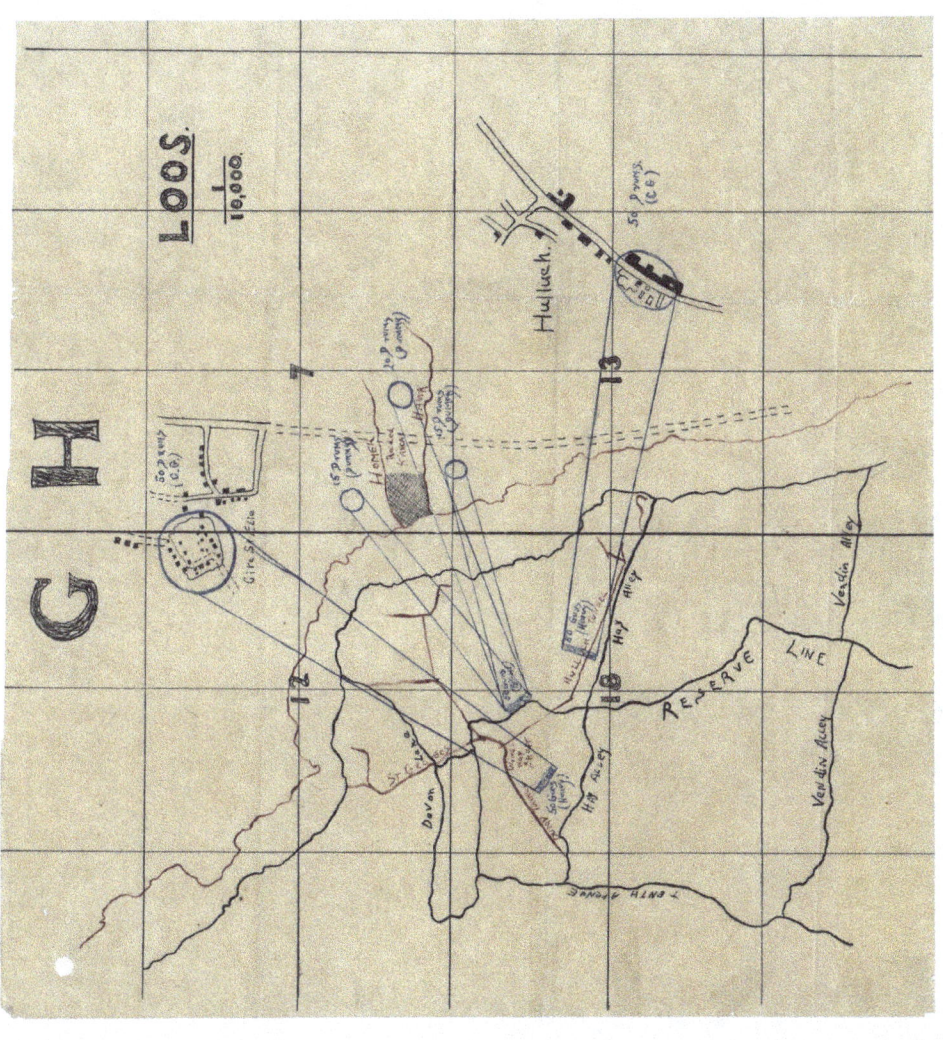

SECRET.

138th. Inf. Bde.
No. G.146/7.

46TH DIVISION,
GENERAL STAFF.
No. M742/234
Date 5.11.17

H.Q. 46th Division

Reference 138th. Infantry Brigade Orders Nos. 175, 175/1 and 175/2.

1. The Operations detailed therein will be carried out tonight if weather conditions are favourable.

2. ZERO HOUR will be 10-5 P.M. 5th. November '17.

3. Same Codes will be used.

ACKNOWLEDGE.

Captain,
Brigade Major, 138th. Infantry Brigade.

Issued at 10.30 a.m. to -
All recipients of 138th. Inf. Bde. Order No. 175.

SECRET.

46TH DIVISION, GENERAL STAFF.
No. M742/232
Date 4.11.17

Copy No. 15

138th. INFANTRY BRIGADE ORDER NO. 175/2.

Headquarters,
4th. Novr, 1917.

1.   Reference 138th. Infantry Brigade Order No.175, para. 12.

SIGNALS.   (ii) The Signal for the pre-arranged barrage of Artillery, Trench Mortars and Machine Guns will be as follows :-

    (a) Telephone.

    (b) Thermite Bomb will be fired straight up in the air from top of BCKAU 78 - G.12.d.69.12.

    (iv) Three white Very lights will be fired from the Support Company Headquarters at G.12.c.5.1. to indicate that all the Raiding Party have returned to our lines.

2.   O.C. 4th. LINCOLNSHIRE REGT. will decide in conjunction with an Officer of 'K' Special Company, R.E. whether wind is favourable for the Raid and notify Brigade Headquarters by 'Priority Wire' by Zero minus 2 hours.

    The following code will be used :-
    RAID will take place   - IRELAND.
    RAID will NOT Take place - SCOTLAND.

ACKNOWLEDGE.

Captain,
Brigade Major, 138th. Infantry Brigade....

Issued by Orderly at 2-0 p.m. to -
All recipients of 138th. Infantry Brigade Order No.175.

SECRET.

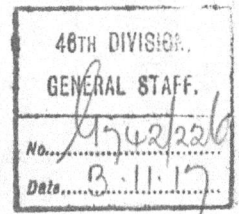

Copy No. 15

138th. INFANTRY BRIGADE ORDER No.175/1.

Ref. maps :-
LOOS, 1/10,000 36 C.N.W.
QUARRIES (2)

Headquarters,

3rd. Novr. '17.

1. Reference 138th. Infantry Brigade Order No.175.

    (a) Cancel para. 7.
    (b) Cancel para 16.

2. Para 11.

Delete line 6 to end of para and substitute :-

'Z' DAY - At Zero, projectors filled with water will be fired on line H.7.c.50.05. to H.7.c.80.70., also (wind permitting) gas will be projected on to H.13.d.central and G.12.b.8.7.

The following gas precautions will be taken from Zero minus 5 minutes till Special Company Officer reports 'ALL CLEAR'.

All personnel, with the exception of the Raiding Party, will wear Box Respirators and all dugout and tunnel entrance blankets and gas doors will be closed in the area contained within the following points :-
    G.18.a.central - G.12.c.5.8. - G.12.d.8.0.

In connection with this operation the following code will be used :-

GAS will NOT be projected on H.13.d. = BEEF
GAS will NOT be projected on G.12.b. = HAM
    'ALL CLEAR' = BREAD

O.C. RIGHT SUB-SECTION will notify Brigade H.Q. by Priority wire when all is clear.

ACKNOWLEDGE.

Captain,

Brigade Major, 138th. Infantry Brigade....

Issued by Orderly at 8-0 p.m. to -

    All recipients of 138th. Infantry Brigade Order No.175.

S E C R E T.

G. 742/233.

1. With reference to 46th Division Order No. 251 dated 17th October.
    The 4th Lincoln Regiment, 138th Infantry Brigade, raid will not take place tonight unless the wind is favourable.

2. The following codes will be sent out 1½ hours previous to Zero :-

    Raid will take place..........IRELAND.
    Raid will not take place......SCOTLAND.

(signed) G.P. Sandeman. Col.

Lieut-Colonel,
General Staff, 46th Division.

Issued at 5 pm, 4th November, 1917,
to all recipients of Div: Order No. 251.

S E C R E T.

G. 742/229.

With reference to 46th Division Order No. 251 dated 17th October, 1917.-

Para. 4.- The signal for pre-arranged barrage of artillery, Trench Mortars and Machine Guns will be as follows :-

(a) Thermite bomb will be fired straight up in the air from top of BOYAU 74 - G 12 d 69.12.

(b) Telephone.

— amended by G 861

G.R. Thurman Capt.

Lieut-Colonel,
General Staff, 46th Division.

Issued at 11.15 am, 4th November, 1917, to-

46th D.A.	I Corps H.A.
O.C, Signals.	I Corps R.A.
137th I.Bde.	I Corps (2)
138th :	I Corps C.B.O.
139th :	11th Division.
178th M.G. Co.	25th Division.
D.M.G.O.	
A.D.C. for G.O.C.	
No. 4 Special Co, R.E.	

Secret.   G.742/228.

1. With reference to 46th DIVISION ORDER No. 254 and G.742/217.

Zero hour for 8th Bn. Sherwood Foresters, 139th Infantry Brigade, Raid will be 8.40 pm., 4th November, 1917.

2. With reference to 46th DIVISION ORDER No. 251 dated 17th October and G.742/195.

Zero hour for 4th Bn. Lincolnshire Regiment, 138th Inf. Bde, Raid will be 9.5 pm., 4th November, /'17.

3. ACKNOWLEDGE.

                                    Lieut-Colonel,
                        General Staff, 46th Division.

Issued at 7 a.m., 4th November, 1917
to all recipients of D.O's No. 254 and
No. 251.

SECRET.

138th. Inf. Bde.
No.G.146/6.

Headquarters,
46th. Division.

Order No.175.

Reference 138th. Infantry Brigade

ZERO HOUR will be 9.5 P.M., November 4th. 1917.

[signature]
Brig. Genl.,
Commanding 138th. Infantry Bde.

3/11/17.

SECRET.

[Stamp: 46TH DIVISION, GENERAL STAFF. No. 4742/220 Date 2.11.17]

Copy No. 15

138th. INFANTRY BRIGADE ORDER NO. 175.

Reference maps:-
1/10,000 36 C.N.W.
QUARRIES (2)

Headquarters,
Novr. 1st. 1917.

1. A Raid will be carried out by the 4th. Battalion LINCOLNSHIRE REGIMENT, on night 4th/5th November 1917.

2. **OBJECTIVE.** Enemy first and second line trenches between HAWK and HOMER ALLEYS, both inclusive.

3. **OBJECT.**
   To kill and capture enemy.
   To obtain identifications.
   To damage and destroy enemy trenches, dugouts and material.
   Special parties being detailed to secure and bring back identifications.

4. **STRENGTH OF PARTY.** Three Officers and Eighty Other Ranks.

5. **ASSEMBLY.**
   The Raiders will be assembled between G.12.d.72.42. and G.12.d.75.10. by Zero minus 15'.

6. **ACTION OF RAIDERS.** The Company will be divided into two parties A and B.
   PARTY A - will proceed through the two gaps at H.7.c.10.14 and H.7.c.05.27. and go through to their final objectives, forming blocks at about H.7.c.50.20. and H.7.c.38.48, but will not proceed further than the LENS - ST ELIE Road. On securing an identification it will return without delay to our own lines.

   PARTY B - will follow party A and enter by same gaps and then lie concealed in the vicinity of derelict trench running from H.7.c.22.19. to H.7.c.10.40.
   Blocks will be formed at -
   H.7.c.22.18   H.7.c.10.10.
   H.7.c.10.40,   H.7.c.02.30.

   In the event of party A obtaining an identification, party B will return to our own lines as soon as party A has passed through. If party A is unsuccessful, party B will continue to lie up for any enemy returning to their forward posts, but will in any case return to our lines before daylight.

P.T.O./

- 2 -

7.	R.E.	1 N.C.O. and 4 men, 466th. Field Company R.E. will accompany the 1st. Line with mobile charges for the destruction of enemy dugouts, Machine Gun and Trench Mortar emplacements.
8.	H.Q.	Battalion Headquarters will move to Centre Company Headquarters in Tunnels. H.Q. of O.C. Raid will be at about H.7.c.15.40
9.	LIAISON.	The Brigade Intelligence Officer will report to O.C. 4th. LINCOLNSHIRE REGT. at Battalion H.Q. at ZERO minus 30 minutes, remaining till ALL CLEAR. O.C. St ELIE GROUP R.F.A. will detail a special LIAISON Officer to report to O.C. 4th. LINCOLNSHIRE REGT. at Battalion H.Q. at ZERO minus 30 minutes
10.	WIRE CUTTING.	(a) Enemy First and Second line wire is being cut by 2" Trench Mortars up to 'Z' DAY inclusive. Gaps at - H.7.c.10.14 - H.7.c.05.27. H.7.c.42.22. - H.7.c.35.38. (b) O.C. RIGHT SUBSECTION will arrange to cut the necessary gaps in our own wire on the night of 'Z' minus ONE DAY.
11.	SPECIAL COY. R.E.	'K' Special Company are co-operating on W/X night by projecting gas on the South end of HULLUCH, and a less heavy projection on the trenches in H.13.a. These projections will not be accompanied by Artillery fire. 'Z' DAY - At Zero projectors filled with water will be fired on line H.7.c.50.05. to H.7.c.20.70., at the same time a small number of smoke projectiles to be fired on H.13.a. central and G.12.b. central, also (wind permitting) gas to be projected on H.13.d. central.
12.	SIGNALS.	(i) RED LIGHTS from Electric torches will be shown from STONE O.P. to guide parties back. (ii) In the event of a protective barrage being required the Signal will be a coloured Very Light fired by Raiding party straight into our own wire in front of 78 POST, on which, the signal will be passed back by - (a) Telephone. (b) Firing of Thermite Bomb from 78. (iii) A Special telephone line to be laid to the top of 78 Exit, Teed into an Artillery line to give direct communication with Group.
13.	PRISONERS.	Any Prisoners captured will be sent under escort to Brigade Headquarters

14. SYNCHRONIZATION /

- 3 -

14.	SYNCHRONIZATION.	A watch will be sent to Headquarters, 4th. Bn. LINCOLNSHIRE REGT. at 6 P.M. A representative from ST ELIE GROUP, 138th. M.G. COY., 138th. T.M. BTY. and 'K' SPECIAL COMPANY R.E. will be at Brigade Headquarters to synchronize watches at 6 p.m. on 'Z' Day. O.C. ST ELIE GROUP, R.F.A. will arrange to synchronize with HULLUCH Group R.F.A.
15.	ARTILLERY.	There will be no Artillery fire unless specially called for to assist the raiders, when the ST ELIE GROUP assisted by the HULLUCH GROUP will form a protective barrage of 18 pdrs and 4.5 Hows. as follows :-

        H.13.a.20.65.   to   H.13.b.01.65.
        H.13.b.01.65.   to   H.7.c.30.65.
        H.7.c.60.35.   to   H.7.c.15.70.
        H.7.c.15.70.   to   H.12.d.80.70.

4.5 Hows. to fire on Trench junctions outside box barrage.
The Corps Heavy Artillery will bombard the following points :-
    (a) Group of houses containing T.M. emplacements round G.12.b.90.55.
    (b) Houses from H.7.a.35.30. to H.7.a.53.30.
    (c) FOSSE 13 in H.7.a.
    (d) Houses containing Machine Guns at F.13.b.67.80.
(Copy of Artillery Programme attached)

16.	SMOKE.	If the barrage is asked for smoke will be fired by Special Company R.E. over the following points :-
		   H.13.a. central. H.7.a.30.25.
		   H.7.a. central. I.12.b.50.15.

17.	STOKES MORTARS.	In the event of a barrage being asked for the 138th. Trench Mortar Battery will put down a Dummy Barrage about points -
		   H.13.a.20.70.
		   I.12.a.44.86.
		   G.5.d.05.16.
		   G.11.b.90.55.
		with two guns, with the object of confusing the enemy as to the extent of the Raid Front.

18.	MACHINE GUNS.	The 138th. Machine Gun Company is putting a Machine Gun into BOYAU 76, to cover the HULLUCH ROAD after Party A has withdrawn and is arranging to thicken the Artillery Barrage and engage enemy emplacements if called on to do so.

Acknowledge

Captain,

for Brigade Major, 138th. Infantry Brigade.

To accompany 138th. Infantry Brigade Order No.175.

ARTILLERY PROGRAMME.

HEAVY ARTILLERY.

1. The I Corps H.A. will stand by to bombard the following points if called upon :-
   (a) Group of Houses containing Trench Mortar emplacements round d.12.b.90.55.
   (b) Houses from H.7.a.30.80. to H.7.a.83.80.
   (c) FOSSE 13 in H.7.a.
   (d) Houses containing Machine Gun H.7.b.67.50.

2. Stand by for Counter Battery work if called upon.

DIVISIONAL ARTILLERY.

The ST ELIE GROUP assisted by the HULLUCH GROUP, R.F.A. will barrage as follows, if called upon to do so :-

18 POUNDERS — From 'OPEN FIRE' to 'STOP'

Guns.	Task.
4 Guns	Barrage H.13.a.19.93 to H.13.a.60.85.
1 Gun	Enfilade trench H.13.a.60.85. to H.13.a.67.88.
1 Gun	Enfilade trench H.13.a.67.88. to H.13.a.75.92.
5 Guns	Barrage H.13.a.75.92. to H.7.c.85.21.
5 Guns	Barrage H.7.c.85.21 to H.7.c.77.52.
4 Guns	Barrage H.7.c.77.52. to H.7.c.50.63.
3 Guns	Barrage H.7.c.50.63 to H.7.c.21.67.
3 Guns	Barrage H.7.c.21.67. to G.12.d.87.65.

4.5 HOWITZERS.

1 How.	Machine Gun and Post at G.12.d.75.82.
1 How.	Trench Junction at H.7.c.01.82.
1 How.	Trench Junction at H.7.c.90.60.
1 How.	Bombard Trench H.7.d.11.48. to H.7.d.21.35.
1 How.	Machine Gun at H.13.a.30.61.
1 How.	Bombard Trench from H.13.a.60.86. to H.13.a.62.75.

MEDIUM TRENCH MORTARS — Machine Gun at G.12.d.61.65. Bombard Machine Gun at H.13.a.29.29.

HEAVY TRENCH MORTARS — Bombard Machine Guns etc, in houses H.7.a.30.30.

RATES OF FIRE. For 18 pdrs and) 3 minutes INTENSE
                4.5 Hows   ) 7 minutes NORMAL

after which Batteries will continue at a SLOW RATE until further orders.

For HEAVY T.Ms.   1 round per 3 mins. for 15 minutes.
For MEDIUM T.Ms. 2 rounds per minute for 15 minutes.

1/11/1917.

DISTRIBUTION TABLE of 138th. Infantry Brigade Order No.175.

Issued by Orderly at 8 p.m. to :-

- Copy No. 1. Bde Major for B.G.C.
- 2. Staff Captain.
- 3. Intelligence Officer.
- 4. 4th. Lincs. Regt.
- 5. 5th. Lincs. Regt.
- 6. 4th. Leics. Regt.
- 7. 5th. Leics. Regt.
- 8. 138th. M.G. Coy.
- 9. 138th. T.M. Bty.
- 10. 468th. Fd. Coy. R.E.
- 11. St Elie Group, R.F.A.
- 12. Hulluch Group, R.F.A.
- 13. 137th. Inf. Bde.
- 14. 74th. Inf. Bde.
- 15. 46th. Division.
- 16. 'K' Special Company R.E.
- 17. 1/1st. N. Mid. Fd. Amb.
- 18. Brigade Signals.
- 19. War Diary.
- 20. War Diary.

SECRET.   Copy No. ___

46TH DIVISION ORDER No. 259.

****

Ref: Maps:- QUARRIES (2) and HULLUCH (2) and
Secret Trench Maps, 1/10,000.   2nd November, 1917.

1.   With reference to 46th Division Order No. 251 dated 17th October, 1917. The following Machine Gun arrangements will be made in connection with the 138th Infantry Brigade Raid.-

   137th Machine Gun Company.-

   (a)   2 guns from G 18 b will be laid on fortified crater at H 7 c 56.00 and will form protective right flank barrage.

   (b)   1 gun from R.46 will be laid on HABORN ALLEY at H 13 a 95.95.

   (c)   2 guns from CURZON Battery will be prepared to sweep HAMLET Trench from H 7 d 05.52 to H 7 d 40.20.

   (d)   1 gun CURZON Battery will be laid on trench junction at H 7 d 11.84.

   (e)   1 gun CURZON Battery will be laid on Trench junction at H 7 d 55.57.

   (f)   1 gun from G 24 b will be laid on H 7 d 22.23.

   138th Machine Gun Company.-

   (a)   1 gun at or near front line will protect the right flank of Raiding Party.

   (b)   1 gun R.52 will be laid on Crater at H 7 c 60.65.

   (c)   1 gun R.53 will be laid on trench junction at H 7 c 16.70.

   (d)   1 gun R.55 will be laid on point H 7 c 00.81 and traverse allowed of 1° both ways.

   (e)   2 guns from G 11 c will be prepared to barrage HAMLET Trench from H 7 a 35.10 to H 7 c 80.83.

   (f)   1 gun DEVON DUMP will engage hostile machine guns on locating flashes.

   (g)   1 gun from R.51 will be laid on point H 7 c 95.84.

   (h)   2 guns V.35 if necessary will open fire on G 12 b 53.12 and G 12 d 41.96 to deceive the enemy.

   (k)   1 gun R.54 will be laid on trench junction H 7 c 90.60.

   178th Machine Gun Company.-

        1 gun at POSEN ALLEY will be laid on H 7 c 70.37.

                                                              P.T.O.

(2)

2. Guns will not fire but will be ready to fire on observing pre-arranged signal. Further information as to this signal will be communicated later.

3. In case guns have to fire the rate of fire will be as follows :-

   First 5 minutes - RAPID.
   Afterwards intermittent fire until ALL CLEAR.

   ALL CLEAR signal will be communicated later.

4. ACKNOWLEDGE.

[signature]
Lieut-Colonel,
General Staff, 46th Division...

Issued at 8 pm.-

Copy No.		
1	to	C.R.A.
2		C.R.E.
3		O.C. Signals.
4/5		137th Infantry Brigade.
6/8		138th : :
9		139th Infantry Brigade.
10		178th M.E. Co.
11		D.M.G.O.
12		A.D.C. for G.O.C.
13		I Corps H.A.
14		I Corps R.A.
15/16		I Corps.
17		I Corps C.B.O.
18		File.
19/20		War Diary.

GOC. to see

GSO. 1. to

Not proposed to
issue any further
Div orders on this.

See Div order No 251
para 4.

4th Lincoln Raid File.

SECRET.

"K" SPECIAL COMPANY R.E.   OPERATION ORDER No.21.

"K" SPECIAL COMPANY, R.E.
No. K.O/62
Date 1.11.17

46TH DIVISION, GENERAL STAFF.
No. G.727/253
Date 1.11.17

Copy No. 2.

Map Reference LOOS 1/10,000.

1. INTENTION

Sections 47,48 and 49 will carry out a combined projector and dummy projector attack in support of a raid by the 4th.Battalion Lincolnshire Regiment, on the night of Nov.4/5.1917.

2. TARGETS AND AMMUNITION.

(a). 15 dummy drums will be fired on to H.7.c.2.7.
    15 .. .. H.7.c.4.0.
    20 .. .. H.7.c.9.4.
The dummy drums will be filled with water except 5 containing smoke mixture.

(b). 50 drums filled C.G. on to CITÉ ST.ÉLIE, G.12.b.8.7.

(c). 50 drums filled C.G. on to HULLUCH, H.13.d.5.8.

3. OFFICER i/c OPERATION

Lt.C.D.STORRS,R.E. will be in command of the firing and will establish his Headquarters at Battalion H.Q. in HULLUCH TUNNEL at G.18.a.0.2.

4. ZERO.

Zero hour will be notified later.

5. WIND LIMITS.

No projectors will be fired on to CITÉ ST.ÉLIE or HULLUCH unless the wind is N.W. through W. to S.
The dummy attack will take place, except if the raid is cancelled.

6. PRECAUTIONS.

Arrangements are being made with 46th.Division that all personnel will wear box respirators and all gas doors will be closed from zero minus 5 minutes till "ALL CLEAR" is given within the two triangles G.18.a.central, G.12.c.5.8., G.12.d.8.0. and G.18.b.3.3.; G.18.b.8.8., H.13.c.3.3.
Lt.C.D.STORRS,R.E. will report "ALL CLEAR" to the Battalion Headquarters where he is and by priority wire to 138 Brigade Headquarters and will also send a priority wire to Divisional Headquarters reporting number fired and retaliation, if any.

7. SYNCHRONISATION. Lt.C.D.STORRS,R.E. will synchronise his time with that of 138 Brigade Headquarters four hours previous to zero. He will also get in touch with the O i/c Raid as early as possible.

8. CODE. The code as regards the operation taking or not taking place will be the same as that used by O i/c Raid. (Orders not yet received).

9. ACKNOWLEDGE.

Issued at 10 a.m. 1ˢᵗ Nov~~October~~ 1917.

Capt.
O.C."K" Special Company, R.E.

Copies to :-

    No. 1. I Corps
        2. 46. Division.
        3. 138. Infantry Brigade.
        4. Lt.C.D.STORRS.
        5. O.C.No.4.Special Company,R.E.
        6. C.S.C.,R.E. First Army.
        7. File.
        8. War Diary.
        9. War Diary.

Secret.   G.742/195.

With reference to 46th DIVISION ORDER NO: 251, para. 1., dated 17th October, 1917.

1. The 138th Infantry Brigade raid will be carried out by the 4th Bn. Lincolnshire Regiment on night 4th/5th November, 1917.

2. Zero hour will be notified later.

3. ACKNOWLEDGE.

Captain,
General Staff, 46th Division.

Issued at 2.30 p.m., 25th October, 1917 to all recipients of D:O: 251.

Secret.

G.742/192.

With reference to 46th DIVISION ORDER No. 251, dated 17th October, 1917.

Erase para. 6. - There will be no bombardment of raid front either with artillery or gas previous to Z day.

Paras. 7 and 8 should now read 6 and 7.

(signed)

Captain,
General Staff, 46th Division.

Issued at 8 p.m., 23rd October, 1917 to all recipients of 46th D:O: No.251.

Secret.

Headquarters,

46th Division.

> 46TH DIVISION, GENERAL STAFF.
> No. 4742/191
> Date 23.X.17

138th Inf Bde.
No. G.146/2.

Reference your G.742/174.

There are no points directly connected with the raid front which require previous bombardment, but it is desirable to have the H.A., standing by for counter-battery work in the event of artillery assistance being required by the raiding party.

22nd Oct.1917.

Brig. General,
Commanding 138th Inf Bde.

No action. see CRA 568.
(138. Bde raid file.)

MESSAGES AND SIGNALS.

Army Form C. 2121 (in pads of 100).

TO: K Special Co RE

Sender's Number: G650
Day of Month: 23
In reply to Number: KO/913
AAA

Issue approved

From Place: 46th Division
Time: 3.50 pm

"C" Form.
MESSAGES AND SIGNALS.

Army Form C. 2123
(In books of 100).
No. of Message..........

Prefix	Code	Words 16	Received From	Sent, or sent out. At .... m.	Office Stamp
Charges to collect £ s. d.			By	To	
Service Instructions.				By	

Handed in at .... Office ....m. Received ....m.

TO VI Div

Sender's Number	Day of Month	In reply to Number	A A A
G1086	23	G669	

Issue of 600 rounds of approved

FROM 1st Corps
PLACE & TIME 3.10 pm

* This line should be erased if not required.
(6334). Wt. W7496/M857. 500,000 Pads. 10/16.—D. D. & L. (E 489). Forms C/2123/3.

"A" Form
MESSAGES AND SIGNALS.

Army Form C. 2121 (in pads of 100).

TO | I Corps

Sender's Number: G 661
Day of Month: 23

Ref 46th Division Order 251 para 6

may authority be given
for issue 600 drums
(C G)

From: 46th Division
Time: 10.42 am

SECRET.

46" "Dw"
G.

Would you please
order 600 drums (CG)
through I Corps
for the proposed
operation on HULLUCH.

H.R. Wright Capt
OC K Special Coy RE

"K"
SPECIAL COMPANY,
R.E.
No. K0/903
Date 10·17

SECRET

46TH DIVISION, GENERAL STAFF.
No. G 742/185
Date 18.X.17

Headquarters,
R.A. I Corps.

H.A. I Corps.   ) For information.
46th: Division)

(1)   Can the I Corps H.A. be prepared to support a raid by 4th: Battalion Lincolnshire Regiment against trenches between HOMER and HAWK ALLEYS, to be carried out during the first week in November as follows?

It is intended that the Raiding Party shall go in under a Dummy Gas Barrage without Artillery fire.
The assistance asked for will only be required if called for.

Engage:-

(1) Group of Houses around G.12.b.90.55.
(2) Houses H.7.a.35.60. - H.7.a.53.60.
(3) FOSSE 13 in H.7.a.
(4) House at H.13.b.67.80.

and Counter Battery work if called for.

H M Campbell
Brigadier General.
C.R.A. 46th: Division.

Headquarters R.A.
18/10/17

S E C R E T.   Copy No. 25

46TH DIVISION ORDER No. 251.

****

Ref: Maps - QUARRIES (2) and HULLUCH (2)
and Secret Trench Maps, 1/10,000.   17th October, 1917.

1. 138th Infantry Brigade will raid the enemy's front and second line trenches between HAWK and HOMER ALLEYS, both inclusive.
    The raid will take place during the first week in November: the exact date will be notified later.

2. Object of the raid will be to kill or capture any enemy encountered and to obtain identification.

3. Wire cutting will be carried out by 4.5" Howitzers and 6" Stokes Mortars as follows :-

    (a) Gaps to be cut on raid front at the following points :-
        H 7 c 10.14 - H 7 c 05.27.-
        H 7 c 42.22 - H 7 c 35.38.

    (b) Gaps to be cut off raid front at :-
        H 13 a 10.84 - G 12 d 42.94.

4. The raiding party will go over at Zero under a "dummy" gas barrage, with no artillery, machine gun or trench mortar action.
    Artillery, machine guns and trench mortars will stand by on a pre-arranged barrage, which will be put down on a given signal being sent up - Thermite bomb to be fired by No. 4 Special Company, R.E.

5. (a) The artillery programme will be drawn up by the C.R.A.

   (b) Arrangements will be made for Heavy Artillery to bombard machine gun and trench mortar emplacements in the vicinity of raid front previous to Z Day as required by G.O.C., 138th Infantry Brigade.

6. Previous to Z Day the following action will be taken in connection with this raid :-

    'B' Special Company, R.E., (Projectors) will bombard raid front and enemy's trenches opposite, where gaps in wire have been cut to the north and south of actual raid front, for two nights previous to Z Day.
    These bombardments will be accompanied by a two minutes intense 18-pdr barrage: at Zero plus 2' the 18-pdr barrage will lift on to enemy's C.Ts to Zero plus 5' when it will cease altogether.

P.T.O.

(2)

7. Watches will be synchronized at 138th Infantry Brigade Headquarters four hours previous to Zero on Z Day.
O.C., "K" Special Company, R.E., will send a representative to 138th Infantry Brigade Headquarters at this time.

8. ACKNOWLEDGE.

G.R. Trendman.
Captain,
General Staff, 46th Division.

Issued at 1.30 pm.-

    No. 1.
    Copy to 46th Div'l Art'y.
    No. 2 to C.R.E.
       3   O.C., Signals.
       4   137th Inf: Bde.
       5   138th : :
       6   139th : :
       7   1st Monmouths.
       8   178th M.G. Co.
       9   D.M.G.O.
     10   A.A. & Q.M.G.
     11   A.P.M.
     12   A.D.M.S.
     13   A.D.C for G.O.C.
     14   "B" Special Co, R.E.
     15   No. 4 Special Co, R.E.
     16   3rd Australian Tunnelling Co,.
     17   Major Evans.
     18   I Corps R.A.
     19   I Corps H.A.
   20/21   I Corps.
     22   I Corps C.B.O.
     23   6th Division.
     24   25th Division.
     25   File.
   26/27   War Diary.

S E C R E T.

G. 742/174.

Headquarters,
138th Infantry Brigade.
****

Reference your No. G. 146 dated 13th October, 1917,- para. 10.

Please let me know points you wish bombarded previous to Z Day. I should like this information as soon as possible.

Captain,
General Staff, 46th Division.

15/10/1917.

S E C R E T.
[Stamp: 46TH DIVISION, GENERAL STAFF. No. G.742/174 Date 14.X.17]
138th. Inf. Bde.
G.146.

Headquarters,

46th. Division.

Reference map QUARRIES (2). 1/10,000.

        It is proposed to carry out a raid with the 4th. Battalion, LINCOLNSHIRE REGT., about the first week of November '17.

1. **OBJECTIVE.** German First and Second Line trenches between HAWK and HOMER ALLEYS, both inclusive.

2. **OBJECT.** To obtain an identification.

3. **STRENGTH OF PARTY.** One Company about 80 strong.

4. **WIRE.** Points of entry at which gaps must be cut :-

    (i)   H.7.c.10.14.
    (ii)   H.7.c.05.27.
    (iii) H.7.c.42.22.
    (iv)   H.7.c.35.38.

Dummy gaps to be cut :-

    (i)   H.13.a.10.84. (on 137th. Bde.'s Front.)
    (ii) G.12.d.42.94.

5. **SCHEME FOR RAID.** It is proposed that the Raiding party go over and into the Objective under a 'Dummy' Gas Barrage, without any Artillery, Machine Gun or Trench Mortar action.
A protective 18 pdr, Machine Gun and Trench Mortar Barrage will be worked out and all concerned will stand by and be prepared to put it down on a given signal being sent up.

[Handwritten: 2 Projectors]

6. **ACTION OF RAIDERS.** The Company will be divided into two parties 'A' and 'B'.

    Party 'A' will follow 'Dummy' Gas Barrage through the two gaps in front line wire, and go through to the final Objective, forming blocks at about H.7.c.50.20. and H.7.c.38.48. but will not proceed further than the LENS-ST ELIE Road. On securing an identification it will return without delay to our own lines.

    Party 'B' will follow party 'A' as a 2nd wave and enter by same gaps and will then lie concealed in the vicinity of derelict trench running from H.7.c.22.19 to H.7.c.10.40. Blocks will be formed at H.7.c.22.18., H.7.c.10.10., H.7.c.10.40., H.7.c.02.30.
In the event of party 'A' obtaining an identification party 'B' will return to our lines as soon as 'A' has passed through.

                              If party 'A'/

- 2 -

If Party 'A' is unsuccessful, party 'B' will continue to lie up for any enemy returning to their forward posts, but will in any case return to our lines before daylight.

7. SPECIAL COMPANY R.E.
(a) To bombard Raid Objectives with Gas Mortar Shells and Dummy Gaps on one or two occasions before 'Z' Day, and also on the night before 'Z' Day. These bombardments to be accompanied by a 2 minute 18 pdr barrage, which will then lift onto Communication Trenches to inflict casualties on enemy, should their forward posts be withdrawn in anticipation of a raid.

(b) At Zero Hour on 'Z' Day to fire "Smell Bombs" under cover of which Raiders will enter objective.

(c) On 'Z' Day be prepared to fire Thermite Bombs as Signal to call down protective barrage if required.

8. MACHINE GUNS.
Protective Barrage to be arranged by D.M.G.O.

9. DIVISIONAL ARTILLERY.
Protective Barrage will be arranged with O.C. ST ELIE Group.

10. HEAVY ARTILLERY.
Requested that Heavy Artillery Stand by for counter-battery work if required. Also to bombard certain points previous to 'Z' Day.

11. STOKES MORTARS.
Will assist on flanks of protective barrage if required.

F. Rowley   Brig. Genl.,
Commanding 138th. Infantry Brigade.

13th. Octr. 1917.

Approved.

Find out how much wire can be cut by mortars before demanding help from howies.

The wire being cut on (3) front ought to help to blind the Boche — we might cut in G.R.d. a wire cutting [to commence at once]

Position of 4" mortars for gas with (3) said should function for this raid too.

WT

WAR DIARY
or
INTELLIGENCE SUMMARY.

Army Form C. 2118.

1/4 BATTN LINES REGT

32.E

DECEMBER.

Place	Date	Hour	Summary of Events and Information	Remarks and references to Appendices
	1		We move from our rest billets at VAUDRICOURT to our new Divisional Reserve at BEUVRY. The C.O., Coy Commanders and Intelligence Officer push on to reconnoitre the new sector (CAMBRIN). Our particular sub-sector is CAMBRIN LEFT.	
	2		On our reaching BEUVRY we are rejoined by Lt. Col G.A. Yool who resumes command of the battalion after 15 days leave. Another move is made, this time direct to the trenches. A daylight relief is possible and we set off at 9.40 A.M. to relieve the 13th CHESH-IRES in the line. The Portuguese have been holding the line with 13th CHESH-IRES in close support but to simplify matters for us a relief has taken place the day previous and we are able to take over in our own language. Lt. Col. T.P. Fielding Johnson, LEICESTERSHIRE REGT. leaves us to take over command of 4th	
	3		Our first day in the line are very quiet. We are able to reconnoitre to our hearts content. One regrettable incident happens. A Rode trench Mortar Bomb falls near a group of men burying 13 of them. As a result one man dies and 7 are wounded. 2/Lt R.D. Utting returns from F.A. & takes over command of B Coy.	

Army Form C. 2118.

WAR DIARY
or
INTELLIGENCE SUMMARY.
(Erase heading not required.)

Place	Date	Hour	Summary of Events and Information	Remarks and references to Appendices
	4th		At 6.30 p.m. the enemy bombarded our front line with T.M's. We had one man killed.	
	5th		2/Lt J.W. BRETT returns for duty with A Coy. Capt. LUDOLF, our M.O. returns from leave and Capt. ULMAN of the American Army returns to F.A. In his short stay with us he proved himself an efficient and hardworking medical officer and a genial companion.	
	6th		Enemy trench mortars fire intermittently throughout the day, but happily we suffer no casualties.	
	7th		Very quiet. Capt. A.H. CLARKE arrives from ENGLAND and assumes command of D Coy. Lieut H.O. SIMPSON relinquishes the acting rank of Capt. and is posted to A Coy. Capt. A.H. CLARKE has previously served in 2/4th Bn LINCS REGT	
	8th		We are relieved in the line by the 5th Lincs Regt and march to BETHUNE where the whole battalion is billeted in the TOBACCO FACTORY.	
	9th		After Church Parade we march to BEUVRY and take over our normal Divisional Reserve billets.	

Army Form C. 2118.

WAR DIARY
or
INTELLIGENCE SUMMARY.
(Erase heading not required.)

Instructions regarding War Diaries and Intelligence Summaries are contained in F. S. Regs., Part II. and the Staff Manual respectively. Title pages will be prepared in manuscript.

Place	Date	Hour	Summary of Events and Information	Remarks and references to Appendices
	10th		Rest at BEUVRY. Bathing, Kit Inspections &c. Then accommodated in excellent billets - in their opinion the best Divisional Reserve we have had. 2/Lt. E.A. DENNIS arrived from ENGLAND - posted to D Coy [Lyet had]. Bathing continued and completed.	
	11th			
	12th		Platoon training on ground immediately north of BEUVRY.	
	13th		We are allotted the 300x Rifle Range but on arriving there we find it has been allotted to the Brigade on our left also. As they are the first comers we are forced to yield and continue our platoon training	
	14th		On the morning of the 14th we set out to relieve the 5th Lancs Regt in the line. An enemy plane, flying very low passes directly over us whilst in the open, but happily no enemy activity follows.	
	15th		Change in Dispositions. We have taken over from the 5th lines with a two company front and now have to readjust our front line to accommodate three companies. Our front line system consists of a series of defended localities organised in depth.	

A 5834 Wt. W 4973 M687 750,000 8/16 D. D. & L. Ltd. Forms/C.2118/13.

Army Form C. 2118.

WAR DIARY
or
INTELLIGENCE SUMMARY.
(Erase heading not required.)

Place	Date	Hour	Summary of Events and Information	Remarks and references to Appendices
	16th		2/Lt BAIN On night of 16th was sent on patrol, when an unlucky "pineapple" descends on the party. Two of the patrol were killed outright and the officer, himself, was slightly wounded.	
	17th		Very quiet — nothing of importance to report	
	18th		At about 8 P.M. the enemy opened rapid fire from his gas trench mortars. The gas bombs fell between our frontline and supportlines and in the first few moments of the attack we had 2/Lt HAYSEY and 8 O.Rks. gassed. Once those respirators were fitted no further casualties were suffered.	
	19th		Very quiet.	
	20th		We are relieved by the 5th Lines Regt. and move to Bde Support at ANNEQUIN. Two coys are forward in immediate support, HQrs in FACTORY DUG OUTS and B Coy in MAISON ROUGE ALLEY.	
	21st		The battalion enjoys an excellent rest at ANNEQUIN, few carrying and working parties are required and we almost have a monopoly of the excellent baths there.	
	22nd		(On 22nd 2/Lt F.G. BAKER is appointed Asistant Coy Light Railway Officer and in charge of the strength of the Battalion.	
	23rd		2/Lt Few proceeds to England for transfer to Tank Corps.	

Army Form C. 2118.

WAR DIARY
or
INTELLIGENCE SUMMARY.
(Erase heading not required.)

Instructions regarding War Diaries and Intelligence Summaries are contained in F. S. Regs. Part II. and the Staff Manual respectively. Title pages will be prepared in manuscript.

Place	Date	Hour	Summary of Events and Information	Remarks and references to Appendices
	24th		The arrival of numerous parcels from home makes it possible for the men to celebrate Xmas Eve, but unfortunately, although the estimated hours are extended for the French Civilians on the 24th and 25th, this does not apply to the British Tommy.	
	25th		Christmas Day. All working parties are cancelled for the day. Due to the distribution of the battalion, we are unable to have our Xmas dinner but the mens rations are improved, cigarettes are distributed and a liberal supply of coal adds to the cheeriness of the atmosphere.	
	26th		We relieve the 5th Lines Regt in the line, the 4th Lines Regt taking our place in Support. The relief is completed by 3.30 p.m.	
	27th		The frost still holds and the trenches are in excellent condition. The moon is approaching to full, and with a good evening of snow on the ground the nights are intensely light. A man would be plainly seen against the snow at a distance of 400 yds.	
	28th		The days continue very quiet. By night the enemy bombing machines fly over in force and their bombs can be heard dropping on LES MINES and BETHUNE.	

WAR DIARY
or
INTELLIGENCE SUMMARY.
(Erase heading not required.)

Army Form C. 2118.

Place	Date	Hour	Summary of Events and Information	Remarks and references to Appendices
	29th	8 P.M.	On the night of the 29th the enemy sent over several gas bombs accompanied by shelling of communication trenches. Happily no casualties were suffered.	
	30th		An R.F.C. liaison officer is attached for three days and in return we send 2/Lt R.E. CREASEY as liaison officer to the R.F.C. at HESDIGNEUL. Nothing of importance happens during the day but at night, on two separate occasions small enemy patrols are seen near our wire. The sentry posts immediately take front fired on them and we sent out patrol to cut them off but unfortunately no identification was obtained. Once discovered the enemy were in too great a hurry to gain their own lines.	
	31st		Except for occasional heavy trench mortars on our battalion front there is remarkable quiet. Evidently the enemy wishes the year to end peacefully and our present policy allows him to do so. The trench strength of the battalion on the last day of the year is 25 Officers and 420 Other Ranks. Only small reinforcements have been obtained during the month of December, totalling 2 Officers and 24 Other Ranks.	

7TH LINCOLNSHIRE REGT

WAR DIARY or INTELLIGENCE SUMMARY

Army Form C. 2118.

JANUARY

Place	Date	Hour	Summary of Events and Information	Remarks and references to Appendices
	1st		We are relieved in the line by the 5th Lincolnshire Regt and move to BEUVRY in Divisional Reserve. Roads are in a treacherous condition and a very north wind is blowing at present. The tour has been a very quiet one. Spent in bathing and general cleaning up. The Battalion is to hold a Christmas Dinner for the men on the night of January 3rd. Much good work has already been done by Major J.C.P. Howis and his committee. Provisions have been bought, marquees procured on loan and altogether the plans are now almost complete.	
	2nd		On this day commence the more material preparations. Each company has applied a large working party and all are busy erecting the marquees, fitting them up with electric light and decorating them. Tables are loaned by D.A.D.O.S. and plates are hired from BETHUNE.	
	3rd		On this day final adjustments are made, cookers are installed in the schoolyard and provisions are brought in. At 5 P.M. the whole battalion is present. A goodly host of men is seated at the tables, eager anticipation of the good things showing on their faces. Meanwhile officers and sergeants are rushing about to serve them. Piled up plates of steaming roast pork and vegetables are brought in and the men soon fall to. There is plenty of good beer and plenty of approximations of it. The plum pudding is voted excellent and when this is followed	

by units, fruit and cake, the men begin to show little desire for more. The officers and sergeants show much interest in the washing of plates and other such unusual tasks, a spirit for which the men show their good humoured appreciation.

A very enjoyable sing-song follows the dinner and representatives of both Divisional and Brigade Staffs are present. Such a gathering together of the whole battalion has not taken place since their crossing to France and when the gathering breaks up at 9 p.m. one feels what an immense amount of good has been done. For once at least the men have realised that the battalion is a <u>unit</u> and the <u>unit</u>.

WAR DIARY or INTELLIGENCE SUMMARY

Army Form C. 2118.

(Erase heading not required.)

Instructions regarding War Diaries and Intelligence Summaries are contained in F. S. Regs. Part II. and the Staff Manual respectively. Title pages will be prepared in manuscript.

Place	Date	Hour	Summary of Events and Information	Remarks and references to Appendices
	4th		The greater portion of the day is occupied in clearing away the marquees, tables etc borrowed for the previous night. All Coys, less the men employed on this work, turn out for training. In the evening the sergeants held their dinner, to which the officers pay a brief visit.	
	5th		Route march by companies through SAILLY, LABOURSE, VERQUIGNEUL, VERQUIN and by direct route back to BEUVRY. In the evening the officers held their dinner at the BOITE D'OR Estaminet. It is the first time for two years that all the officers of the battalion have assembled together.	
	6th		Church Parade — preceded by an address by Capt MITCHELL A.S.C. on National War Bonds. Capt W.C. HEER returns from leave.	
	7th		We relieve the 5th Lincs Regt in the line. Except for a heavy trench mortar bombardment on night of 6th they have had a quiet time.	
TRENCHES	8th		A cold north wind blowing all day with occasional falls of snow. The activity on part of own & enemy artillery.	
	9th		The enemy artillery suddenly subjects MUNSTER PARADE to a few salvos of ft. 2.s — a most unusual target for him. Four direct hits are obtained.	

A5834 Wt. W4973 M687 730,000 8/16 D. D. & L. Ltd. Forms/C.2118/13.

WAR DIARY
or
INTELLIGENCE SUMMARY.
(Erase heading not required.)

Army Form C. 2118.

Place	Date	Hour	Summary of Events and Information	Remarks and references to Appendices
	10TH		Arrival of Capt E.E. Elliot from 2/4th Lines Regt. He takes over the duties of acting adjutant in the temporary absence in F.A. of Capt W. Cheer. One night receives a few rounds from a Boche trench mortar firing from the Corons de Maroc. These are intended for the battalion on our right who receive quite 40 rounds.	
	11TH		Very quiet - nothing to report. Capt A.E. Stephenson proceeds on leave and 2/Lt R.D. Utting temporarily takes over command of B Coy.	
	12TH		There are no enemy aeroplanes are continually over our lines and no combats but meant aeroplanes ventured over our heads but take place.	
	13TH		We are relieved in the line by 5th Lincolnshire Regt. "B" and "D" Companies go to Factory Trench and Maison Rouge respectively and "A" and "C" Companies to Annequin.	
Annequin	14TH		"A" and "C" Companies spend most of the day in bathing and cleaning up, and in being medically inspected. The C.O. and acting Adjutant reconnoitre the 42nd Divisional Village Line Reserve. There was a fairly heavy fall of snow during the night 13/14th 2nd forwarded to O.C.	

WAR DIARY
or
INTELLIGENCE SUMMARY.

(Erase heading not required.)

Army Form C. 2118.

Place	Date	Hour	Summary of Events and Information	Remarks and references to Appendices
	15th		A very wet day. Very little can be done except clearing up preparatory to moving to BETHUNE on 16th.	
	16th		Owing to a thaw and the heavy rain the move to BETHUNE is cancelled. Companies working on RAILWAY ALLEY as most of the trenches are falling in. Proposed relief by 11th Division is postponed much to our chagrin.	
TRENCHES	17th		Relieved the 5th Lincolnshire Regt in the line. They have had a very hard time owing to the severity of the weather. It was a very quick relief considering the bad state of the trenches, many parts of which are knee-deep in mud. RAILWAY ALLEY is closed to traffic. CAPT R.N HOLMES rejoins battalion.	
	18th		Parties are hard at work on the trenches and the MONMOUTHS are working on RAILWAY ALLEY. Can officer A.W. aeroplanes are brought down by a Boche Fokker machine, falling well behind our lines.	
	19th		Fairly quiet. Our observers report activity behind the enemy lines which points to his being relieved. Boche are seen walking about on the top. Our trenches are evidently in a bad state.	
BETHUNE	20th		We are relieved in the morning by the 6th YORK & LANCS Regt 11th Division and move to billets in BETHUNE. The men have tea as they pass ANNEQUIN. CAPT R.N HOLMES takes up his duties as Adjt.	

Army Form C. 2113.

WAR DIARY
or
INTELLIGENCE SUMMARY.
(Erase heading not required.)

Place	Date	Hour	Summary of Events and Information	Remarks and references to Appendices
CANTRAINNE	21st		The Battalion left BETHUNE at 9 o'clock en route for CANTRAINNE via VENDIN LES BETHUNE, ANNEZIN, CHOCQUES, and BUSNETTES, arriving at 12.30 p.m. The billets are by no means good and it is a poor training area.	
	22nd		Companies spent the day in cleaning up and washing equipment.	
	23rd		"A" and "B" were firing on the range at ALLOUAGNE. Remainder of Battalion under Company Commanders in the vicinity of billets. The surrounding district is waterlogged and training had to be carried on along the roads.	
BUSNES	24th		Battalion moved to BUSNES. The first intimation of the scheme for a drastic reorganisation of the whole army reaches us to-day. In each brigade one battalion is to be disbanded, and no outsider can appreciate the gloom that is cast over the Battalion when we hear that we are to make the sacrifice. The Battalion is to be divided as under:—	
			12 Officers & 300 Other Ranks, including H.Q. & complete to 52/4th Lincolnshire Regt	
			12 " & 250 " to 1/5th Rn Lincolnshire Regt	
			12 " & 260 " to 2/5th " "	
			The Battalion continues its normal training for the next few days but work at Battalion H.Q. is far from normal	

Army Form C. 2118.

WAR DIARY
or
INTELLIGENCE SUMMARY.

(Erase heading not required.)

Instructions regarding War Diaries and Intelligence Summaries are contained in F. S. Regs., Part II. and the Staff Manual respectively. Title pages will be prepared in manuscript.

Place	Date	Hour	Summary of Events and Information	Remarks and references to Appendices
	28th		The task of allotting officers drawn to their respective units is most trying and at the same time most distasteful. Although most of the officers have joined the battalion since the war there are number of permanent officers' men who have served in no other battalion and who look back to the camp training of pre-war days. It is these men who must feel the unrest, for the others the disappointment is more or less temporary although acute. The G.O.C. addressed the battalion and in few words expressed his great regret that they should have to suffer. In a letter which he read to the battalion, he explained and shewed the necessity for the drastic measures which were being taken, and lastly he called upon to remember that though the 1/4th Bn Lines Regt was no longer, yet they belonged to the same army and must continue bearing on in the same spirit.	
AMBRINES.	29th		On this day began the actual breaking up. 12 officers and 260 Other Ranks set off to join the 2/5th Bn Lincolnshire Regt stationed at AMBRINES.	

WAR DIARY
or
INTELLIGENCE SUMMARY.

Army Form C. 2118.

Place	Date	Hour	Summary of Events and Information	Remarks and references to Appendices
	30th		The Colonel, Adjutant, Quartermaster and 9 other Officers with 200 men set out for the 2/4th R'n Lincolnshire Regt with whom they will amalgamate and form the 4th Battalion, Lincolnshire Regt. Lt Col H.A. Waring, D.S.O. commanding 1/5 R'Rn Lincolnshire Regt called for a voluntary parade of his battalion to give us a send off, and every available man attended. The spirit which prompted this voluntary parade to see us off was very much appreciated demonstrating, as it did, the splendid feeling of kinship which has always existed between us and our sister battalion, a feeling which the two colonels have always done their best to foster. Our journey is by St. Pol, Frevent, Le Cauray, and we arrive at Maizieres at 6 p.m. Lt.Col. G.A. Yool takes over command of the 4th Battalion Lincolnshire Regt. and Capt. R.N. Holmes is appointed Adjutant.	

Lt Col Whitbread
1/4 Lincolnshire

WAR DIARY or INTELLIGENCE SUMMARY.

Army Form C. 2118.

(Erase heading not required.)

Summary of Events and Information

Disposition of Officers in Detail.

To 4th Bn Lincolnshire Regt.	To 1/5th Lincs Regt.	To 2/5th Lincs Regt.
Lt.Col. G.A. Yool	Capt G.H. Marris	Lt. A.W. Wilson
Capt & Adjt. R.N. Holmes	Lieut F. Day	2/Lt. E.A. Dennis
Capt A.H. Clark	2/Lt. R.D. Utting	,, R.E. Creasey
,, E. Elliot	,, A.G. Black	,, C.V. Longland
,, S. Lee	,, E. Tomlinson	,, E.J.V. Righton
,, A.E. Stephenson	,, P. Sharpe	,, R.G. Eedes
,, H.G. Ludolf R.A.M.C.	,, J.P. Murray	,, G. Taylor
Lieut & Q.M. J.W. Upex	,, J.W. Brett	,, F.R. Gibbons
2/Lt. J.R. Neave	,, A.C. Fisher	,, A.J. Elston
,, A.M.H. Bain	,, R.G. Harris	,, F.J. Levi
,, W. Phypers	,, F. Dawson	,, A.R. Lunn
,, H.L. Hubble	Capt. W.R. Myers	
,, H.R. Greenwood		Lt. H.O. Simpson

Unposted Major J.C.P. Howis
 Capt R.J.C. Crowden
 2/Lt. W. Cheer
 Lt. A.G. Vivian.

(War diary)   Copy No 10

1/4th BATTALION LINCOLNSHIRE REGT.
ORDER No. 171.

                                                    In the Field 6.7.1916.
Ref.Map : Bethune Canh.Sheet.
         Sheet 36 N.W. (1:20,000)

1. **Relief.**   The Battalion will relieve the 5th Lincs. Regt. in the
                line on the 7th inst. Relief to be complete by 8 p.m.

2. **March.**   Coys. will pass the starting point P.?.a.9.35
                (Road Junction) at the following times :-
                    D Coy. 10.15 p.m.   B Coy. 11.15 p.m.
                    A Coy. 10.45 p.m.   C Coy. 10.45 p.m.
                    H.Q. Details : 11.05 p.m.
                March will be by platoons at 100 yds. interval.
                Movement of Advanced troops Ahead will not take place
                before ?, and platoons will move in single file on
                either side and clear of the road.
                All necessary precautions will be taken against observation
                by hostile aircraft.

3. **Disposition on relief** will be as follows :-
                    Right   D Coy.   Centre   C Coy.
                    Left   A Coy.   Support   B Coy.

4. **Advance Party.**   The C.O., Sgt.Maj., 2 signallers per Coy. & 2
                for Bn.Hrs., water duty men and 1 cook per Coy. will
                report to Bn.Hqrs. at ? p.m. and proceed to the line.

5. **Lewis Guns and Ammunition** will be attached at respective Coy. Hqrs.
                (except C Coy. which will be attached at B Coy.) by 11 a.m.
                and collected by transport. One Lewis Gunner per Coy.
                will accompany Lewis Gun limber. ? Sgt. ? will be in
                charge.
                Lewis Guns will be carried from LEFT LANE.
                L.G.Ammunition will be handed over to 5th Lincs. at
                ? and receipt obtained.
                L.G. Ammunition will be taken over in the line

6. **Boiler fire.** It will be taken over from 5th Lincs. in the line.

7. **Stores.** Blankets will be neatly tied in bundles of 10,
                securely tied, and handed ?
                A, B, C Coys at H.Q. Mess Yard by ?. Qtr. Sgt. Daubney in charge
                D Coys at Coy. HQ. Hrs. by 3.30 p.m.
                Palliasses will be tied in bundles of 10 and dumped
                respective Coy. Qtr. ?. Recpts. to will be obtained and
                forwarded to B.Mess.
                Officers valises and all stores for ?.Q. Mess will
                be dumped by 11 a.m. as follows :-
                A, B, C Coys .Hd.Qrs., in H.Q. Mess Yard.
                D Coy. at Coy. H.Q.
                Trench Mess Gear and all stores for trenches to be
                dumped in H.Q. Mess Yard by 12 noon. ? Qtr. Sgt. will be
                in charge.

8. **Billets.** Billets must be left scrupulously clean and inspected
                by a Coy. officer before leaving.

9. **Canteen.** All Canteen Stores will be ready to be put on limber
                at 10.30 a.m.

10. **Relief Complete.** to be notified by signalling the name of Coy.
                 2nd in Command.

                              (Sd) J R NEAVE
                                                    ?/Lt. & a/Adjt.
                                                  1/4th Bn. Lincolnshire Regt.

4th Bn. Lincolnshire Regiment   No. 10.
                    6 th. July. 1916.

To: ETTRICK Comdr. ...
    2 C. ... .

1.   The Battalion will be relieved in the line by the 5th Battn.
        LINCOLNSHIRE Regiment on the 13th instant and on completion
        of relief will move into CLOSE SUPPORT.

2. Dispositions will be as follows:
        RIGHT FORWARD Support   - B Company FACTORY DUGOUTS
        LEFT   "   "   - D Company MAISON ROUGE DUGOUTS
        ANNEQUIN   - A and C Companies.
        B and D Companies will send parties to reconnoitre routes to
        respective dispositions to act as guides to Companies.

3. On relief: Companies will move independently to ... relief
        ... ... on the BETHUNE-CAMBRIN ... will march in file on
        ... side ... ... of the road.
                All necessary precautions will be taken against observation
        by hostile aircraft and balloons.

4. Ammunition. All small arm ammunition will be handed over in the line,
        and a similar quantity taken over in CLOSE SUPPORT. receipts
        will be exchanged.

5. ...   ...

6. Stores.   ...
               ...
               ...
               ... will be sent to CAMBRIN ... ... dark.
               ... O.C. will arrange for Transport to
        remove stores from CAMBRIN to ANNEQUIN.

7. ...   . KHAKI ... ... MINSTER ... ...
               ... from ... ...

8. Advance   ... Officer and one Sergeant per Company and one NCO per
   Party   ... ... from ... ... BATTN ... ... for
               ... ... report to Orderly Room at 2 a.m. they will
        ... ... take over billets and all stores and accoutre ...
        from 5th Bttn. LINCOLNSHIRE Regt.

9. Trucking   To reach Orderly Room by 9 a.m. on day of relief.
   out list

10. Relief   Will be notified by signalling KNOBETO ... by Company
    Complete   Commanders reporting personally at HQ Qrs.

                                    E. Elliott
                                              Capt. & Adjt.
                        4th Bn. Lincolnshire Regiment.

    Issued by Orderly or ...
        Copy No. 1. O/C 1 Coy.
                2. " A Coy.
                3. " A Coy.
                4. " B Coy.
                5. " C Coy.
                6. " D Coy.
                7. T. + Q.M.
                8. 138 Inf Bde.
                9. 5th Lincolns
            10 & 11. War Diary
                    R.S.M.

Copy No. 9

1/4th Bn. LINCOLNSHIRE REGIMENT.

Order No. 173.

Ref.Maps: BETHUNE Comb. Sheet.   In the Field 18.1.17.

1. **Relief.** The Bn. will be relieved in Support by the 6th YORK & LANCASTER REGIMENT on 19th January 1917. Relief will commence at 1 p.m.

2. **March.** On completion of relief, companies will move by platoons at 200 yards interval to BETHUNE. Steel helmets will be worn.
   All necessary precautions will be taken against observation by hostile aircraft and balloons.

3. **Dispositions.** A Coy. 6th YORK & LANCASTER Regt. will relieve B Coy. 4th LINC
   B Coy.   do.   do.   A do.
   C Coy.   do.   do.   D do.
   D Coy.   do.   do.   C do.

4. **Guides.** Four guides per Coy., and one for Hd.Qrs. will be outside C Coy.H.Q. at 1 p.m. to meet incoming Bn.

5. **Billetting Party.** One N.C.O. per Coy., and C.S.M. BILTON for Hd.Qrs. together with one man per platoon will report to Lieut. F. DAY at Bn.H.Q. at 8 a.m. to proceed to BETHUNE to billet Bn.

6. **Stores.** Blankets will be neatly rolled in bundles of 10, securely tied and stacked in Hut at Bn.Hd.Qrs. by 10 a.m. Sergt. DANBURY in charge.
   Officers valises, shoemakers and tailors gear, and Orderly Room boxes will be dumped at Bn.H.Q. by 10 a.m.
   Mess Gear to be at Bn.H.Q. by 12.30 p.m.
   Canteen stores to be ready by 10 a.m.
   All stores from B & D Coys., including Officers Mess Gear will be brought to CAMBRIN DUMP by 1 p.m., and placed on limber.

7. **Lewis Guns & ammunition.** Lewis guns and ammunition of A & C Coys. will be dumped at Bn.H.Q. by 10 a.m., and collected by limber.
   One Lewis Gunner per Coy. will accompany limber.
   Guns and ammunition of B & D Coys. will be brought out to CAMBRIN DUMP, and placed on limber there. One Lewis Gunner per Coy. will accompany limber.
   Sgt. F.F. DON will be in charge.

8. **Cooker Tins.** The six cooker tins with Support Companies will be brought to CAMBRIN by 1 p.m., and placed on limber.

9. **Handing over lists.** Lists of all stores, maps and documents to be handed over will reach Orderly Room by 8 p.m. tonight.

10. **Relief complete.** of Support Companies to be signalled by "BUFF AND"

11. **Returns.** Marching in state, position of Coy.H.Q., time of arrival in billets, and numbers falling out on march to be sent to Bn.H.Q. as soon as possible on arrival in billets.

(sd)   H.F. ELLIOTT, Capt. & Adj
1/4th Bn. Lincolnshire Regiment.

(over)

Issued by Orderly to:-
Copy No.1   Officer Cmdg.
     2.   H.J.Moss.
     3.   A Coy.
     4.   B Coy.
     5.   C Coy.
     6.   D Coy.
     7.   T.M.B.
     8.   114th Inf.Bde.
     9.   War Diary.
    10.   War Diary.
    11.   R.S.M.

Copy No. 11

1/4th BATTALION LINCOLNSHIRE REGIMENT
ORDER NO. 174.--

In the Field 16th January 18.

1. **Relief.** The Battalion will relieve the 5th LINCS REGT. in the Line on the 17th January ~~Relief to be complete by~~

2. **Move.** Coys. will move at the following times :
    A Coy   4. P.M.   B Coy   4.15 P.M.
    C Coy   4.10 "   D Coy   4.15 P.M.
    Headquarter Details 4.30 p.m.
    All movement will be by platoons at 200 yds. interval.
    Coys. will use MAISON ROUGE ALLEY or Overland Tracks.
    B Coy. will use Overland Tracks.
    RAILWAY ALLEY from entrance in A 26 c to Reserve Line is closed to all traffic tomorrow.

3. **Disposition.** Right Front A Coy.   Centre Front D Coy.
                     Left Front   B Coy.   Support   C Coy.

4. **Advance Party** 1 Officer per Coy. and 1 N.C.O. per platoon will go on in advance to take over.

5. **Stores.** All blankets, rolled neatly in bundles of 10, will be dumped at Bn. Hd. Qrs. by 10 a.m.
    All stores for trenches will be dumped at Bn.Hd.Qrs. by 12.30 p.m.
    Stores for Transport Lines will be handed in to R.S.M. by 3.15 p.m.

6. **Lewis Guns.** Lewis Guns will be carried into the Line.
    Lewis Gun Ammunition of A & C Coys. will be dumped at Bn.Hd.Qrs. by 10 a.m.
    The Transport Officer will make arrangements for handing over same and will obtain receipt.
    B & D Coys. will stack their ammunition at Coy.Hd.Qrs and will detail pushing parties to transport it to CAMBRIN Dump where it will be handed over to 5th LINCS REGT and receipts obtained.
    All Lewis Gun AMMUNITION will be taken over in the Line

7. **Boiler Tins.** Boiler Tins of B & D Coys. will accompany Lewis Gun Ammunition. 12 boiler tins will be taken over in the line

8. **Relief Complete** will be wired by "FED UP".

(Sd). E.Elliott Capt. & a/Adjt.,
1/4th Bn. Lincolnshire Regt.--

Copy No. 1 Retained.
        2 C.O.
        3 138th Inf.Bde.
        4 C.O., 5th Lincolns.
        5 O.C. A Coy.
        6 "   B Coy.
        7 "   C Coy.
        8 "   D Coy.
        9 T.O. & Q.M.
       10 R.S.M.
       11 War Diary.
       12 War Diary.

Copy No. 11

1/5th BATTALION LINCOLNSHIRE REGIMENT

ORDER No. 171.

In the Field.

Ref.Map BETHUNE Combined
    Sheet 1/40,000.

1. Move.   The Battalion will move to billets at CANTAINE to-morrow
           31st inst. and will be clear of BETHUNE by 10 a.m.
                The Battalion will move off in the following order:-
                H.Qrs., A. B. C. D Coys. 2nd Line Transport.
           Companies will march with intervals of 100 yards between
           platoons.
                The leading platoon will pass starting point at 9 a.m.
                When the Battalion is clear of BETHUNE platoons on
           receiving the order will close up and Companies will march
           at 100 yards interval.

           Starting Point: TOBACCO FACTORY.

           Route: VENDHILes-BETHUNE, CHOQUES, BUSNETTES, Road
                     Junction V.3.d.6.3. CANTAINE.

2. Lewis Guns. Lewis guns and Ammunition limbers will leave at 8 a.m.
                Sgt. DOE in charge, and 1 Lewis Gunner per Company will
                accompany the limbers.

3. Cookers.   Will leave at 8 a.m. Dinners to be ready at 14.30 p.m.
                at CANTAINE.

4. Stores.   Stores will be delivered to Pioneer Sergeant in
                Factory Yard as under:-
                    Blankets   7.30 a.m.
                    Valises   7.30 a.m.
                    Officers Mess Gear   8. 0 a.m.
                    Orderly Room Gear   8. 0 a.m.

5. Loading Party. Provost Sergeant, Police & Pioneers will report
                   to Pioneer Sergeant at 7.30 a.m. and act as loading party.

6. Baggage Guard. 'D' Company will detail 1 Platoon under an Officer
                   as Baggage Guard. This platoon will report to Transport
                   Officer at 8 a.m. and march in rear of 2nd Line Transport.

7. Billeting Party. Lieut. F.DAY & Cpl BIRCH have proceeded to
                    CANTAINE to-day to arrange billets.
                         C.Q.M.S's will proceed to CANTAINE on bicycles
                    and report to Lieut. F.DAY by 9 a.m. Bicycles will be
                    drawn from Q.M. Stores.

8. Parade States.   To be in Orderly Room by 8.15 a.m.

9. Marching In States showing usual particulars to be sent to Orderly
                     Room immediately Companies are in billets.

10.Orderly Room will close at BETHUNE at 8 a.m. and re-open at
                 CANTAINE on arrival.

Copy No 1 Retained
        2 H.Q.Mess   (Sd) E. N. Holmes, Capt. & Adjt.,
        3 O.C. A Coy   1/5th Bn. LINCOLNSHIRE REGIMENT.
        4 O.C. B Coy
        5 O.C. C Coy
        6 O.C. D Coy
        7 Transport Officer
        8 Quartermaster
        9 138th Inf.Bde
       10 & 11 War Diary
       12 R.S.M.

Copy No. 10

1/5th BATTALION LINCOLNSHIRE REGIMENT

ORDER No. 176.

In the Field 20.1.18.

Ref.Map BETHUNE Combined
Sheet 1/40,000.

1. **Move.** The Battalion will move to billets at CANTRAINE tomorrow 21st inst; and will be clear of BETHUNE by 10 a.m.
   The Battalion will move off in the following order:-
   Bd.Qrs., A, B, C, D Coys, 2nd Line Transport.
   Companies will march with intervals of 100 yards between platoons.
   The leading platoon will pass starting point at 8 a.m.
   When the Battalion is clear of BETHUNE platoons on receiving the order will close up and Companies will march at 100 yards interval.

   Starting Point: TOBACCO FACTORY.

   Route: VENDIN-les-BETHUNE, CHOCQUES, BUSNETTES, Road Junction V.7.d.6.5, CANTRAINE.

2. **Lewis Guns.** Lewis guns and Ammunition limbers will leave at 6 a.m.
   Sgt. COX in charge, and 1 Lewis Gunner per Company will accompany the limbers.

3. **Cookers.** Will leave at 6 a.m. Dinners to be ready at 12.55 p.m. at CANTRAINE.

4. **Stores.** Stores will be delivered to Pioneer Sergeant in Factory Yard as under:-
   Blankets   7.30 a.m.
   Valises   7.30 a.m.
   Officers Mess Gear   6.0 a.m.
   Orderly Room Gear   6.0 a.m.

5. **Loading Party.** Provost Sergeant, Police & Pioneers will report to Pioneer Sergeant at 7.30 a.m. and act as loading party.

6. **Baggage Guard.** 'D' Company will detail 1 platoon under an Officer as Baggage Guard. This platoon will report to Transport Officer at 6 a.m. and march in rear of 2nd Line Transport.

7. **Billeting Party.** Lieut. F.DAY & Cpl ALLTON have proceeded to CANTRAINE today to arrange billets.
   C.Q.M.S's will proceed to CANTRAINE on bicycles and report to Lieut.F.DAY by 8 a.m. Bicycles will be drawn from Q.M. Stores.

8. **Guard States.** To be in Orderly Room by 8.15 a.m.

9. **Marching In States** showing usual particulars to be sent to Orderly Room immediately Companies are in billets.

10. **Orderly Room** will close at BETHUNE at 8 a.m. and re-open at CANTRAINE on arrival.

Copy No 1 Retained
2 H.Q. Mess
3 O.C. A Coy
4 O.C. B Coy
5 O.C. C Coy
6 O.C. D Coy
7 Transport Officer
8 Quartermaster
9 138th Inf.Bde
10 & 11 War Diary
12 R.S.M.

(Sd) E. H. Holmes, Capt. & Adjt.,
1/5th Bn. LINCOLNSHIRE REGIMENT.

Copy No.

1/4th BATTALION LINCOLNSHIRE REGT.
ORDER No. 17

Ref. Map 36A S.E.   In the Field 23.1.18.

1. **Move.**   The Battalion will move to billets at HINGES tomorrow
                24th inst. and will move off in the following order:-
                Hd.Qrs, B, D, A Coys. All available 1st Line
                Transport and 2nd Line Transport.
                Coys will march at intervals of 100 yards. Leading
                platoon will pass starting point at 10 a.m.
                STARTING POINT: On road 100 yards N.E. of Orderly
                                Room V.7.b.4.6.
                ROUTE: D'ELLES. Road Junction V. .... HINGES.

                'C' Company will proceed to HINGES as per Battalion Orders.

2. **Lewis Guns.** Lewis Gun Limbers will be outside Orderly Room at
                8 a.m. and guides will be sent from each Company to
                guide the limbers to the Lewis gun billet where they
                will be loaded.   Sgt.FOX in charge and 1 Lewis gunner
                per Company will accompany the limbers.

3. **Stores.** Stores will be delivered as under:-
                Blankets (with the exception of D Coy) 8 a.m.) To Pioneer Sgt
                Valises   8.30 a.m.)in Yard of
                                                                 'C'Coy Mess.
                Tailors & Shoemakers Gear) Delivered to Q.M.
                Orderly Room Gear   ) Stores at 8.30 a.m.
                D Coy Blankets & Valises will be dumped at Billet No.226
                at 7.30 a.m.

                Mess Cart will call for Officers Mess Gear commencing
                with 'B' Coy at 8.30 a.m.

                Canteen Stock will be collected later.

4. **Loading Party.** The Police & Pioneers will report to Pioneer Sgt.
                at 8 a.m. to act as the loading party.

5. **Baggage Guard.** 'A' Coy will detail 1 Platoon under an Officer
                as baggage guard. This platoon will report to Transport
                Officer at 10 a.m. and march in rear of 2nd Line
                Transport.

6. **Billeting Party.** Billeting party under Lieut.P.FAY has arranged
                billets today.

7. **Parade States** to be in the Orderly Room at 8.15 a.m.

8. **Marching In States** to be sent to Orderly Room on arrival in billets.

9. **Orderly Room** will close at CAUCHADME at 10 a.m. and re-open at
                HINGES on arrival.

Copy No. 1 Retained
        2 Hd.Qr Mess
        3 O.C. 'A' Coy   (Sd) R.N. HOLMES
        4 O.C. 'B' Coy   Capt. & Adjt.
        5 O.C. 'C' Coy   1/4th BN. LINCOLNSHIRE REGIMENT.
        6 O.C. 'D' Coy
        7 Transport Officer
        8 Quartermaster
        9 138th Inf. Bde
       10 & 11 War Diary
       12 R.S.M.

www.ingramcontent.com/pod-product-compliance
Lightning Source LLC
Chambersburg PA
CBHW080828010526
44112CB00015B/2476